Urban Computing

Series editors
Antonio A. F. Loureiro, Federal University of Minas Gerais, Computer Science
Department, Netivot, Minas Gerais, Brazil
Thiago H. Silva, Federal University of Technology, Department of Informatics,
Paraná, Brazil

The Urban Computing book series publishes high-quality research devoted to the study and application of computing technology in urban areas. The main scope is on current scientific developments and innovative techniques in urban computing, bringing to light methods from computer science, social sciences, statistics, urban planning, health care, civil engineering, anthropology, geography, and other fields that directly address urban problems using computer-based strategies. The series offers publications that present the state-of-the-art regarding the problems in question.

Suggested topics for prospective titles for the Urban Computing series include:

Architectures and Protocols for Urban Environments
Case studies in Urban Environments
City Life Improvement through Mobile Services and Big Data
Crowdsourced data acquisition in Urban Environments
Cyber-physical systems
e-Health and m-Health
e-Government
Green Computing in Urban Environments
Human Mobility
Intelligent Transportation Systems
Internet of Things in Urban Areas
Location-based Services in Urban Environments
Metering Infrastructures in Urban Environments
Mobile Cloud Computing
Mobile Sensing
Navigation in the Urban Environment
Recommendation Systems in Urban Spaces
Reliability and Security/Trust in Urban Computing
Semantic Sensing for Urban Information Gathering
Smart Cities
Smart Environment
Smart Grid and Urban Energy Distribution
Social Computing
Standards for Urban Computing
Urban Computing
Urban Economy Based on Big Data
Urban Heterogeneous Data Management
Urban Human-Computer Interaction
Urban Planning using Big Data
User-data interaction in Urban Environments
Using data in heterogeneous environments and Vehicular Sensor Networks

More information about this series at http://www.springer.com/series/15552

Rodolfo I. Meneguette
Robson E. De Grande
Antonio A. F. Loureiro

Intelligent Transport System in Smart Cities

Aspects and Challenges of Vehicular Networks and Cloud

 Springer

Rodolfo I. Meneguette
Federal Institute of São Paulo
Catanduva, São Paulo, Brazil

Antonio A. F. Loureiro
Instituto de Ciências Exatas
Departamento de Ciôncia da
Universidade Federal de Minas Gerais
Belo Horizonte, Minas Gerais, Brazil

Robson E. De Grande
Department of Computer Science
Brock University
St. Catharines, Ontario, Canada

ISSN 2510-2575   ISSN 2510-2583 (electronic)
Urban Computing
ISBN 978-3-030-06641-3 ISBN 978-3-319-93332-0 (eBook)
https://doi.org/10.1007/978-3-319-93332-0

This Springer imprint is published by the registered company Springer Nature Switzerland AG
The registered company address is: Gewerbestrasse 11, 6330 Cham, Switzerland

Contents

Acronyms

A-STAR	Anchor-Based Street and Traffic Aware Routing
ACC	Adaptive Cruise Control
AI	Artificial Intelligence
ANN	Artificial Neural Network
AP	Access point
ARC-IT	Architecture Reference for Cooperative and Intelligent Transportation
ATL	Arterial Traffic Light
BCE	Binding Catch Entry
BCG	Bayesian Coalition Game
CA-TLS	Context-Aware Traffic Light Scheduling
CaaS	Cooperation as a Service
CAN	Controller Area Network
CBF	Contention-Based Forwarding
CC	Cruise Control
CCH	Control Channel
CN	Corresponding Node
CR	Cognitive Radio
CRM	Cloud Resource Management
DDR	Distributed Dynamic Routing
DFD	Data Flow Diagram
DLSDP	Distributed Location-Based Service Discovery Protocol
DMM	Distributed Mobility Management
DNER	National Department of Roads
DoS	Denial of Service
DV-CAST	Distributed Vehicular Broadcast
ECU	Engine Control Unit
EDR	Event Data Recorder
ENaaS	Entertainment as a Service
EV	Electric Vehicle
FCC	Federal Communications Commission

FPMIPv6	Fast Handover Protocol PMIPv6
GDP	Gross Domestic Product
GeoDTN	Hybrid Geographic and DTN Routing
GPCR	Greedy Perimeter Coordinator Routing
GPGR	Grid-Based Predictive Geographical Routing
GPSR	Greedy Perimeter Stateless Routing
GR	Geocast Region
GSR	Geographic Source Routing
HA	Home agent
HACK	Handover Acknowledgment Message
HARP	Hybrid Ad Hoc Routing Protocol
HI	Handover Initiate
HIF	Handover Initiation for Flow Mobility
HLA	High Level Architecture
HNP	Home Network Prefix
HUA	HNP Update Acknowledge
HUR	HNP Update Request
HyDi	Hybrid Data Dissemination
ICT	Information and Communication Technologies
IE	Information Element
IEEE	Institute of Electrical and Electronics Engineers
IETF	Internet Engineering Task Force
IF	Intersection-Based Forwarding
ILP	Integer Linear Programming
INaaS	Information as a Service
ISA	Interface-Status-and-Action
iTETRIS	Integrated Wireless and Traffic Platform for Real-Time Road Traffic Management Solution
ITLC	Intelligent Traffic Light Controlling
ITS	Intelligent Transportation System
ITS-S	ITS Station
JVM	Java Virtual Machine
LACADF	Learning Automata-Based Contention Aware Data Forwarding
LC	Local Controller
LIN	Local Interconnect Network
LLC	Logical-Link Layer
LMA	Local Mobility Anchor
MAC	Media Access Control
MAG	Mobile Access Gateway
MANET	Wireless Network
MAV-AODV	Multicast with Mechanisms of Ant Colony Optimization
MCA-VANET	Multihoming Clustering Algorithm for Vehicular Ad Hoc Networks
MCTP	Mobile Control Transport Protocol
MDP	Markov Decision Process

MEXT	IETF Mobility Extensions for IPv6
MIB	Management Information Base
MICS	Media Independent Command Service
MIES	Media Independent Event Service
MIH	Media Independent Handover
MIHF	Media Independent Handover Function
MIIS	Media Independent Information Service
MLME	ML Layer Management Entity
MN	Mobile Node
MOVE	MObility Model Generator for VEhicular Networks
MoZo	Moving Zone Based Routing Protocol
MPR	Multipoint Relay
MSM	Multilink Striping Management
MVC	Military Vehicular Clouds
NAm	Network Animator
NEP	Nash Equilibrium Point
NetFC	Networked Fog Center
NS	Network Simulation
OBD	Onboard Diagnostics
OBU	Onboard Unit
OLSR	Optimized Link State Routing
ONF	Open Networking Forum
OSI	Open Systems Interconnection
OTCL	Object-Oriented Tool Command Language
P2P	Peer-to-Peer
PBA	Proxy Binding Acknowledge
PBU	Proxy Binding Update
PGB	Preferred Group Broadcasting
PKI	Public Key Infrastructure
PKSP	Probabilistic k-Shortest Path
PLC	Programmable Logic Controller
PLME	Physical Layer Management Entity
PMIPv6	Proxy Mobile IPv6
PoA	Point of Access
PoS	Point of Service
QoS	Quality of Service
RA	Router Advertisement
RC	Regional Controller
RFID	Radio Frequency Identification
ROVER	Robust Vehicular Routing
RS	Router Solicitation
RSU	Roadside Unit
SCH	Service Channel
SDN	Software Defined Networking
SENaaS	Sense-as-a-Service

SFMMA	Seamless Flow Mobility Management Architecture
SIPTO	Selective IP Traffic Offload
SMDP	Semi-Markov Decision Process
SNR	Signal-to-Noise Ratio
SRD	Simple and Robust Dissemination
STAR	tranSporTAtion seRver
SUMO	Simulation of Urban Mobility
TBRPF	Topology Dissemination Based on Reverse-Path Forwarding
TraCI	Traffic Control Interface
TraNS	Traffic and Network Simulation Environment
UE	User Equipment
UMB	Urban Multi-Hop Broadcast
US	United States
V2I	Vehicle-to-Infrastructure
V2V	Vehicle-to-Vehicle
VADD	Vehicle-Assisted Data Delivery
VANET	Vehicle Ad Hoc Network
VINT	Virtual InterNetwork Testbed
VM	Virtual Machine
VNI	Virtual Navigation Interface
VRC	Virtual Resource Counter
VSimRTI	V2X Simulation Runtime Infrastructure
VTP	Vehicle Transport Protocol
VVMM	Vehicular Virtual Machine Migration
WAVE	Wireless Access in Vehicular Environments
WBSS	WAVE Basic Service Set
WME	WAVE Management Entity
WMP	WMP Short Message Protocol
WSMP	WAVE Short Message Protocol
WWM	Weighted Waypoint Model
ZOA	Zone of Approach
ZOF	Zone of Forwarding

Chapter 1
Intelligent Transportation Systems

Abstract Transportation systems constitute an essential part of modern life and large urban centers. These systems have emerged as major players in enabling the mobility of not only vehicles but also people residing in cities, playing a part in all issues related to mobility within urban environments. Owing to the unprecedented growth of urban centers and the introduction of new services that have emerged as a result of technological advancements, these systems have been increasingly requiring considerable support to manage resources and vehicles. Transportation systems play a role in coordinating vehicle traffic and guaranteeing safety, which involves tackling many challenging issues commonly observed in large urban centers. The advancements and support of information and communication technologies have enabled the design and implementation of transportation solutions, which led to the development of intelligent transportation systems (ITSs) and the provision of many innovative services, such as those related to guaranteeing safety, providing useful information to drivers, enabling greater flow of movement on streets, and avoiding congestion. ITSs combine various technologies and services to optimize urban mobility and reduce both the financial and environmental damage caused by the demand for vehicles in urban centers. This chapter describes the fundamental concept of ITSs in the context of big cities.

1.1 Introduction

Communication and information technology are the driving force behind some of the most notable innovations in the automotive industry and modern society. In the last two decades, mobile communications have transformed our lives by allowing the exchange of information, anywhere and anytime. The use of such mobile communications systems in vehicles is expected to become a reality in the near future, as industries, universities, and governments around the world devote significant efforts and resources to the development of safer vehicles and infrastructure for road transport. These investments can be verified through many national and international initiatives dedicated to vehicular networks [3, 19, 24].

© Springer International Publishing AG, part of Springer Nature 2018
R. I. Meneguette et al., *Intelligent Transport System in Smart Cities*, Urban Computing, https://doi.org/10.1007/978-3-319-93332-0_1

We can observe through these initiatives, whereby vehicles gradually incorporate embedded features and devices, such as sensors, cameras, computers, and communications resources. These features are causing vehicles to have an impact on existing systems with the transmission and real-time interpretation of information, supporting data acquisition and decision making to assist drivers and devices to take proper, timely actions [14]. Vehicles have become a relevant tool for smart cities because they have the ability to sense objects and events in the environment and respond appropriately; they not only assist in vehicle traffic management but also represent a tool for capturing real-time, relevant information used in resource management.

Among its existing definitions, a smart city can be defined as an intelligent environment that embeds information and communication technologies and creates interactive systems. These systems bring communication to the physical world to solve inhabitants' problems in their urban conglomerations and ensure better management of public resources and space. From this perspective, a smart city, more generally referred to as an intelligent space, relates to a physical environment in which communication and information technologies, as well as sensor systems, are imperceptible as they become transparently embedded in physical objects and the environment in which people live, travel, and work [21]. An intelligent city, like any other urban center, needs careful attention to a series of mobility and management problems, such as traffic, surveillance, natural disasters, and sustainability. To support such solutions, many urban data need to be collected and disseminated through communication infrastructures, which in turn require integrated, heterogeneous, and intelligent forms of wireless communication.

Thus, in this context of smart systems, ITSs comprise the union of several technologies with the aim of providing comprehensive optimization of the urban mobility of a city and bringing greater safety to drivers and comfort and entertainment to passengers [1]. As a result, ITSs employ data, communication, and computation to provide services and applications for addressing and possibly solving a wide range of transportation problems in modern large cities [5]. These applications rely on collaboration among elements that integrate urban and transportation systems, such as sensors, mobile devices, and vehicles, to introduce real-time awareness of the environment. The appropriate junction of all these factors significantly contributes to the sensing and gathering of data for evaluation and subsequent implementation of appropriate responses by a control system [6].

The services and applications provided by ITSs have particular characteristics and peculiarities, which distinguish them from more traditional applications [15]. They are services that generate and consume a high volume of disparate data and use specialized communication technologies with different bandwidths, reach, and latency. These characteristics face restrictive, challenging issues since ITSs also hold a wide range of restrictions and levels of quality of service that vary dramatically according to each application. For this reason, designing a service that is part of these systems represents a major challenge.

This chapter outlines the concepts of an ITS that offers services and applications to smart cities, which includes pedestrians and vehicles. These services seek to provide higher road safety, efficient mobility, and comfort to drivers and passengers of vehicles traveling on city streets. The rest of the chapter is organized as follows. In Sect. 1.2, we describe the concepts of an intelligent transport system and present the principal ITS architectures and applications. We also explain the various issues involved with security and privacy in an ITS. Finally, we discuss the most significant challenges involved in integrating ITSs into smart urban centers.

1.2 Intelligent Transportation System Concepts

An ITS comprises a set of technologies and applications aimed at improving transport safety and mobility, as well as increasing people's productivity and reducing the harmful effects of traffic. The initial ITS concept was proposed by researchers in the United States (US) in the twentieth century [1]. However, ITSs are now attracting a great deal of attention from academia and industry because such systems not only improve vehicle traffic conditions but may ultimately make the transportation sector safer and more sustainable and efficient, avoiding the inconveniences caused by traffic congestion and the effects of climate problems on traffic.

ITSs integrate information and communication technologies (ICT) and apply them to the transport sector [4]. These systems collect data from sensors and equipment implanted in vehicles and infrastructures to merge the data so that it is possible to contextualize the information, which will allow for making inferences about the state of the transportation system of a given city. With this information it is possible to offer services and applications that aim to improve the management of urban resources and increase the convenience of people through the use of information and alert services. Thus, ITSs help to ease traffic flow in cities by reducing the time spent in traffic jams, in turn reducing fuel consumption, CO emissions, and monetary losses.

In the following sections, we present the main ITS architectures and their components, highlighting the main differences between each proposed model. In addition, some projects aimed at the development of an ITS and the challenges of ITSs are described.

1.2.1 ITS Integration with Smart Cities

Modern vehicles come equipped with a series of sensors, cameras, processing units, and communication resources. All these embedded capabilities enable vehicles to collect, transmit, and interpret information to assist in the acquisition of data and in taking some action to help the driver and devices take action. These features turn vehicles into a valuable tool for smart cities, serving as a source for capturing real-time, relevant information used in the management of either traffic or resources. A smart city can be defined as an intelligent environment that embeds information and communication technologies that create interactive environments that bring communication to the physical world to solve daily problems of inhabitants in their urban conglomerations, ensuring better public management.

From this perspective, an intelligent city, or more generally an intelligent space, refers to a physical environment in which communication and information technologies, as well as sensor systems, disappear as they become embedded in physical objects and the environment in which people live, travel, and work [21]. An intelligent city requires solutions to several problems, such as traffic, surveillance, natural disasters, and environmental monitoring. Urban data need to be collected and disseminated through communication infrastructures to support such solutions. This data flow, in turn, requires integrated, heterogeneous, and intelligent forms of wireless communication.

Among the services employed in an intelligent city, we can include the coordination of traffic lights, parking, location services, weather services, tourist services, and emergency services. All services should be integrated to improve the accuracy of the information delivered to drivers [16]. Another useful service consists of the deployment of sensors in streets to track and alert drivers of dangers ahead. In addition, autonomous vehicles can make use of these sensors to guide passengers to their destination. One framework explored the communication between sensors and vehicles to enable a car to be moved between source and destination safely [12].

With the emergence of electric vehicles (EVs), new services have arisen to provide shorter route planning with the aim of minimizing costs and avoiding traffic jams, emphasizing recharging points along the way when needed [20]. Another relevant aspect to smart cities revolves around the concern with sustainability and related actions performed by humans to reduce their impact on the global environment. Many traffic routing services and applications are already available to the population to favor the movement of people, thereby decreasing fuel consumption and vehicle emissions of carbon dioxide. Also, route- and ride-sharing services have received significant attention and supporters [25] because these strategies reduce the number of vehicles in circulation and, consequently, emissions of gases into the atmosphere.

In intelligent cities, one challenge is the analysis and interpretation of data obtained from various mobile and fixed devices that have localization and communication mechanisms, such as GPS, WIFI, 3G, and 4G. The mobility of individuals must be taken into account in such environments to track the movement of vehicles and pedestrians for maximizing connectivity and forecasting. Thus, this urban dynamicity requires identifying mobility patterns, social events, routines, and the interactions of individuals with the surrounding environment and with other individuals [18]. Equipped with the urban geographical characteristics, the microscopic factors linked to human behavior make it possible to define macroscopic trends and flow aspects of individuals over a period of time in a given region, evidencing critical regions in a street network. In other words, deep analysis can identify those regions that are most frequented and why these regions, for instance, receive a given stream of people at a given time [18].

One of the most challenging aspects in smart cities is to design a robust and reliable solution that can cope with the diversity and volume of data collected in real time. Another part of the challenge relates to the precision of such a solution regarding the monitoring and interpretation of data that can be used in decision making. The analysis output should be usable in a large variety of applications, such as allocating or moving physical resources not only for citizens but also for municipal services, such as fire departments, ambulances, and police.

1.2.2 Architecture

The recent evolution of computing and communication technologies in the last decade has boosted the development of ITS services, matching against increasing demands, which come with a variety of requirements. The high diversity of factors has prompted the need for standardization to define a general method by which devices and components can interact with each other. Among the existing architectures, we describe the architecture adopted in Canada, the United States, Europe, and Japan.

1.2.2.1 North American ITS Architecture

The architecture used in the United States has been developed by the U.S. Department of Transportation [22]. Its design focuses on assisting urban mobility through a cooperative system. The architecture is referred to as the Architecture Reference for Cooperative and Intelligent Transportation (ARC-IT); it consists of a set of interconnected components organized into four views, as we can see in Fig. 1.1. We describe each of the views as follows:

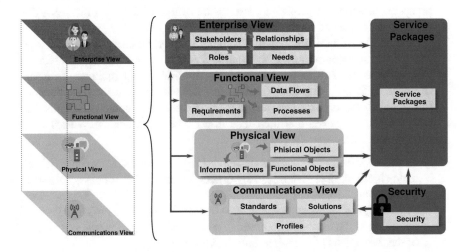

Fig. 1.1 Architectural reference for cooperative and intelligent transportation [22]

- **Enterprise View** deals with the relationship between users and organizations, establishing rules that such organizations follow within the cooperative ITS environment. Therefore, the relationships between an entity, user, and system depend on the roles that entities receive when interacting with user services. Enterprise View consists of a set of objects such as:

  - *Enterprise Object* is an individual or organization that interacts with an object. An Enterprise Object can comprise several other objects by participating in the interaction of various functionalities. For instance, Device Developer is a component of Auto Manufacturer, but it also participates in Standards Body [22];
  - *Resource* supports the execution of some object. It may be a physical or virtual element with limited dispersion;
  - *Relationship* defines the coordination between Enterprise Objects, for example, a contract;
  - *Role* consists of a set of actions, functions, and rules that an object participating in a relationship carries out or follows.

  Thus, in summary, the Enterprise View is composed of Enterprise Objects that cooperate and interact to exchange information, manage systems, and operate actions. Also, Enterprise View establishes relationships among those Enterprise Objects, defining the method for Enterprise Objects to interact with other objects that may appear in the View as Resources. The relationships among Enterprise Objects establish a contract or agreement that seeks to find common purposes necessary to implement and deliver an ITS service.

- **Functional View** focuses on the functioning of the abstract elements and their logical interactions. Therefore, Functional View defines the functional requirements to support the needs of ITS users. For this, the data flows and processes provide a structure of presentation of interactions and functions that preserve the requested requirements.

  The ARC-IT functional model falls under a structural analysis methodology. The methodology employs the National ITS Architecture's logical architecture. The architecture applies the work of Hatley/Pirbhai and includes Yourdon-Demarco data flow diagrams (DFDs) to illustrate the flow of data between functional elements [22]. The functional model does not include diagrams, just collections of processes and their data flows. The Functional View uses some structural artifacts, described as follows:

  - *Process* consists of a function or activity that is required to perform actions and achieve an objective or to support actions of another process, such as to collect data and generate data;
  - *Process Specification* corresponds to a function primitive, which is the textual definition of the most detailed processes, including a set of inputs and outputs of the functions, their requirements, and an overview;
  - *Data Flows* comprise the flow of information among processes and an object within a process;

- *Terminator* represents an external device that belongs to the architecture, such as source and a sink for information.

The Functional View uses processes to manage and control the behavior of the system, a type of monitoring. These processes execute a set of predefined actions to achieve the goals of an application or to support the operations of another process. The Functional View also provides data processing functions, data stores, and the logical flows of information among these elements that establishes the flow of data that move between processes.

- **Physical View** describes the physical elements, such as devices and systems, that provide ITS functionality. This functionality contains the roles of elements involved in delivering user services, the respective capabilities of such elements, and the connections between them. Therefore, the Physical View describes the transportation systems and the information exchanges that ITSs support. The Physical View consists of seven main objects:

  - *Physical Object* represents people, places, or objects that participate in the ITS. These objects can be expressed according to their application, their processing, and their interface with other objects. A Physical Object is divided into five classes, as shown in Fig. 1.2:

    Center defines the center of control and management of the system, which provides application, management, administrative, and support functions from a fixed location not in proximity to the road network;

    Field encompasses all the infrastructure of the environment, such as traffic detectors, cameras, signal controllers, dynamic message signs, and parking. The Field class also includes communication equipment between vehicles and the shoreline infrastructure, as well as other communication mechanisms that provide communications between mobile elements and fixed infrastructure;

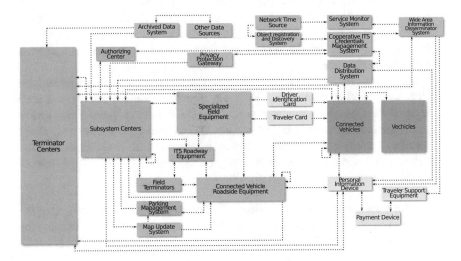

Fig. 1.2 Diagram describing major physical components in ARC-IT [22]

Support consists of a center that presents non-transportation-specific services, such as security and communications facilitation;

Traveler corresponds to the devices used by people on a trip to gain access to transport services during their journey;

Vehicle represents vehicles and embedded sensors;

Mobile encompasses all Vehicles and mobile Travelers.

- *Functional Object* comprises the building blocks of the physical objects in the Physical View. Functional objects group similar processes of a particular Physical Object together into a package.
- *Information Flow* contains the information exchanged between a physical object and a view. This information meets the communication requirements provided by the interface. The Information Flow uses flow characteristics that imply a series of communication protocol standards, in which provision of the agreement relationship determines the role and use of those standards.
- *Triple* represents the junction of a Physical Object source and destination with the Information Flow and Physical Object destination. It is used to define an interface.
- *Subsystem* consists of a Physical Object with a specified functionality inside the ARC-IT system boundary.
- *Terminator* represents a Physical Object without a specified functionality, outside the ARC-IT system boundary.
- *Service Package Diagram* illustrates all Physical Object diagrams.

- **Communication View** defines how physical objects communicate. It describes communication protocols to provide interoperability between Physical Objects in the Physical View. These protocols need to map the system requirements with the constraints imposed by physical connectivity, among other aspects.

  The ARC-IT can be represented as an integrated set of physical objects that interact and exchange information to support the architecture service packages. Physical Objects consist of subsystems and of terminators, in which they provide a set of capabilities that can be implemented at any one place or time. Communication between these elements is carried out by Information Flows, in which are included the source and destination Physical Objects and the Information Flow that is exchanged, as depicted in Fig. 1.3.

  Additionally, ARC-IT includes dozens of communication profiles that support all links defined in the Physical View. Each profile identifies standards at each layer of the Open Systems Interconnection (OSI) communication stack and in particular includes standards that support ITS communications. Security Plane specifies security policies, authentication mechanisms, and encryption of data. Figure 1.4 describes a three-stack configuration based on the type of network element used by the ARC-IT architecture.

- Service Package represents a service-oriented entry point that shares each of the four views. The Service Packages specify not only the technologies but also the views that involve the ARC-IT architecture.

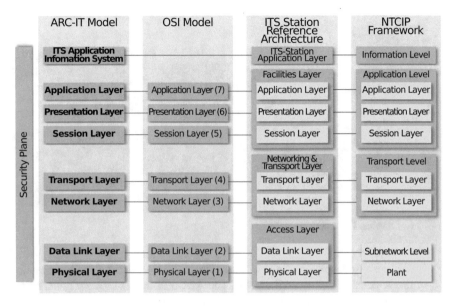

Fig. 1.3 Difference between ARC-IT, OSI model, and NTCI

RSE Gateway						
OBE status						
Vehicle OBE		**Roadside Equipement**				**Service Monitor System**
ITS Application Information Layer Undefined	Security Plane IEEE 1609.2				Security Plane IETF DTLS	**ITS Application Information Layer** Undefined
Application Layer Undefined						**Application Layer** Undefined
Presentation Layer ISO ANS.1 UPER						**Presentation Layer** ISO ANS.1 UPER
Session Layer IETF DTLS	Security Plane IETF DTLS	**Session Layer** IETF DTLS	**Session Layer** IETF DTLS			**Session Layer** IETF DTLS
Transport Layer IETF UDP		**Transport Layer** IETF UDP	**Transport Layer** IETF UDP			**Transport Layer** IETF UDP
Network Layer IETF IPv6		**Network Layer** IETF IPv6	**Network Layer** IETF IPv6			**Network Layer** IETF IPv6
Data Link Layer IEEE 1609.4, IEEE 802.11		**Data Link Layer** IEEE 1609.4, IEEE 802.11	**Data Link Layer** LLC and MAc compatible			**Data Link Layer** LLC and MAc compatible
Physical Layer IEEE 802.11		**Physical Layer** IEEE 802.11	**Physical Layer** Backhaul PHY			**Physical Layer** Backhaul PHY

Fig. 1.4 Example of communication diagram [22]

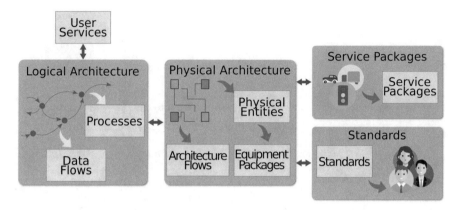

Fig. 1.5 Canadian ITS architecture [2]

- Security is responsible not only for the safety of the system but also for the safety of the vehicles' mobility on the roads. The ARC-IT handles security holistically, addressing security concerns spanning all four views.

The USA architecture provides the framework for the description of ITSs, which defines the functions that must be performed by Physical Objects. Although the architecture supplies several services to its users, it does not clarify the support of the simultaneous use of various communication technologies to meet the needs of its users. Another limitation of this architecture is related to the flexibility of the system with respect to using new computing paradigms, such as cloud computing and fog computing.

1.2.2.2 Canadian ITS Architecture

Transport Canada introduced the Canadian ITS architecture [2] and provided a framework for planning, defining, and integrating ITSs. The architecture contains the follows elements:

- The functions reflect the actions required for ITS, such as gathering traffic information or requesting a route;
- The physical entities or subsystems correspond to the elements affected by the functions, such as the field or the vehicle;
- The information flows and data flows are the connections between these functions and physical subsystems together in an integrated system.

This framework contains a clear description of each element and subsystem. The architecture is divided into five distinct components, as shown in Fig. 1.5. We review each component in what follows.

- **User Services** describe the services offered in the platform and accessed by users. The platform provides 37 services to its users. These services present a set of functions that allow the user to travel quietly and securely. Among the provided services, we mention Traffic Management, Traveler Information, and Emergency Management;
- **Logical Architecture** defines the functions and activities of each process to meet the requirements of the user services. This architecture also seeks to help identify the system functions and information flows and attempts to guide the development of functional requirements for new systems. The Logical Architecture provides a graphical view that shows the fit between processes and data flows. However, this architecture does not define where or by whom functions are performed in the system, nor does it describe how to implement a function.

  Therefore, in the Canadian framework, the architecture defines the set of information and data flows and processes that meet user service requirements. Processes and data flows are grouped to form particular transportation management functions and are represented graphically by bubble charts, which decompose into several levels of detail.

- **Physical Architecture** describes the physical entities that define subsystems and Terminators. The architecture specifies Architecture Flows that detail the integration of subsystems and Terminators in the system. However, this architecture provides agencies with a physical representation of how the system should provide the required functionality. Thus, the architecture takes the processes identified in the Logical Architecture and assigns them to physical entities.

  The subsystems represent a set of capabilities, corresponding to the principal structural elements of the ITS physical architecture. These subsystems are divided into four classes, as shown in Fig. 1.6. Center defines the control and management center of the entire system, which executes the services. Field encompasses all the infrastructure of the environment, such as roadside units (RSUs), monitoring sensors, and cameras. Vehicles represent vehicles and onboard sensors. Travelers correspond to the devices used by people during a trip. Terminators describe the boundary of an architecture and represent people, systems, and the general environment that interface to an ITS.

  Physical Architecture also uses an entity called Equipment Packages that divides the subsystems into deployment-sized pieces. Equipment Packages serve to group functions of a particular subsystem together into an "implementable" software package and hardware capabilities.

- **Service Packages** consist of slices of the Physical Architecture that deal with specific services related to transportation problems, such as surface control. A service involves a set of Equipment Packages required to work together and deliver a given transportation service. Therefore, a service collects different information from many subsystems, Equipment Packages, and Terminators to provide the required service output.

- **Standards** are methods that facilitate the deployment of interoperable systems at local, regional, and national levels without impeding an innovation as technology

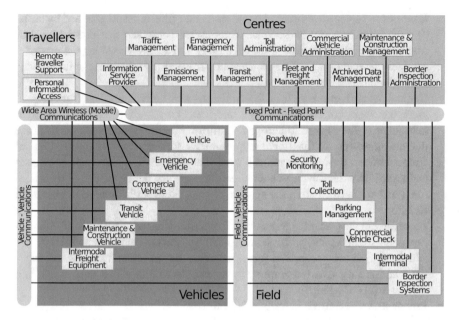

Fig. 1.6 ITS architecture for Canada subsystems and communications [2]

advances and new approaches evolve. Therefore, Standards are fundamental to the establishment of an open ITS environment.

The Canadian architecture provides a standard structure for the design of ITSs, defining functions that must be performed by components and subsystems. The used information flow employs a communication mechanism that allows for the mapping of the requirements of each function with the need for each service offered to its users. Although the architecture provides several services to its users, it is unclear how the architecture allows for the simultaneous use of various communication technologies to meet user needs. Another limitation of this architecture relates to the availability of the resources; all services lie in Centers, and the communication between the two Center and Vehicle classes occurs through an interface, which limits the use of new paradigms.

1.2.2.3 European ITS Architecture

The ETSI Technical Committee on Intelligent Transport Systems [7] is responsible for the development of the European ITS architecture, which consists of four subsystems, as shown in Fig. 1.7.

- **Personal** provides access to service in ITSs from mobile devices to users, such as by smartphone;

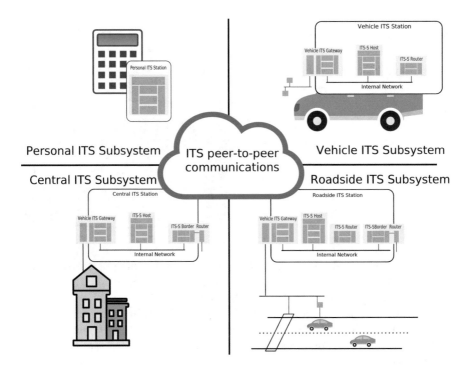

Fig. 1.7 European ITS architecture: communication subsystems [7]

- **Vehicle** corresponds to devices embedded in a vehicle, such as the onboard unit (OBU), which hosts ITS applications. These applications consider information about the vehicle and the environment in which it is located. They receive information from, send it to, and exchange it with other drivers;
- **Central** defines a central device that manages, monitors, and makes available ITS services to users;
- **Roadside** represents devices installed along the roadside that drive ITS applications. These devices collect information about vehicle flow and road conditions; they also control roadside equipment and establish communication among vehicles with the objective of enabling the exchange of information between them.

These subsystems comprise a standard architecture known as an ITS station (ITS-S). This architecture is based on the OSI model for which it establishes layers of communication. However, this architecture includes one more layer interfacing with ITS applications. Figure 1.8 describes the ITS-S architecture and shows how it is divided into six elements.

- **Access** corresponds to layers 1 and 2 of the OSI protocol and contains a function to establish access to communication channels;

Fig. 1.8 ITS-S reference
architecture [7]

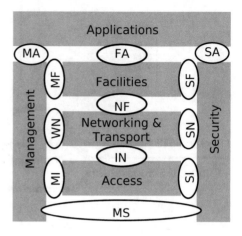

- **Networking** and Transport define the addressing and routing of network information, as well as the sending of information over the network. This module corresponds to layers 3 and 4 of the OSI model;
- **Facilities** comprise layers 5, 6, and 7 of the OSI model and are intended to assist ITS applications that share functions and information according to their functionality and application. They manage all data coding and application sessions;
- **Applications** refer to ITS applications. These applications may contain features of more than one service, and one service may be the result of a combination of other applications;
- **Management** is in charge of managing communications within the ITS-S;
- **Security Entity** provides security services.

Therefore, an ITS-S hosts a variety of ITS applications and communicates with other components within the subsystem and other ITS-Ss [7]. An ITS-S can be composed of the following functional elements:

- **ITS Station Host** provides access to ITS applications through personal devices;
- **ITS Station Gateway** supports external communication. It connects two different OSI protocol stacks at layers 5–7;
- **ITS Station Router** establishes a vehicle-to-vehicle (V2V) or vehicle-to-infrastructure (V2I) communication or communication between ITS-Ss, meaning an interconnection between OSI layer 4 (transport) and 3 (network) of the OSI model;
- **ITS Station Border Router** provides nearly the same functionality as ITS-S routers, with the difference that the external network may not support the same management and security principles of the ITS [1].

The European architecture presents a set of subsystems that offer ITS services. Like the architectures mentioned previously, this one also has limitations, such as the use of a centralized control element and the lack of integration with new communication paradigms. These restrictions reduce its flexibility with respect to the inclusion of new technologies, which may emerge in the future, or even current technologies, such as cloud computing and fog computing.

1.2.2.4 Challenges in ITS Architectures

Nowadays we see a significant dynamism in urban mobility due to the number of vehicles on urban roads and the daily routines and particular characteristics of urban road networks. The growth of traffic flows has led to an increase in issues related to transportation systems, such as congestion and higher rates of traffic accidents. Advancements in communication technology, in loco sensing, and in-vehicle monitoring have engendered a host of smart services that rely on more immediate and dynamic communication, enabling an abstraction of the state of mobility in a given city.

ITSs can use heterogeneous means of communication, including mobile devices, that are not restricted to vehicular networks. This broader access to networks allows for greater scalability and a reduction in delays in sending and receiving information regarding services related to the transport system. However, the architecture for such systems faces several challenges in acting efficiently and guaranteeing quality and safety, entailing additional costs, which means the implementation of such services will not always be feasible.

As with previous descriptions of existing ITS architectures, we can highlight several critical components in these architectures, such as sensors, OBUs, RSUs, GPS, intelligent traffic lights, access points, portable devices, satellites, and specialized servers. Communication among the devices and even subsystems of this architecture is critical and largely determines the feasibility and performance of ITS solutions. The heterogeneity of communication requires dealing with several adopted technologies, such as Wi-Fi, WiMAX, LTE, GSM, 3G, 4G, satellite, and Bluetooth, which directly increases the flexibility and complexity of the design.

The communication and abstraction of data between technologies of different networks represent one of the great challenges in designing a transport system architecture. This challenge stems from the complexity of establishing a heterogeneous connection, as mentioned earlier. For a system to operate collaboratively, it needs to develop standards that facilitate the integration of components. Also, the distinct characteristics of the urban environment and high mobility of vehicles require additional attention for an adequate implementation of the infrastructure, taking into consideration the transportation system as a whole, as well as tolerance for delays and failures.

An ITS, which includes vehicles, devices, and infrastructure, can contain a diversity of wireless communication technologies that allow communication over more than one data channel. The work presented in [8] confirms the importance and role of the Internet's infrastructure in the context of vehicular networks. According to the study, the benefits of the Internet's infrastructure are that it is ubiquitous, provides ready access to services in several urban environments, and establishes interconnections among vehicles. Future trends for the Internet consist of peer-to-peer (P2P) wireless communications and a support infrastructure for the proper provisioning of applications and services. In what follows, we highlight some works that make use of infrastructure integrated with ad hoc networks, demonstrating how an ITS can become complete and more efficient through the use of hybrid architectures, and discussing the challenges that need to be overcome.

An analysis of the impact of urban features [9] has shown that the appropriate placement and installation of RSUs, together with the corresponding communication configurations, could ensure successful V2I communications. The study made use of tests in a real urban scenario, the city of Bologna, where experiments employed the IEEE 802.11p protocol for V2I communication. The obtained results demonstrated that the use of the IEEE 802.11p protocol was strongly affected by the layout of the streets, elevation of the terrain, traffic density, presence of heavy vehicles, and other obstacles, such as trees and vegetation. These enforced the suggestion that these environmental elements must be taken into consideration for adequate deployment of RSUs and for the configuration of radio communication.

We may observe in several works in the literature [10, 11, 17, 23] the use of infrastructure in the design of ITSs in which RSUs extend the primary communication mechanisms to serve as devices with the computational power to assist in the ITS architecture. More recent works show a growing trend toward merging vehicular networks with cloud computing. This merging of the two technologies aims to provide greater scalability for transportation services. These joint technologies also make it possible to increase the computational power of ITS architectures through mobile cloud communication brought about dynamically among devices, vehicles, and the static cloud, which corresponds to control centers or data centers [14].

1.2.3 ITS Applications

With the ease of communication between vehicles and with a road infrastructure, vehicular networks provide diverse applications and services for users. The design of ITS services and applications aim to assist drivers and passengers during their travels, with a focus on reducing accidents and managing traffic in large cities. In addition, other types of applications help and promote services to drivers, making their travel more peaceful and enjoyable. The main applications focused on ITS are as follows:

- **Safety applications** are intended to alert drivers to the possibility of imminent collisions with other vehicles or with obstacles ahead. In some scenarios, a driver needs to react by making a quick decision to avoid a collision. For this reason, this type of application has severe restrictions on delay and reliability. Some types of this class of applications involve alerting drivers to hazards on highways, warning of collisions, notifying about accidents on the road, and informing drivers about construction work ahead. All services aim at avoiding collisions between vehicles and supporting efficient access for first responders;

- **Traffic efficiency applications** aim to improve the flow of vehicles, reducing travel time and traffic congestion. These applications also indirectly provide economic and environmental benefits. They typically use data dissemination techniques and roadside infrastructures to obtain and propagate traffic condition information from vehicles. This class of applications includes adaptive electronic traffic signs, route guidance and navigation services, traffic flow optimization services, and management of hazardous goods vehicles;
- **Entertainment and comfort applications** attempt to make passengers more comfortable in their vehicles by reducing the driving burden. In such applications, network elements, such as vehicles, sensors installed on highways or traffic lights, access points, and mobile/pedestrian devices, sense the environment and provide traffic information on streets, avenues, and highways. After collecting this information, it is disseminated to vehicles by the system. Applications in this class include interactive games, content sharing, yellow pages, and notification services.

Applications classified in these three major classes have been explored in a wide variety of works, and all these works, in their particular context, attempt to improve efficiency and comfort in urban mobility. Chapter 7 explores and describes these applications in detail, discussing the challenges they face and future trends. However, in this chapter, we would like to emphasize an especially challenging issue, which is present not only in ITS applications but also in any current smart mobile application: information security. This particular aspect involves access to systems and the information contained in applications; it also concerns the introduction of erroneous information into the system.

1.2.4 Security and Privacy in an ITS

Concerns about ITS safety focus on information protection and the transportation infrastructure. More than ever, information-based transportation systems have become inherently accounted for to detect, collect, process, and disseminate data and essential to improving the efficiency of moving goods and people, enhancing the safety of our transportation system, and providing travel alternatives. The vast collection and dissemination of information raises significant security and privacy issues due to the large-scale exchange of sensitive data.

Security concerns have been addressed in the ITS architecture using two approaches [22]:

- ITS Security Areas discretize and classify security issues that might arise in ITS environments. As previously described, ITSs can be used to improve the safety of the surface transportation system. Figure 1.9 shows eight security applications defined for an ITS that can be used to detect, respond to, and recover from threats against the transport system.

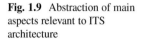

Fig. 1.9 Abstraction of main aspects relevant to ITS architecture

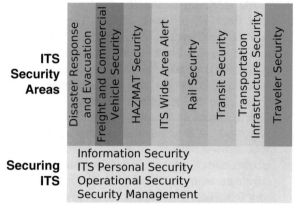

• Securing an ITS addresses the issue of protecting information from the ITS to safeguard ITS applications so that they are reliable and available when needed. Owing to the nature of communication, the information exchanged between the elements of an ITS is subject to tampering and unauthorized use, in which false or erroneous information can cause a severe accident to the driver or passengers in a vehicle. Thus, security is concerned with not only preventing unauthorized disclosure of confidential information but also covering a wide range of threats that may disrupt or change the operation of the system. For these aspects, information security is one of the great challenges for an ITS operating in a city.

When considering the security aspect of information in an ITS, the safety components need to be explicitly established. Some research works, such as that presented in [13], describe several components that smart transportation systems need to consider. These elements include keeping the system secure, addressing the threats faced by the system, and providing security services to protect against threats while allowing the system to perform in line with its objectives.

In securing an ITS, we can highlight the following contextual aspects:

• **Confidentiality** aims to ensure that data and the system are not accessible to unauthorized entities, processes, or systems;
• **Availability** refers to allowing access to data and the system to authorized entities, as well as other processes and even systems;
• **Integrity** involves ensuring that ITS data retain their meaning, completeness, and consistency.

The design of an ITS must be such that possible threats are avoided so that the aforementioned security requirements are met. We can broadly define a threat as anything that might cause an issue in the system and arise accidentally or intentionally due to a natural disaster. Threats are also present in ITSs, and the following list summarizes the major ones in the context of ITSs:

- **Disclosure** entails the interception of sensitive data by unauthorized entities. In the context of an ITS, data disclosure can occur, for example, when vehicles exchange information between each other or with the infrastructure, which creates vulnerabilities in the ITS that can be exploited;
- **Information change** relates to adding, modifying, or removing system information to produce unauthorized system effects. An example of the negative potential of this threat in an ITS consists of the change of information displayed on highways to incorrect or inappropriate content;
- **Masquerading** refers to the unauthorized access of a user or process to the system so that it perceives the access as authentic. If unauthorized users gain access to the system, they can obtain confidential information and unique permissions to change the system. In an ITS, unauthorized users may, for example, change data on highways, send erroneous information to system users, and even interrupt the proper functioning of the system;
- **Repudiation** consists of denying an action. Repudiation enables the transmitter or receiver to block the execution of an action. Repudiation can usually occur in electronic transactions. For instance, suppose that the payment of a toll is automated. In this case, nonauthorization of the toll payment, even if accidental, may occur, which will result in the user's being denied further passage;
- **Denial of service** (DoS) happens when actions are taken to block access to or disrupt the proper functioning of a system. Usually, a DoS is caused by the introduction of malicious code or the execution of unauthorized actions that make the system unavailable. In the context of an ITS, DoS can be critical; for example, accidents are most likely to happen if a safe direction detection system becomes unavailable;
- **Replay** involves the repetition of valid information under invalid circumstances to bring about unauthorized effects on the system. This type of threat can impact system integrity, especially with respect to the meaning and consistency of information within the system. In the context of an ITS, this threat can be used to relay identity and credit data from valid users to benefit those who illegally obtained valid information.

After threats are identified and properly managed, it is natural to develop protection mechanisms to establish system confidentiality, availability, and integrity. Although a single tool or service cannot eliminate security threats, the application of security services, such as those described in what follows, can prevent or mitigate threats.

- An **access control service** aims to provide distinct permissions for each entity, given the function it serves in the system. Usually, an access control service runs after user authentication, so rules that limit access to system information apply. This service aims to reduce disclosure, information changes, and DoSs.
- An **authentication service** consists of a means of verifying the identity of entities that operate in the system. Typically, the identity itself is a form of identification to the system.

- An **integrity service** supports the analysis of the integrity of information flowing through the system and aims to minimize the manipulation of information.

In addition to these services, it is also possible to use cryptographic mechanisms to mask the original information that ITS applications transmit.

1.3   Final Discussion

In this chapter, we have described the concept of an ITS. First, we described the concept of smart cities and how they relate to ITSs. We discussed the main architecture used in an ITS, presented its main components and the main features of each architecture, and described the challenges encountered in proposing an architecture. Finally, we identified the main functions of ITS applications and the security requirements that these applications need to meet.

References

1. Alam M, Ferreira J, Fonseca J (2016) Introduction to intelligent transportation systems. Springer, Cham, pp 1–17
2. Transportation Association of Canada (2017) ITS architecture for Canada
3. CICAS (2017) Official website Cooperative Intersection Collision Avoidance Systems (CICAS) project
4. European Commission (2019) European commission mandate m/453 en
5. Cunha F, Villas L, Boukerche A, Maia G, Viana A, Mini RA, Loureiro AA (2016) Data communication in VANETs: protocols, applications and challenges. Ad Hoc Netw 44:90–103
6. Dimitrakopoulos G, Demestichas P (2010) Intelligent transportation systems. IEEE Veh Technol Mag 5(1):77–84
7. European Telecommunications Standards Institute (2010) Intelligent Transport Systems (ITS) communications architecture
8. Gerla M, Kleinrock L (2011) Vehicular networks and the future of the mobile internet. Comput Netw 55(2):457–469
9. Gozalvez J, Sepulcre M, Bauza R (2012) IEEE 802.11p vehicle to infrastructure communications in urban environments. IEEE Commun Mag 50(5):176–183
10. He W, Yan G, Xu LD (2014) Developing vehicular data cloud services in the IoT environment. IEEE Trans Ind Inf 10(2):1587–1595
11. Hussain R, Son J, Eun H, Kim S, Oh H (2012) Rethinking vehicular communications: merging VANET with cloud computing. In: Proceedings of the 4th IEEE international conference on cloud computing technology and science proceedings, pp 606–609
12. Kumar S, Shi L, Ahmed N, Gil S, Katabi D, Rus D (2012) Carspeak: a content-centric network for autonomous driving. SIGCOMM Comput Commun Rev 42(4):259–270
13. Levy-Bencheton C, Darra E (2015) Cyber security and resilience of intelligent public transport: good practices and recommendations. European Union Agency for Network and Information Security
14. Meneguette RI (2016) A vehicular cloud-based framework for the intelligent transport management of big cities. Int J Distrib Sens Netw 12(5):8198597

15. Mutalik P, Nagaraj S, Vedavyas J, Biradar RV, Patil VGC (2016) A comparative study on AODV, DSR and DSDV routing protocols for Intelligent Transportation System (ITS) in metro cities for road traffic safety using VANET route traffic analysis (VRTA). In: Proceedings of the IEEE international conference on advances in electronics, communication and computer technology. IEEE, Piscataway, pp 383–386

16. Nam T, Aldama FA, Chourabi H, Mellouli S, Pardo TA, Gil-Garcia JR, Scholl HJ, Ojo A, Estevez E, Zheng L (2011) Smart cities and service integration. In: Proceedings of the 12th annual international digital government research conference: digital government innovation in challenging times, dg.o'11. ACM, New York, pp 333–334

17. Olariu S, Khalil I, Abuelela M (2011) Taking VANET to the clouds. Int J Pervasive Comput Commun 7(1):7–21

18. Pan G, Qi G, Zhang W, Li S, Wu Z, Yang L (2013) Trace analysis and mining for smart cities: issues, methods, and applications. IEEE Commun Mag 51(6):120–126

19. PATH (2017) Official website path

20. Qin H, Zhang W (2011) Charging scheduling with minimal waiting in a network of electric vehicles and charging stations. In: Proceedings of the eighth ACM international workshop on vehicular inter-networking, VANET '11. ACM, New York, pp 51–60

21. Steventon A, Wright S (eds) (2006) Intelligent spaces: the application of pervasive ICT. Computer communications and networks, vol XVIII

22. U.S. Department of Transportation (2017) Architecture reference for cooperative and intelligent transportation

23. Trullols O, Fiore M, Casetti C, Chiasserini C, Ordinas JB (2010) Planning roadside infrastructure for information dissemination in intelligent transportation systems. Comput Commun 33(4):432–442

24. VICS (2017) Official web site of vehicle information and communication system (VICS) Japan

25. Zhu J, Feng Y, Liu B (2013) Pass: parking-lot-assisted carpool over vehicular ad hoc networks. Int J Distrib Sens Netw 9(1):1–9

Chapter 2
Vehicular Networks

Abstract The automotive industry has been incorporating several technological advances in vehicles to improve the safety and experience of drivers and passengers. In general, the systems that have grown out of these advances are based on increasingly sophisticated sensors and actuators, which enable vehicles to detect signals in the environment and pass on information to drivers. For this, communication systems are necessary to allow interactions between different vehicles. Communication systems that rely on vehicles as data transmitters and receivers form a so-called vehicular ad hoc network. Vehicular networks are a type of emerging network. Vehicles that compose these networks possess processing and wireless communication capacity, so they move along streets and highways, sending and receiving information from other vehicles. A vehicle with these capabilities can serve as a monitoring and sensing agent, which can help cities to control transportation and traffic better. This chapter describes the concept of smart connected vehicles, as well as the concept and features of a vehicular network.

2.1 Introduction

Information and communication technology is the driving force behind some of the most important innovations in the automotive industry, as well as society more generally. In the last two decades, mobile communications have changed our lifestyles by allowing the exchange of information, anywhere, anytime [22]. The use of such mobile communication systems in vehicles is expected to be a reality in the coming years, as industries, universities, and governments around the world devote significant resources to the development of safer vehicles and infrastructure for road transport [7].

Automobiles have been incorporating various technological advances that improve the experience of drivers and passengers. Examples include the use of braking systems, sensors capable of detecting and warning drivers of the proximity of other vehicles, and speed alarms. In general, these systems are based on increasingly sophisticated sensors and actuators that enable vehicles to detect signals in the environment and inform their drivers. This technological evolution

© Springer International Publishing AG, part of Springer Nature 2018   23
R. I. Meneguette et al., *Intelligent Transport System in Smart Cities*, Urban
Computing, https://doi.org/10.1007/978-3-319-93332-0_2

is now converging to communication systems that enable interactions between vehicles. The primary objective of these systems is to allow communication of mobile users and provide the necessary conditions for applications with different requirements to be met satisfactorily. Communication systems that have vehicles such as transmitters and data receivers form so-called vehicular ad hoc networks [10].

Vehicular networks are a type of emerging network that rely on vehicles and their embedded intelligent capabilities. The dynamicity of these vehicles in urban environments presents itself as a feature and challenge that allows data propagation and heterogeneous connectivity with different network technologies. These networks differ from traditional networks in many ways. The first difference lies in the nature of the nodes that form them, such as automobiles, trucks, buses, and taxis, as well as equipment attached to roads where they all have wireless communication interfaces. Also, these nodes have high mobility, and their trajectory follows the limits and direction defined by public pathways [2, 9].

Therefore, vehicular networks present many challenges that must be addressed before their large-scale adoption. The high mobility of nodes, the dynamism of scenarios, and the scalability regarding the number of nodes are among the main challenges. The loss of connectivity during data transmission and the reduced time that two nodes stay in contact are other challenges. As a result, to promote proper development of services and applications for these networks, it is necessary to consider not only the requirements of each application but also the conditions and characteristics of vehicular networks.

Other related technologies can help in enabling the connectivity of vehicles and supporting the infrastructure created to provide information and services for these networks. The combination of vehicular networks with other technologies, such as resource management and predictive tools, offers the ability to optimize the mobility of vehicles and people in a city [21]. For instance, new services, such as the detection of hazardous road conditions and calculation of possible detours, can promote safer and more reliable urban mobility. The set of these new services supports intelligent transport systems (ITSs), which aim to optimize the flow of vehicles on the streets of a city and to provide comfort to drivers and passengers during their journey.

This chapter focuses on providing a description of the fundamental aspects of a smart vehicle and a broad definition of a vehicular network, its characteristics, and the technologies involved in such a network. The remainder of this chapter is organized as follows. Section 2.2 introduces and defines a smart vehicle. Section 2.3 presents the concept and characteristics of vehicular networks. Finally, Sect. 2.4 briefly summarizes the chapter.

2.2 Smart Vehicle

Supported by several advancements in technology in recent decades and motivated by a desire to make transportation safer and more comfortable, the automotive industry has designed vehicles with increasing sophistication. These modern, intelligent vehicles are equipped with a series of sensors, several networking interfaces, and a central processing unit for coordinating the execution and communication of applications. The networking is facilitated through wireless communication devices or wireless transceivers, which allow vehicles to establish communication between other elements of the network and transfer information among themselves. These vehicles also come equipped with the Global Positioning System (GPS), which establishes their position and allows for the creation of navigation services. The several different sensors present inside and outside vehicles make it possible to measure various parameters, such as speed, acceleration, and distance from nearby obstacles. Finally, vehicles contain input/output devices to promote fast and intuitive human interactions with their system.

Thus, all these interconnected processing, sensing, and communication capabilities allow for more precise control and for the development of intelligent vehicles capable of monitoring and being aware of both the environment and other vehicles. This intelligence can be vividly illustrated through the implementation of self-driving vehicles on roads and highways. Figure 2.1 shows the complexity of a vehicle through the interconnection between sensors and embedded devices in the interior of an intelligent vehicle.

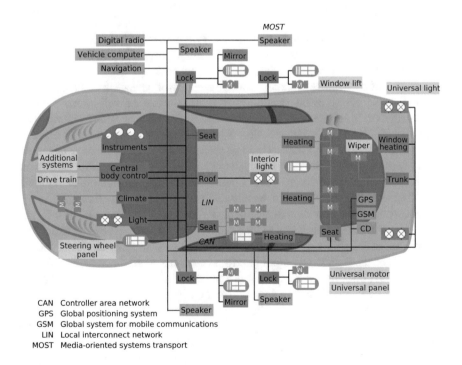

CAN Controller area network
GPS Global positioning system
GSM Global system for mobile communications
LIN Local interconnect network
MOST Media-oriented systems transport

Fig. 2.1 Design of a modern vehicle's network architecture [18]

   These vehicles are composed of an internal communication mechanism called the Controller Area Network (CAN), developed by Bosch [29]. CAN is a robust vehicle bus standard designed to allow microcontrollers and devices to communicate with each other in applications without a host computer. It is a message-based protocol, designed originally for multiplex electrical wiring within automobiles. CAN has a data transmission rate of up to 1 Mbit/s and has an error detection system. A vehicle can contain two or three separate CANs working at different rates of transmission. Thus, it is possible to establish higher transmission rates according to the particular component characteristics; for instance, comfort-related electronics, such as those controlling window movement and seat adjustment, can work at a rate below 125 Kbps. These control applications, which do not depend on device response time, normally use a lower transfer rate to conserve a vehicle's battery lifetime. However, components that rely on fast response, such as antilock brakes and cruise control, have a higher communication rate. As of 2011, a new version of this bus was released that allowed greater flexibility of its components through payloads higher than 8 bytes per frame. This addition to its payloads allowed it to specify the operating modes, such as software download at end-of-line programming.

   Another component embedded in vehicles is the Local Interconnect Network (LIN) bus ([26]), which was developed by the LIN Consortium. The LIN Consortium was founded by five automakers, BMW, Volkswagen Group, Audi Group, Volvo Cars, and Mercedes-Benz, and had the development of technologies supplied through networking and hardware expertise from Volcano Automotive Group and Motorola. The LIN bus is a small and slow network system that is used as a subnetwork of a CAN bus to integrate intelligent sensor devices or actuators.

   FlexRay, developed by the FlexRay Consortium, is another well-known communication system in automobiles [6]. The consortium consists of BMW, Daimler AG, Motorola, Phillips, Bosch, General Motors, and Volkswagen. Its protocol is based on CAN protocols; however, FlexRay has two transmission channels, each with a transmission capacity of 10 Mb/s. FlexRay uses several engine control units (ECUs), but only one communicates at a time; this condition means that the protocol has an emitter ECU and a receiver ECU, which communicate with each other through a bus.

   Thus, these buses and sensors enable the collection of a wide range of information, which ultimately is relevant to the state of vehicles and can be used to perform the sensing and monitoring of the mobility of vehicles in urban contexts. For the abstraction of these data, an output interface called on-board diagnostics (OBD) is used to extract information from sensors embedded in a vehicle. A standard called OBD-II has been established to standardize the connection with this interface and the format of the messages with which these devices need to deal. OBD-II makes it possible to monitor and regulate gas emissions, and it is present in all vehicles produced in Europe and the United States since 1996. The OBD interface also facilitates maintenance services by tracking the origin of mechanical problems [20]. By enabling the storage of engine failure codes, this information provides mechanics with a history of vehicle problems and possible associated sources.

   The combination of sensors from several vehicles, as well as the communication among vehicles and vehicles with an infrastructure of roadblocks, gives rise to an immense set of services and applications not only for the monitoring of urban mobility but also driver comfort. These devices require an efficient connection system. In the following sections, we describe vehicular networks.

2.3 Vehicular Networks

From a definitional perspective, VANETs belong to a subclass of mobile ad hoc networks (MANETs) that, in simple terms, provide a wireless connection among vehicles and between vehicles and roadway devices. These networks have attracted special attention from the research community for the opportunities they provide with respect to connected vehicles and the networks' applicability to vehicles. The benefit of the research in this area is related to two aspects: (1) Communication and automatic partnering between vehicles offer great potential in reducing the number of accidents involving vehicles and (2) some applications can improve passenger comfort in vehicles, buses, and trains, and they can help drivers to travel more efficiently on roads [23].

In a VANET, vehicles communicate with each other through short-range radio and with road infrastructures through short-range radio or any other available wireless technology, such as WiMax, 3G, and LTE. Advances in mobile communications and the current trend in ad hoc networks allow the use of many architectures for vehicular networks in urban, rural, and highway environments to support existing applications. The goal of a VANET architecture is to allow communication between nearby vehicles and between vehicles and fixed devices on the road, leading to three possible scenarios, as shown in Fig. 2.2.

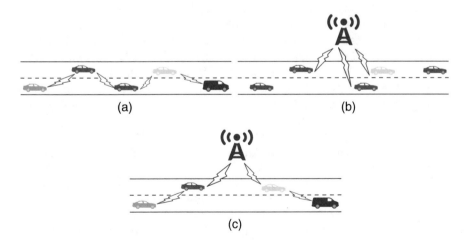

Fig. 2.2 VANET architectures. (**a**) Vehicle-to-vehicle. (**b**) Vehicle-to-infrastructure. (**c**) Hybrid

- **Vehicle-to-vehicle (V2V)** architecture allows for direct communication of vehicles without relying on fixed infrastructure support;
- **Vehicle-to-infrastructure (V2I)** architecture enables a vehicle to communicate with the road infrastructure;
- **Hybrid architecture** combines both V2V and V2I solutions. In this case, a vehicle can communicate with the road infrastructure in a single hop or multiple hops, depending on its location in relation to the point of connection with the infrastructure for different purposes.

In VANETs, vehicles are the network nodes that can be the source or destination of data transmissions, or they can work as network routers [30]. VANETs and MANETs share some similar features, such as low bandwidth, short-range transmission, and omnidirectional broadcast. However, VANETs have some unique characteristics, which are described in what follows.

2.3.1 Characteristics of a Vehicular Network

The development of applications or services for VANETs makes use of proprietary or modified techniques of wireless networks since these networks are different from conventional wireless networks. VANETs not only suffer from rapid changes in their connections but must also deal with diverse types of network densities.

What follows are the characteristics of a VANET and their differences and similarities with a traditional wireless network:

- **Self-Organization**. This feature was inherited from wireless networks, of which vehicular networks are a subclass; it allows a network to self-organize.
- **Mobility**. The nodes of a vehicular network may present a wide range of movement speeds, having high mobility in most situations compared with other wireless networks, for instance, cars that can attain high speeds on highways. However, nodes have limitations in their trajectory; they are restricted to public roads, garages, and highways, for example. Such nodes can move only in places where cars can travel. Unlike conventional wired networks, traditional ones have no geographical limits, and they can be carried anywhere, which means that there are no limitations on the trajectory of their nodes.
- **Transmission Speed**. The speed of transmission in VANETs must be fast. Vehicles can reach a high and inconstant speed and may also travel in opposite directions, which reduces the time of *contact* to only a few seconds to transmit data. Owing to the mobility of their nodes, VANETs suffer from a lack of connectivity, and they needs to deal with different types of network densities [15].
- **Topology**. Even though the location of vehicles follows the layout of streets and roads, again, their relatively high mobility leads to fast changes in topology, which might be challenging to manage.
- **Energy**. In a wireless network (MANET), nodes are limited in power; handheld devices, like smartphones, notebooks, or sensors, are rely entirely on the life

Table 2.1 Comparison of VANETs and traditional wireless networks

Characteristics	VANET	Traditional wireless
Auto-configurable	Yes	Yes
Mobility	Fast, with restrictions	Relatively low, without restriction
Transmissions	Fast, different densities	Relatively low, different densities
Topology	High dynamics	Dynamics
Energy	Constant	Depends on battery
Band	Restricted	Restricted
Fragmentation	Frequent	Random

of their batteries in places where there is no source of electricity [24]. Their computational power is limited because their hardware architecture is restricted. In VANETs, vehicles can rely on relatively ample power/energy, so they can be equipped with significant computational resources [12].

- **Bandwidth**. A node may possess a level of sophistication whereby it can contain hardware to support several wireless devices, making it possible to reach different networks and make use of more powerful communication strategies, such as vertical handoff, to cope with connectivity loss and boost bandwidth.
- **Network Fragmentation**. The fragmentation of a network occurs due to the reach of the communication radius and the high dynamism of vehicles.

While MANETs may experience transient periods of connectivity loss, VANETs might undergo frequent extended periods of disconnection, especially under low urban traffic conditions [13]. Table 2.1 summarily presents a comparison of VANETs and traditional wireless networks.

We can observe from Table 2.1 that there exist significant differences between these networks. Among the differences, some stand out for their more severe consequences with respect to enabling ITS services and applications. As discussed earlier in this chapter, the main differences consist of the movement speed of vehicles, the very short transmission times, and a highly dynamic and frequent network fragmentation.

2.3.2 VANET Applications

Although the initial purpose of VANETs was to promote safer driving conditions, other concerns have also emerged. Current examples of VANET applications are classified into two major classes, as follows [17].

- **Safety**. These applications aim to increase driver safety by disseminating information about accidents or any other information that concerns the safety of drivers and passengers. Perhaps an accident, for instance, has occurred on a certain road or street with respect to a vehicle's location, and traffic conditions are hazardous. This information may help the driver or activate certain traffic signals. An emergency warning system, for example, would notify drivers about the accident.

- **Nonsafety**. Applications in this class focus on passenger comfort, traffic efficiency, and route optimization. Examples include traffic information systems for aiding traffic flow controls and applications that promote interactions between vehicle passengers through entertainment and communication software, such as enabling downloads of songs, chats, and voice messages.

In Chap. 7, we describe in more detail each aspect of vehicular applications and their challenges.

2.3.3 Involved Technologies

In this section, we examine the principal technologies used for the development of communication solutions with VANETs, ranging from the physical layer to the transport layer.

2.3.3.1 Physical Layer

In 1999, the US Federal Communications Commission (FCC) allocated a frequency spectrum for vehicular communication with a shoreline infrastructure, establishing DSRC service and licensing rules in 2003 [5]. DSRC is a communication service that employs a 5.85–5.95 GHz band (5.9 GHz band) of a 75 MHz spectrum, aiming to provide wireless communication capability for transport applications at a distance of up to 1 km [31]. DSRC allows two types of operation modes [25]:

- **Ad hoc mode**, which is characterized by a network of several distributed jumps, typically in communication between vehicles;
- **Infrastructure mode**, which is designated by a centralized, one-hop mobile network. This mode commonly defines communication between a vehicle and a gateway.

The DSRC spectrum is structured in seven channels of 10 MHz, as shown in Fig. 2.3. Channel 178 is the control channel (CCH), which is solely for safety

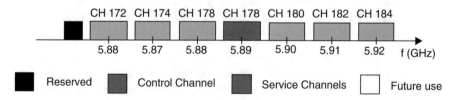

Fig. 2.3 DSRC spectrum allocation for vehicular communications

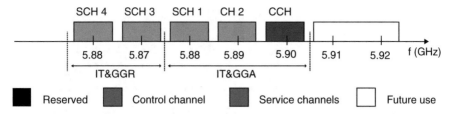

Fig. 2.4 ETSI ITS-G5 spectrum allocation for vehicular communications

communications. Only high-priority short messages and management data are passed through this channel. The two end channels are reserved for particular uses. The other channels are service channels (SCH), and they are available for use in safety and comfort service communications.

The FCC allocated 75 MHz of spectrum in the range of 5.85–5.925 GHz to be used exclusively for V2V or V2I communications. On the other hand, European regulators assigned 50 MHz, which was split into smaller 10 MHz slots. As a result, there are five different channels for the ETSI ITS-G5 [8], as shown in Fig. 2.4. In the European allocation model, three channels (30 MHz) were reserved for road safety, and two channels (20 MHz) are intended for general-purpose ITS services.

The American model is also known as IEEE 802.11p WAVE (Wireless Access in Vehicular Environments), which was standardized by the Institute of Electrical and Electronics Engineers (IEEE) in 2004. This standard is based on the preset standards for wireless LANs and is defined in five documents: IEEE 1609.1, IEEE 1609.2, IEEE 1609.3, IEEE 1609.4, and IEEE 802.11p (IEEE, 2011). The IEEE 802.11p standard defines physical and media access control (MAC) layers for vehicular networks. Also, the WAVE architecture designates a family of patterns that are not restricted to MAC and physical layers, as shown in Fig. 2.5. IEEE 1609 family standards define other layers of the protocol stack. These layers include an alternative network layer to the IP layer, security features for DSRC applications, and multichannel operation of IP layer communication.

The IEEE 1609.1 standard specifies services and interfaces for the resource management application of the WAVE architecture. This pattern synchronizes OBUs and RSUs from a VANET to remain aware of the use of resources, such as memory and processing. This management, which is specified in IEEE 1609.1, aims at the better scheduling of tasks and performance for VANETs.

IEEE 1609.2 defines secure message formats and processing. It also specifies when and how security messages should be processed. Security is provided through issuing and revoking security certificates, as well as employing traditional security tools; for instance, these tools involve the use of a public key infrastructure (PKI), which is also defined by this standard. IEEE 1609.2 also determines a particular type of OBU, public safety OBUs (PSOBUs), which are used in higher-priority government vehicles, such as police and fire department vehicles.

IEEE 1609.3 specifies network and transport layer services, including addressing and routing by defining which stack to use on the logical-link layer (LLC).

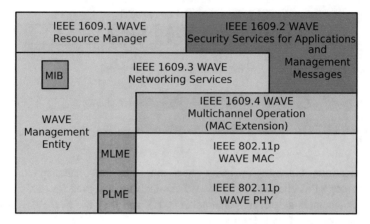

Fig. 2.5   IEEE 1609 (WAVE) reference architecture and its relationship to the IEEE 802.11p MAC and physical layers [11]

The LLC may choose to use the WMP Short Message Protocol (WSMP) or the TCP/IP or UDP/IP stack. In addition, the 1609.3 standard defines the Management Information Base (MIB) for the WAVE stack. This standard is also responsible for setting up and maintaining the system through the management plan. An entity defined by this standard (WME—WAVE Management Entity) is responsible for gathering the information of management entities from other layers, such as the ML Layer Management Entity (MLME) and the Physical Layer Management Entity (PLME). WME implements a broad set of services, such as application registration, WAVE Basic Service Set (WBSS) management, channel usage monitoring, and management database maintenance. In addition to managing the network (IP—version 6) and transport (TCP and UDP) layers, IEEE 1609.3 offers an alternative to using these layers by defining the WSMP. The reason for using this new protocol is that it provides greater efficiency in the WAVE environment, where it is expected that most applications require, among other things, very low latency.

The IEEE 1609.4 standard defines modifications to the IEEE 802.11 standard for multichannel operation. To achieve this operation, the standard defines how switching between channels is done. The classification of packets indicates whether they are switched to the control channel or one of the service channels. The packets also receive forwarding priorities, which are specified by the IEEE 1609.4 standard. IEEE 1609.4 also provides the definition of a time division between channels and synchronization of their respective times in all network devices.

2.3.3.2   Network Layer

Traditionally, the network layer is responsible for addressing (naming network elements), routing (finding good paths), and transmitting (circulating packets in the network) data between the source and destination. Addressing consists of properly naming network elements, routing entails finding useful communication paths, and transmitting data involves effectively circulating packets in the network. In a wireless network, several techniques can be used to carry out addressing of the nodes in the network, but the most relevant strategies for a network are as follows [28]:

- **Fixed Addressing**. Each node has a fixed address assigned by some mechanism at the time the node enters the network. Most applications of ad hoc networks and existing protocols use this addressing technique [28].
- **Geographic Addressing**. Each node is characterized by its geographic position. The address of a node changes every time it moves. Additional attributes can be used to address the node, such as speed, direction, and type of car.

The network layer provides an address mapping service on the network, avoiding an address conflict in the network. The address must be unique for each node, and no two nodes can have the same address.

Another function of the network layer is to provide the best route between the source and the destination so that data are delivered in full and in the shortest possible time. Vehicular networks support different communication paradigms, as shown in Fig. 2.6. These can be categorized as follows:

- Unicast allows communication between two nodes directly, which can be between a vehicle and other vehicles through the dissemination of data using multihop communication. The location of the vehicle that needs to be communicated with must be known in order to carry out this communication.
- Multicast/geocast allows communication between a source with a group of nodes that may or may not be located in a particular area. An example of this would be a vehicle that wants to share its data vehicles, which are delimited in a group that is essentially in a region of interest of the sender vehicle, such as targeting a sporting event or vehicles nearby a risky area.
- Broadcast allows a vehicle to communicate with all its neighbors. Once these neighboring vehicles receive the information, they propagate it to their neighbors. The purpose of this type of communication is to disseminate certain information.

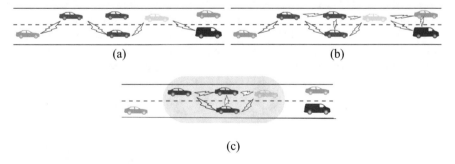

Fig. 2.6 Different communication scenarios in VANETs. (**a**) Unicast communication. (**b**) Broadcast communication. (**c**) Multicast communication

This mechanism is widely used for the discovery of network nodes in routing protocols in order to find the best path between source and destination.

In a vehicular network, routing protocols can be classified in many ways [3, 4, 16]. These protocols are described in both Chap. 4, which details V2I communication, and Chap. 5, which describes V2V communication.

2.3.3.3 Transport Layer

Although the fixed-network TCP can achieve good throughput, its performance in the middle of wireless networks has been shown to be low. This low performance originates from the interpretation TCP gives to packet loss, which is treated as a signal of network congestion. In wireless networks, however, losses can happen for other reasons, such as channel conditions or collisions. As a result of a loss, TCP reduces the size of the congestion window and decreases throughput. Also, owing to the features of VANETs, path symmetry is not guaranteed. Therefore, TCP performance can be further reduced owing to incorrect estimation of round-trip times, resulting in unnecessary retransmissions [4].

A study [14] was conducted to examine the difference in performance between UDP and TCP in VANETs using two real scenarios: interstate highways 80 (I-80) and 5 (I-5) and suburban areas in Sacramento, California. The study has shown that TCP throughput decreases on highways. However, it is more efficient than UDP because TCP source nodes can detect a disconnected receiver and stop transmitting data to intermediate nodes faster than UDP source nodes. Unlike the TCP sending process, where the sender sends some of the data and waits for the receiver to respond before sending additional data to the intermediate nodes, the sender UDP continues to send data to the intermediate nodes regardless of whether or not the receiver is still receiving. In this way, senders can waste the bandwidth of intermediate nodes for a period.

To summarize the performance of TCP and UDP, we can refer to Table 2.2, which demonstrates that these protocols suffer from the high mobility of nodes and the long distances between them. Therefore, vehicular networks can benefit from the development of new transport protocols or changes to existing protocols.

An analysis [27] was carried out to investigate the characteristic paths that are relevant to a transport protocol for a vehicular network. As a follow-up on this study, a vehicle transport protocol (VTP) was developed that observes networks

Table 2.2 Results that evaluated the transport protocols [28]

Works	Number of nodes	MAC	Type of protocol	Speed	Distance	Throughput
Chuang et al.	4	802.11b	TCP	40 km/h	N/A	~ 800 kb/s
Watanabe et al.	3	802.11b	UDP	8–113 km/h	<145 m	500–2300 kb/s
Hui and Mohapatra,	3	802.11g	UDP	<5 km/h	N/A	1–5 Mb/s

and uses statistical data to improve performance when disconnections occur. The Mobile Control Transport Protocol (MCTP) [1] was proposed based on principles similar to those of ad hoc TCP [19]. MCTP aims to provide end-to-end quality of service between a vehicle and an Internet host via a gateway positioned on roadbeds.

All transport protocols proposed for vehicular networks are designed for applications requiring unicast routing [28]. Since many applications require geocast or multicast routing, there is a clear need for new approaches that are not based on traditional transport protocols.

2.4 Final Discussion

In this chapter, we have introduced the concepts of smart vehicle and vehicular networks. We described the major components within a vehicle, in addition to the features and technologies involved in vehicular networks. It is of interest to highlight the main features of VANETs, which also reflect their main challenges: high speed in node mobility and data transfer, frequent network fragmentation, and rapid topology change. The features of VANETs constitute a significant barrier to the development and implementation of applications for these networks, especially when applications require space–time consistency and scalability.

References

1. Bechler M, Jaap S, Wolf L (2005) An optimized TCP for internet access of vehicular ad hoc networks. Springer, Berlin, pp 869–880
2. Boukerche A, Oliveira HA, Nakamura EF, Loureiro AA (2008) Vehicular ad hoc networks: a new challenge for localization-based systems. Comput Commun 31(12):2838–2849
3. Chaqfeh M, Lakas A, Jawhar I (2014) A survey on data dissemination in vehicular ad hoc networks. Veh Commun 1(4):214–225
4. Chen W, Guha RK, Kwon TJ, Lee J, Hsu YY (2011) A survey and challenges in routing and data dissemination in vehicular ad hoc networks. Wirel Commun Mob Comput 11(7):787–795
5. Federal Communications Commission (2017) Dedicated short range communications (DSRC) service
6. FlexRay Consortium (2005) Flexray communications system-protocol specification version 2(1):198–207
7. de Souza AM, Brennand CA, Yokoyama RS, Donato EA, Madeira ER, Villas LA (2017) Traffic management systems: a classification, review, challenges, and future perspectives. Int J Distrib Sens Netw 13(4):1550147716683, 612
8. ETSI (2016) Etsi en 302 571
9. Faezipour M, Nourani M, Saeed A, Addepalli S (2012) Progress and challenges in intelligent vehicle area networks. Commun ACM 55(2):90–100
10. Giang AT, Busson A, Lambert A, Gruyer D (2016) Spatial capacity of IEEE 802.11 p-based VANET: models, simulations, and experimentations. IEEE Trans Veh Technol 65(8):6454–6467
11. Grafling S, Mahonen P, Riihijarvi J (2010) Performance evaluation of IEEE 1609 wave and IEEE 802.11p for vehicular communications. In: Proceedings of the second international conference on ubiquitous and future networks (ICUFN), pp 344–348

12. Hammad AA, Badawy GH, Todd TD, Sayegh AA, Zhao D (2010) Traffic scheduling for energy sustainable vehicular infrastructure. In: Proceedings of the IEEE global telecommunications conference GLOBECOM, pp 1–6
13. Hartenstein H, Laberteaux LP (2008) A tutorial survey on vehicular ad hoc networks. IEEE Commun Mag 46(6):164–171
14. Hui F, Mohapatra P (2005) Experimental characterization of multi-hop communications in vehicular ad hoc network. In: Proceedings of the 2nd ACM international workshop on vehicular ad hoc networks, VANET '05. ACM, New York, pp 85–86
15. Jarupan B, Ekici E (2011) A survey of cross-layer design for VANETS. Ad Hoc Netw 9(5):966–983
16. Kaur N, Singh A (2015) Article: a survey on data dissemination protocols used in VANETS. Int J Comput Appl 120(23):43–50
17. Khekare GS, Sakhare AV (2012) Intelligent traffic system for VANET: a survey. Int J Adv Comput Res 2:99–102
18. Leen G, Heffernan D (2002) Expanding automotive electronic systems. Computer 35(1):88–93
19. Liu J, Singh S (2001) ATCP: TCP for mobile ad hoc networks. IEEE J Sel Areas Commun 19(7):1300–1315
20. Liu Yj, Yao Y, Liu Cx, Chu Lt, Liu X (2012) A remote on-line diagnostic system for vehicles by integrating OBD, GPS and 3G techniques. Springer, Berlin, pp 607–614
21. Meneguette RI (2016) A vehicular cloud-based framework for the intelligent transport management of big cities. Int J Distrib Sens Netw 12(5):8198597
22. Meneguette RI, Boukerche A (2017) Servites: an efficient search and allocation resource protocol based on v2v communication for vehicular cloud. Comput Netw 123:104–118
23. Meneguette RI, Bittencourt LF, Madeira ERM (2013) A seamless flow mobility management architecture for vehicular communication networks. J Commun Netw 15(2):207–216
24. Mohapatra P, Krishnamurthy S (2004) AD HOC NETWORKS: technologies and protocols. Springer, Berlin
25. Nandan A, Das S, Pau G, Gerla M, Sanadidi MY (2005) Co-operative downloading in vehicular ad-hoc wireless networks. In: Proceedings of the second annual conference on wireless on-demand network systems and services, pp 32–41
26. Ruff M (2003) Evolution of local interconnect network (LIN) solutions. In: Proceedings of the IEEE 58th vehicular technology conference, vol 5, pp 3382–3389
27. Schmitz R, Leiggener A, Festag A, Eggert L, Effelsberg W (2006) Analysis of path characteristics and transport protocol design in vehicular ad hoc networks. In: Proceedings of the IEEE 63rd vehicular technology conference, vol 2, pp 528–532
28. Sichitiu ML, Kihl M (2008) Inter-vehicle communication systems: a survey. IEEE Commun Surv Tutorials 10(2):88–105
29. CAN Specification (1991) Bosch. Robert Bosch GmbH, Postfach 50
30. Wang Y, Li F (2009) Vehicular ad hoc networks. In: Misra S, Woungang I, Misra SC (eds) Guide to wireless ad hoc networks, chap 20. Springer, London, pp 503–525
31. Yousefi S, Altman E, El-Azouzi R (2007) Study of connectivity in vehicular ad hoc networks. In: Proceedings of the 5th international symposium on modeling and optimization in mobile, ad hoc and wireless networks and workshops, pp 1–6

Chapter 3
Autonomous Vehicles

Abstract Autonomous vehicles incorporate a large diversity of cutting-edge technologies to enable self-driving capabilities and enhance the experience of drivers and passengers. In general, systems based on these technologies rely on increasingly sophisticated sensors and actuators, which allow vehicles to detect events in the environment, providing their embedded systems with means to infer and make route and navigation decisions and supporting vehicles with greater driving autonomy. Full implementation of self-driving vehicles still involves several concerns related to the implications and threats that minor faults in the system may pose to safety; these faults could cause accidents and place human lives at high risk. Therefore, the design of a standalone vehicle demands significant attention to the safety and reliability of the driving system. These concerns have led the automotive industry to invest heavily in embedded electronic systems to achieve comprehensive safety, comfort, stability, and performance.

3.1 Introduction

Cars without drivers, standalone vehicles, and robotic cars are names given to a type of transport vehicle, for passengers or goods, equipped with a computerized control system. This control system integrates a set of sensors and actuators that, starting from an initial mission established by the user, serve the function of navigating autonomously and safely over streets, roads, and other terrestrial surfaces [5, 29]. The navigation process combines several automated steps to obtain data from the environment, determine the position of the vehicle, avoid collisions with other elements of the environment, and perform optimal actions in terms of the proposed mission [34].

Robotic vehicles originate from two specific segments: intelligent transportation systems (ITSs) and mobile robotics. Unlike other types of autonomous vehicles, a robotic car has the following main requirements. They are designed for the transport of human beings and goods, demonstrating the possibility of large-scale navigation, and can sense, process, and respond to dynamic and static events in the environment within a suitable time frame similar or superior to that of human drivers [28].

© Springer International Publishing AG, part of Springer Nature 2018
R. I. Meneguette et al., *Intelligent Transport System in Smart Cities*, Urban
Computing, https://doi.org/10.1007/978-3-319-93332-0_3

The development of a robotic car involves design requirements that offer high reliability, redundancy, and conservative security. Robotic cars can originate from vehicles initially developed for this purpose or by the integration of sensors, actuators, and control system with a traditional vehicle [3].

In addition to providing drivers with greater safety in adverse critical conditions, vehicle automation can also assist in the driving of vehicles. This assistance involves one or more tasks that can be automated, such as following lanes, maintaining the correct lane, maintaining a safe distance between other vehicles, automatically regulating vehicle speed according to traffic conditions and road features, safely passing and avoiding obstacles, finding the shortest and safest route to a destination, and moving vehicles and parking them in urban environments [30].

The automotive industry has invested heavily in embedded electronic systems in an effort to enhance vehicle safety, comfort, stability, and performance. To assist drivers, several electronic solutions have been developed and incorporated into vehicles in recent decades, such as antilock braking system brakes and electronic stability program stabilization system. These systems act automatically when the vehicle is in extreme conditions, seeking to minimize the occurrence of accidents. A more recent example is the vehicle released by Mercedez, the S500 Intelligent Drive, which is an intelligent vehicle that traveled 100 km without human intervention. This self-driving demonstration involved dealing with traffic circles, traffic jams, traffic signals, and pedestrians. The vehicle was able to react to these different obstacles thanks to a system of cameras, radar, and geolocation [11].

We can conclude that autonomous vehicles have some advantages, such as greater fluidity in traffic and greater safety, comfort, and fuel economy. Also, in this context specifically, we applaud the possibility of sharing access to vehicles by several users as a more sustainable form of transport. Thus, when considering industrial design, particularly automotive design, it needs to be closely aligned with the special concerns associated with urban mobility as a way to contribute to better quality of life and society.

This chapter describes the structure of standalone vehicles, as well as the components that make up these vehicles, describing the main functions of each component. The rest of the chapter is organized as follows. Section 3.2 describes the technology involving autonomous vehicles. Section 3.3 presents the main components required to support autonomous driving. Finally, Sect. 3.6 briefly summarizes the chapter.

3.2   Intelligent Vehicle

The development of a standalone vehicle requires the aggregation several sensors and actuators to allow inference and independent decision making. As a result, the implementation of such vehicles faces a great challenge in the integration of various devices and technologies to allow abstraction of information and data processing. According to Broggi [5], intelligent vehicle applications require the following:

- Position, kinematic, and dynamic state of a vehicle;
- State of environment surrounding vehicle;
- Access to digital maps and satellite data;
- State of driver and occupants;
- Communication with roadside infrastructure or other vehicles.

A technology that meets these requirements is the drive by wire, which represents a new era in transportation [25]. The possibility of driving a vehicle from electronic signals allows the use of embedded computers, which act as pilot or copilot. These processing units assist the driver in emergency situations or perform tasks such as independently driving vehicles or helping drivers to park a vehicle.

The structure of a smart vehicle with drive-by-wire technology consists of a control unit structured in many hierarchical levels of control. These control units are composed of embedded mechatronics systems, which include an entire set of controllers for embedded electromechanical components and driver support systems developed from applied computing solutions.

Mechatronic systems and driver support systems rely on information that is internal and external to the vehicle, captured through specialized sensors. Using the gathered information, these control systems can identify the state of the vehicle and the conditions of the environment surrounding it. In addition, a communication system complements the integration of the control structure as a whole, allowing the exchange of information between the vehicle and remote supervision and control base, as well as communication between vehicles. This structure provides, for example, the automation of transport systems in controlled environments. Through the communication system, vehicles can be informed about the traffic conditions, permitting optimization of traffic.

The human–machine interface between the driver and an automated vehicle also deserves further study. Through drive-by-wire technology, electronic controls enable self-guided vehicles, so there is no need for a conventional interface based on a steering wheel and pedals.

3.2.1 Embedded Mechatronics Systems

Embedded mechatronic systems consist of electromechanical assemblies available in a vehicle that are responsible for specific functions in the operation of a vehicle. In this context, current developments focus on the fuel injection system, brake system, and angular positioning of the steering column. Each of these subsystems is controlled by an electronic unit, which communicates with the others through a network. In the automotive sector, the controller area network (CAN) has been extensively and widely used to support the communication of applications.

CAN comprises a synchronous serial communication protocol that allows inter-communication between several sensors and systems embedded in a vehicle. CAN works based on the multimaster concept, where all systems can become master at one time and slave at another. Messages are exchanged among these systems on a multicast basis, characterized by the sending of any and all messages to all existing systems in the networking system network.

3.2.2 Sensing

When it comes to sensing internal and external vehicular environments, there are three basic groups of sensors: (1) route recognition sensors, (2) object recognition and obstacle sensors, and (3) navigation sensors. These three categories allow the routes traced to be followed safely through markings on the pavement. The principle behind the recognition of markings may be defined using the following terms:

- **Electromagnetic sensing**. This sensing strategy relies on the magnetic field generated by an electric current injected into a cable placed under the driving lane asphalt, which allows to track the presence of a vehicle;
- **Laser sensing**. This sensing depends on lasers bounced in polarized reflecting bands specially attached to the road;
- **Transponders**. These are optomagnetic or electronically placed on the track; they follow the same principle as radio frequency identification systems;
- **Computational vision**. This strategy makes it possible to identify roadway edges visually, which are usually already painted on highways for driver guidance.

Object sensors, such as laser scanners, ultrasound, radar, and stereoscopic vision, allow for the detection of various different obstacles, causing a vehicle to stop or change direction; this sensing enables drivers to avoid collisions, which are the main type of traffic accident involving victims. A reduction of road accidents, with the consequent decrease in the number of victims as a goal, represents one significant contribution that the development of technologies for vehicle automation can make to society. Navigation sensors, such GPS, gyroscope, accelerometers, and wheel speed sensors, ensure in turn the ability of mechatronic systems to infer a given driving context. The hierarchical basis of the control structure allows vehicles to travel in a safe and controlled manner, maintaining their dynamic stability and tracking predetermined trajectories.

3.3 Control

The autonomous navigation of intelligent vehicles requires the joint work of all embedded computational and electromechanical components. All these combined elements generate a complex vehicle automation system with several levels of control.

The vehicle automation system is composed of control solutions of electrome-chanical subsystems. Many of these subsystems are invisible to the driver, such as electronic injection control, automatic transmission, and electrically assisted steering systems.

The task related to the driving of a vehicle is located in the middle of the hierarchical control structure; the human driver currently performs this task, but this function can also be fully automated. In high-value-added cars, cruise control (CC) speed control systems eliminate the driver's need to be concerned about maintaining constant speeds. With the evolution of this system into adaptive cruise control (ACC), where distance sensors are installed in the rear of the vehicle, the onboard computer is also able to adjust the speed according to the traffic conditions.

The top of the control structure contains embedded computing solutions. Of particular note to these solutions, route optimization systems have steadily developed based on digital maps, which determine how a given travel plan is the best route to follow after departure and arrival points are provided. Routes can also be modified dynamically throughout the trip if any obstacles are encountered in the original route. It is worth mentioning the existing efforts to design systems based on operational research and artificial intelligence (AI), which can indicate new dynamically recalculated routes. These routes are adjusted continuously, according to the appearance of fixed or moving obstacles, which are detected by an integrated system of sensors.

Each control subsystem, depending on its hierarchy in the structure, can be classified as a mechatronic solution, closer to the base of the structure, or as a driver support system. There is no well-defined boundary between the two groups since one complements the other.

3.3.1 Architecture

The development of a control system for an autonomous vehicle initially involves the design and implementation of the lower layers of the control pyramid. The development of lower layers subsequently leads to the implementation of a computer system that manages the various components and modules of this system. A computerized control system can involve simpler tasks, which can be managed only by programmable logic controllers (PLCs). However, more complex systems, designed to control the execution of more complex tasks, require a much more sophisticated computational control architecture [27]. The tasks of this control architecture may involve several abilities:

- Reading and interpreting signals received from vehicle sensors;
- Avoiding obstacles present in the path of the vehicle;
- Reacting to events, including unexpected ones, such as the sudden appearance of mobile obstacles;
- Planning trajectories and performing tasks, such as defining routes from point A to point B without reference to a map of the surroundings;
- Managing the various components of the system to generate commands in the proper order and with the correct parameters so that the planned task can be executed;

- Ensuring the correct positioning of a vehicle;
- Performing a mapping of the surroundings by creating a sketch that represents "memories" of the paths explored;
- Learning about the environment and how to interact with it, adapting when new knowledge is acquired;
- Communicating, interacting, and even cooperating with other computing devices;
- Providing strategies to implement fault-sensing and fault-tolerance when identifying and compensating for localized defects in vehicles' components.

A computational control system must, therefore, perform such tasks as preserving the integrity of a vehicle, conserving the integrity of the objects and entities present in the environment where the vehicle is operating, and identifying solutions for the execution of tasks. This control system, in some cases, even needs to interact with other systems to better plan task execution. The features of such a control system prompt us to study techniques in the field of AI, especially control techniques of so-called autonomous artificial agents and multiagent systems. Some techniques and concepts related to autonomous robotics have been reused in the implementation of AI agents, and vice versa. The main aspects addressed in this chapter relate to perception, reasoning, and action, where the communication aspect appears in a complementary role.

The computational architectures of autonomous vehicle controls are very diverse; this diversity is illustrated by the vast number of existing approaches already proposed and found in the literature [10, 15]. However, some of the approaches describe architectures that have become known and recognized for their characteristics and potentialities, as follows:

- **Reactive control** consists of a sensorimotor reaction system. This type of control is usually the simplest to implement, not requiring many computational resources for its implementation. In reactive control, there is a loop for (1) reading the sensors, (2) immediately processing the information, and (3) generating a response command to the actuators. Usually, a reactive control scheme considers only the sensorial readings performed in the present for purposes of decision making and the generation of action commands [9]. A reactive system is very useful for implementing behaviors, such as avoiding collision.
- **Cognitive control** encompasses the application of a mechanism of action planning. Thus, a previous plan of execution of a sequence of actions can be established based on the knowledge that the system has for a problem to be solved. The deliberative control assumes the existence of a process of high-level reasoning and decision making, usually more complex to implement than reactive control. This process allows actions to be planned in order to handle and perform tasks that require a more sophisticated level of control. These tasks might be the definition of plottings and execution of tasks for moving from one point to another in one's environment by looking at a map. However, pure deliberative control has limitations in the face of unforeseen events, such as an obstacle blocking access to a given route [15]. In this case, pure deliberative control

has a difficult time reacting to a new environmental configuration that had been unforeseen in the initial planning. Ideally, a control system should demonstrate the reactive capabilities of a reactive system, with the ability to plan and execute the complex tasks of a deliberative system, combining reactive and deliberative features in a hierarchical/hybrid system.

- **Hierarchical/hybrid control** consists of combining multiple reactive and deliberative control modules in layers arranged such that they can operate in a hierarchical or parallel fashion. The combination of the different control modules leads to the adoption of a prioritization scheme regarding the multiple layers of the system, where these control systems are commonly found and classified as hierarchical systems with vertical and horizontal decompositions [10]. Hierarchical/hybrid systems have the advantage of being able to combine behaviors acquired from their different modules to produce a more robust behavior and more complex task execution. Hybrid control is implemented through a series of modules that operate in parallel and communicate with each other.

3.3.2 Subsystem

The control of a vehicle must first be separated into two parts. The first part is responsible for speed control, while the second controls lateral deviations. The speed control for vehicles equipped with an internal combustion engine and brakes is based on the structure of the ACC stop-and-go system developed and presented in [20]. This subsystem is divided into two branches, one for accelerating and the other for bringing the vehicle to a stop. Each branch has particular features that are integrated into the mathematical model of the vehicle.

An acceleration branch plant is composed of an injection system, an internal combustion engine coupled to the clutch, and the longitudinal dynamics of the vehicle. The injection system may be represented by a second-order element, while the motor and clutch are respectively represented by a time-delay-proportional element PT1 and a nonlinear element of the dead-zone type. Although the motor also has a nonlinear characteristic curve, only the controller design affects the simplification presented here. A PT1 element can also simplify the longitudinal dynamics of the vehicle. An extra branch containing the characteristic curve of the motor can be added in a feedforward structure to increase the dynamics of the control system. The extra branch, in turn, serves to alleviate the work of the closed-loop controller, ensuring a faster response of the system as a whole.

The brake branch plant is composed of an electromechanical actuator with indirect torque control, the mechanical components of the brake system, and the characteristic braking curve of the vehicle. The mathematical model used for the development of the motion controller side of the vehicle is usually based on the "bicycle model" [20]. Among the different controller structures used for the lateral control of the vehicle, solutions involving classical controllers of the PID family, as well as control structures in cascade or nonlinear control, stand out [19].

Considering the influence of the speed value on the dynamic behavior of a vehicle, the use of adaptive controllers or other modern control techniques is necessary for situations where speed varies significantly. Similarly, systems based on AI can also be used to ensure better operating conditions and vehicle performance [15].

For control of vehicles by train, it is vital to ensure a fixed distance between vehicles. Thus, it is necessary to use an extra controller cascaded with the speed controller. The distance between vehicles can be obtained, for example, from the detection of color-coded markings placed on the front car, and this distance information is then sent to the controller. The system, in turn, sends to the speed controller information about an increase or decrease in its reference value. Likewise, the adopted computer vision system also allows the detection of lateral displacement between vehicles. This information is then sent to the lateral distance controllers, which ensure the alignment of the vehicles on the train.

3.4 Trajectory Planning

The planning of a route involves specifying a trajectory joining two points: origin A to destination B. The planning component is of great importance within a computer system of control of autonomous vehicles. The trajectory planning algorithm must take into account the map, presence of vehicles in road segments, and other available information to define a path to be covered by the vehicle.

Several works have proposed various algorithms to facilitate the planning of trajectories; the best known include [23] search in graphs, Algorithm A*, search based on potential fields, and vector fields. The application of these algorithms usually depends on the type of representation of the given environment and questions related to the performance requirements associated with the complexity of the search for a solution to the trajectory problem.

Existing navigation algorithms are highly dependent on the correct identification and estimation of the current position of vehicles. This dependency is even more evident when starting the control of vehicle displacement based on a particular trajectory. The complexity in determining the navigation relies on the relative positioning of vehicles concerning the map of the environment and its position to the specified trajectory. The navigation commands are generated in the form of a sequence of actions, which allow the vehicle to travel the specified path. Thus, errors in a vehicle's positioning and orientation may imply severe problems in performing the driving task. Because of this, in navigation tasks where there is a prespecified route, it is very important that the robot have a mechanism to guarantee that the estimate of its current position can be maintained. In addition, the robot control system must be sufficiently robust, so it can get passed unforeseen situations, usually represented by the presence of unexpected obstacles in its trajectory.

3.5 Computer Vision

In this section, the application of computer vision techniques in driver support systems and autonomous navigation is addressed. The section focuses on applications developed with the aim of supporting commercial intelligent vehicles; however, the concepts covered in this section can be extended to the navigation of mobile robots in general. Although stationary cameras are also used in traffic monitoring systems and driver support systems [18], this section includes applications that use cameras and other sensors embedded in the vehicle. Track monitoring involves the use of monocular vision through a camera installed inside the vehicle and aligned with its central axis. Stereo vision also enables track monitoring through two cameras positioned on the sides of the vehicle. Stereo vision provides a more significant amount of information because it introduces the notion of depth. However, the synchronization of the cameras adds complexities. Another issue to consider is the use of color or monochrome cameras: color images contain more information than grayscale images, but their processing takes longer.

In the analysis of video sequences obtained from embedded cameras, certain factors hinder proper tracking:

- **Painting Failures**. Many highways have paint that has worn out, making it difficult to determine the boundaries of the road;
- **Shadows**. Trees, buildings, bridges, and vehicles project shadows on a highway and on other vehicles, changing the highway's intensity and texture;
- **Solar Position**. Solar orientation can cause saturation in the image captured by a camera or cause specular reflections;
- **Occlusion**. Vehicles traveling on the same highway may partially or completely occlude a camera's view;
- **Climate Conditions**. Natural phenomena can significantly degrade the quality of acquired images.

The following discussion details the problems of track output detection, obstacle detection, traffic signal detection and recognition, and standalone navigation. For each of these problems, the most appropriate type of camera and how many should be set up is discussed.

3.5.1 Track Output Detection

An important problem in the context of driver support systems is the development of track exit detection systems. The main purpose of such systems is to monitor the position of a vehicle relative to roadway edges and to notify if the vehicle exhibits roadway output tendencies. Early detection of roadway intersections is critical for bus and truck drivers, who drive long-distance trips and at night, with a high possibility of drowsiness at the wheel.

A prerequisite for track exit detection is the robust identification of roadway edges. In the vast majority of applications involving intelligent vehicles, this means detecting the paint that marks the edges of the scrolling track. Some techniques use colored cameras for track detection [33], but the vast majority of techniques recently proposed use monochrome images. One reason for this is that lane paint is usually white, and the cost of processing colored images does not compensate for the gain introduced by color information. Some authors opt for the use of stereo vision [4]; however, the use of only one camera has been the most commonly used option in the majority of roadway edge detection techniques, since the notion of depth does not add relevant information to this problem.

Several approaches have been proposed in the literature. Among the most common hypotheses used to obtain the boundaries of roadway, the following may be highlighted [4]:

- **Road Geometry**. The formulation of a mathematical model of the expected geometry of a road results in robust models with respect to artifacts in images but may be less flexible for applications on highways with different structures;
- **Focus of Attention**. The analysis of a small portion of an image reduces computational costs, but the choice of the region of interest can be a hindering factor.

Several authors have explored the aforementioned features and used a wide variety of image processing and computer vision tools for track detection.

Kluge [22] proposed a technique to estimate the orientation and curvature of roads based on detected edges, without having to group them by contour. Such a solution works well when up to 50% of edge pixels are affected by noise, which may not occur in many practical situations.

Another class of track detectors [21] uses a bird's-eye view obtained from the reverse perspective. Such techniques work with world coordinates and provide a robust estimate of the contours of a track. However, there is an additional computational cost for the reverse perspective calculation for all frames of an image sequence, on top of the need to calibrate the camera. Several models of roadway boundaries have been and are being proposed in the literature [31, 35, 37]. These techniques assume that the track has a specific geometric characteristic, and mathematical curves are adjusted to the acquired images. In general, curves with a higher number of degrees of freedom are more malleable but also more sensitive to noise. On the other hand, simpler curves do not provide such an accurate fit but are more robust to the presence of noise/artifacts. The great advantage of using a smooth curve model to segment lanes is that it makes it possible to quickly obtain information about the orientation and curvature of a lane. Such information is crucial in the development of a track exit detection system. Jung and Kelber [17] proposed a linear parabolic model for roadway boundaries. The linear part of the model is used in the field of view near the camera, and the parabolic part fits the farthest region. Such a model combines the flexibility of a quadratic model with the robustness of a linear model.

For the detection of roadway output, information about the position and orientation of a vehicle relative to the center of the roadway and its edges is required. This analysis can be performed in world coordinates or image coordinates. The use of world coordinates provides information about displacement and actual vehicle orientations, which can be quantified at distances or angles; however, calibration of the camera is required to obtain such coordinates. On the other hand, using only the image coordinates does not require a priori knowledge about the camera's type/position. Some roadway detection techniques are discussed briefly in what follows.

A track exit detection system proposed in [24] estimated the orientation of roadway edges using an edge distribution function. Guidance changes are used to calculate the deviation from the center of the roadway. Although this technique works satisfactorily for well-painted roads, the orientation estimate can fail if the paint is of low quality and the paint marks are spaced. A modification was proposed in [13] to introduce an edge pixel extractor and increase the robustness of the technique. However, failures can still occur in curves, since a linear contour model is used.

Some works [36] use radar, vision, and laser sensors to detect lane changes. Clearly, this is an economically unviable solution given the high cost of laser sensors. Other works [16] use a linear parabolic track model and the guidance provided by the linear part to obtain a track deviation metric. When this metric exceeds a certain threshold, an output track is issued.

Currently, some commercial vehicles already incorporate track exit detection systems. For example, the Citroën C5 has infrared sensors on the lower side of its bumpers that inform the driver if the vehicle is crossing a track marking. This system is relatively simple and alerts drivers when they are already effectively crossing road markings.

3.5.2 Obstacle Detection

A frequent type of traffic accident is a collision between a vehicle and a pedestrian. In this scenario, object tracking systems can be used to detect objects that could be on a collision course with a vehicle, alerting the driver. Although some techniques deal with the obstacle detection problem generically, most authors focus on the detection and tracking of specific objects, taking into account particular geometric characteristics of the object of interest. It should also be noted that the autonomous navigation of robots in unstructured environments is characterized as an obstacle that could disrupt the movement of the robot.

Among the most popular approaches to the detection of obstacles, some stand out [4]:

- **Static Image Analysis**. This technique normally enables fast processing and is independent of vehicle movement; on the other hand, it does not exploit temporal continuity in the movement of an obstacle;
- **Optical Flow**. This strategy allows the detection of generic obstacles and the calculation of relative speeds but usually carries a high computational cost and is sensitive to vehicle movements and camera calibration;
- **Stereo Vision**. This technique introduces the notion of depth, allowing the reconstruction of 3D objects; however, it comes with a high computational cost and is sensitive to camera parameters;
- **Recognition of Objects by Form**. A priori knowledge of the shape of objects to be detected usually entails more robust detection, with few false positives; on the other hand, model-based techniques are rather generic.

In addition, other sensors such as radar and lasers can be combined with visual information; such sensors have the advantage of providing information on the distance of detected objects. On the other hand, the introduction of other sensors has an associated financial cost, besides the difficulty and computational cost of performing the data fusion. Next, some computer vision techniques for obstacle detection are briefly described.

Some works [1, 32] assume a road model and are based on this model to detect possible obstacles. The technique in [32] uses a probabilistic model to detect structures outside this plane that are considered potential obstacles. The method in [1] uses a homogenous formulation for the flow of pixels between consecutive frames, detecting objects off the road plane. Such techniques encounter limitations in slopes. An algorithm based on monocular vision for the detection of obstacles [6] uses a Kalman filter for the tracking of objects; the technique employs a three-dimensional geometric model of the road to obtain the distance to the detected object.

Another work [8] also used monocular vision for obstacle detection. In this approach, the movement of the road relative to the vehicle is calculated through the wavelet transform, and regions with different movement patterns are detected statistically. Although fast, the proposed method does not allow for estimates of distance and velocity in world coordinates. A system for the detection of pedestrians based on stereo vision [14] has been developed based on depth mapping. A depth map is initially calculated, and form search algorithms are used to detect pedestrians. Finally, a bounding box of each pedestrian is used for tracking over time.

The problem of obstacle detection has also been addressed by private companies.

3.5.3 Detection and Recognition of Traffic Signals

Another desirable feature of driver support systems is the inclusion of techniques to enable the detection and recognition of traffic signals. Such techniques allow traffic signs to be observed continuously, informing drivers about the signs in a timely manner, thereby allowing them to follow all driving regulations and adjust to road conditions. To implement such a feature, two steps are required:

- **Detection**. In this step, traffic signals are segmented and isolated from the bottom of an image;
- **Recognition**. In this step, previously segmented traffic signals are recognized, usually through a search in an existing database.

In the context of traffic signal detection, color information plays a key role. For instance, the National Department of Roads (DNER) of Brazil divides Brazilian traffic signs into six classes: warning, educational, name, work, regulatory, and auxiliary service. In general, these signs have a specific color, geometry, and sizes.

Although we do not know whether a detection and recognition system exists for Brazilian traffic signals, several researchers around the world have been proposing solutions to this problem, exploring information, such as color and geometry contextualized for the signaling rules of their respective countries. For the analysis of chromatic information, several color spaces have already been used.

The problem of detecting traffic signals may be seen as a particular case of the problem of obstacle detection, where the search region is a neighborhood on the sides of roadway boundaries. Although a priori knowledge of the color and geometry of traffic signals facilitates detection and recognition processes, the following factors are present in urban and road environments:

- Differences in lighting due to solar position and shadows must be taken into account in the chromatic analysis of images;
- Differences in the angle of view and distance between the camera and traffic signs change the geometry and the expected scale of the board in a projected image.

An additional issue in the detection of traffic signals is the degradation or poor preservation of traffic signals on national highways. Road signs may have paint that is worn out or be faded, rusted, or scratched. With that in mind, we briefly describe some techniques proposed by researchers from various countries for the detection and recognition of traffic signals.

Fang et al. [12] studied the problem of detection and tracking of traffic signals in video sequences. Initially, two neural networks are applied, for color features and shapes, and used for the detection of traffic signs. In subsequent frames of the video, a Kalman filter is used to track the detected traffic signals. The results presented by the authors demonstrated efficient detection and tracking under different lighting conditions and climatic conditions.

Barnes and Zelinsky [2] developed a technique for the rapid detection and recognition of traffic signals. They explored the radial symmetry of traffic signs for gray-scale segmentation and used normalized cross correlation in each chromatic channel in the recognition phase. Although this technique is indeed fast, it is quite limited because it assumes a circular shape of traffic signs.

3.5.4   Visual Navigation

Visual navigation systems usually consist of an image base, which is a sequence of images captured at regular intervals that describe the path to be covered. This sequence can be "annotated," which may include the association of actions to be performed when a certain position is reached. This sequence is the vehicle's so-called path memory. The navigation process starts by capturing an image from the vehicle's camera. Then it identifies which image in the image base most closely resembles the captured image (or the current image can also be considered an initial image as the starting point). A comparison of the image captured by the vehicle and the current image allows the vehicle to determine what command to execute. This command causes the vehicle to rotate or to move forward until both images are correctly framed. After position and orientation adjustments are made, the vehicle executes the command associated with the current reference image or simply continues advancing. As the vehicle reaches the target, the current image is changed by the next image from the image base, and the whole process is repeated. Usually, the comparison of the image captured by the robot and current image base images is done using techniques such as normalized cross correlation [7].

This technique has been enhanced continuously for use in omnidirectional vision systems. Such systems guarantee an additional amount of information and references on the current position of the robot and allow paths to be navigated in both directions, that is, a round trip, using only a single sequence of images [26].

3.6   Final Discussion

In this chapter, we have introduced the concept of the autonomous car and described its main components. We described how computer vision methods, as well as the aggregation of multiple sensors, can help to abstract information, inferences, and decision making based on the response to the information. Such methods allow vehicles to be self-driving or assist the driver in various everyday tasks, such as parking a car, maintaining constant speed, and other functions.

References

1. Alix R, Le Coat F, Aubert D (2003) Flat world homography for non-flat world on-road obstacle detection. In: Proceedings of the IEEE intelligent vehicles symposium. IEEE, Piscataway, pp 310–315
2. Barnes N, Zelinsky A (2004) Real-time radial symmetry for speed sign detection. In: Proceedings of the IEEE intelligent vehicles symposium. IEEE, Piscataway, pp 566–571
3. Benenson R (2008) Perception pour véhicule urbain sans conducteur: conception et implementation. PhD thesis, Tese (Doutorado)-École des Mines de Paris, Paris Tech, Paris

4. Bertozzi M, Broggi A, Cellario M, Fascioli A, Lombardi P, Porta M (2002) Artificial vision in road vehicles. Proc IEEE 90(7):1258–1271
5. Broggi A, Zelinsky A, Özgüner Ü, Laugier C (2016) Intelligent vehicles. Springer, Cham, pp 1627–1656
6. Chuanjin L, Xiaohu Q, Xiyue H, Yi C, Xin Z (2003) A monocular-vision-based driver assistance system for collision avoidance. In: Proceedings of the IEEE intelligent transportation systems, vol 1. IEEE, Piscataway, pp 463–468
7. Crowley J, Martin J (1995) Experimental comparison of correlation techniques. In: Proceedings of the international conference on intelligent autonomous systems
8. Demonceaux C, Kachi-Akkouche D (2004) Robust obstacle detection with monocular vision based on motion analysis. In: Proceedings of the IEEE intelligent vehicles symposium. IEEE, Piscataway, pp 527–532
9. dos Santos CT, Osório FS (2004) An intelligent and adaptive virtual environment and its application in distance learning. In: Proceedings of the working conference on advanced visual interfaces. ACM, New York, pp 362–365
10. Dudek G, Jenkin M (2010) Computational principles of mobile robotics. Cambridge University Press, Cambridge
11. Ziegler J, Lategahn H, Schreiber M, Keller CG, Knöppel C, Hipp J, Haueis M, Stiller C (2014) Video based localization for Bertha. In: Proceedings of the IEEE intelligent vehicles symposium proceedings. IEEE, Dearborn, MI, pp 1231–1238
12. Fang CY, Chen SW, Fuh CS (2003) Road-sign detection and tracking. IEEE Trans Veh Technol 52(5):1329–1341
13. Fardi B, Scheunert U, Cramer H, Wanielik G (2003) A new approach for lane departure identification. In: Proceedings of the IEEE intelligent vehicles symposium. IEEE, Piscataway, pp 100–105
14. Gavrila DM, Giebel J, Munder S (2004) Vision-based pedestrian detection: the protector system. In: Proceedings of the IEEE intelligent vehicles symposium. IEEE, Piscataway, pp 13–18
15. Heinen FJ, Osório FS (2002) Hycar-a robust hybrid control architecture for autonomous robots. In: Proceedings of the HIS, pp 830–842
16. Jung CR, Kelber CR (2004) A lane departure warning system based on a linear-parabolic lane model. In: Proceedings of the intelligent vehicles symposium. IEEE, Piscataway, pp 891–895
17. Jung CR, Kelber CR (2004) A robust linear-parabolic model for lane following. In: Proceedings of the Brazilian symposium on computer graphics and image processing. IEEE, Piscataway, pp 72–79
18. Kastrinaki V, Zervakis M, Kalaitzakis K (2003) A survey of video processing techniques for traffic applications. Image Vis Comput 21(4):359–381
19. Kelber CR, Dreger RS, Schirmbeck J, Borges DA (2002) Nonlinear steering control strategy for an optical stripe tracker. In: Proceedings of the 7th international workshop on advanced motion control. IEEE, Piscataway, pp 546–550
20. Kelber CR, Webber W, Gomes GK, Lohmann MA, Rodrigues MS, Ledur D (2004) Active steering unit with integrated ACC for x-by-wire vehicles using a joystick as HMI. In: Proceedings of the IEEE intelligent vehicles symposium. IEEE, Piscataway, pp 173–177
21. Klette R (2015) Vision-based driver assistance. In: Wiley encyclopedia of electrical and electronics engineering. Wiley, Hoboken
22. Kluge K (1994) Extracting road curvature and orientation from image edge points without perceptual grouping into features. In: Proceedings of the intelligent vehicles symposium. IEEE, Piscataway, pp 109–114
23. Latombe JC (2012) Robot motion planning, vol 124. Springer, Berlin
24. Lee JW (2002) A machine vision system for lane-departure detection. Comput Vis Image Underst 86(1):52–78
25. Linfeng L, Hai W, Ping H, Huifang K, Ming Y, Canghua J, Zhihong M (2017) Robust chattering-free sliding mode control of electronic throttle systems in drive-by-wire vehicles. In: Proceedings of the 36th Chinese control conference, pp 9513–9518

26. Matsumoto Y, Ikeda K, Inaba M, Inoue H (1999) Visual navigation using omnidirectional view sequence. In: Proceedings of the IEEE/RSJ international conference on intelligent robots and systems. IEEE, Piscataway, vol 1, pp 317–322
27. Medeiros AA (1998) A survey of control architectures for autonomous mobile robots. J Braz Comput Soc 4(3). http://dx.doi.org/10.1590/S0104-65001998000100004
28. Meneguette RI, Boukerche A, Pimenta AHM, Meneguette M (2017) A resource allocation scheme based on Semi-Markov Decision Process for dynamic vehicular clouds. In: Proceedings of the IEEE international conference on communications, pp 1–6
29. Ozguner U, Stiller C, Redmill K (2007) Systems for safety and autonomous behavior in cars: the DARPA grand challenge experience. Proc IEEE 95(2):397–412
30. Paden B, Cap M, Yong SZ, Yershov D, Frazzoli E (2016) A survey of motion planning and control techniques for self-driving urban vehicles. IEEE Trans Intell Veh 1(1):33–55
31. Risack R, Mohler N, Enkelmann W (2000) A video-based lane keeping assistant. In: Proceedings of the IEEE intelligent vehicles symposium. IEEE, Piscataway, pp 356–361
32. Stein GP, Mano O, Shashua A (2000) A robust method for computing vehicle ego-motion. In: Proceedings of the IEEE intelligent vehicles symposium. IEEE, Piscataway, pp 362–368
33. Thorpe C, Hebert MH, Kanade T, Shafer SA (1988) Vision and navigation for the Carnegie-Mellon Navlab. IEEE Trans Pattern Anal Mach Intell 10(3):362–373
34. Vis IF (2006) Survey of research in the design and control of automated guided vehicle systems. Eur J Oper Res 170(3):677–709
35. Wang Y, Shen D, Teoh EK (2000) Lane detection using spline model. Pattern Recogn Lett 21(8):677–689
36. Weiss K, Kaempchen N, Kirchner A (2004) Multiple-model tracking for the detection of lane change maneuvers. In: Proceedings of the IEEE intelligent vehicles symposium. IEEE, Piscataway, pp 937–942
37. Yue Wang EKT, Shen D (2004) Lane detection and tracking using b-snake, image and vision computer. Image Vis Comput 22:269–280

Chapter 4
Vehicle-to-Infrastructure Communication

Abstract Vehicular ad hoc networks (VANETs) provide applications that focus on driver safety, traffic efficiency of vehicles on public roads, and the comfort and entertainment of passengers throughout their journey. Some of these applications require connections to the Internet via an access point (AP) at roadsides, such as a cell tower or Wi-Fi tower. A connection can generate an overhead of control messages and could suffer a change of AP that would impact application performance. Besides the interface connected to APs, vehicles are equipped with other network interfaces linked to various different technologies. Thus, a vehicular application can take advantage of the simultaneous use of these various network interfaces, thereby maximizing throughput and reducing latency. However, these additional interfaces can also serve as a connection to the APs located at roadsides. These multiple connections further increase the overhead of control messages and the time of change from one AP to another, thereby affecting the network throughput and, consequently, application performance. This chapter describes techniques and architectures that manage the communication among APs and vehicles to allow heterogeneous communications among several network technologies, such as wireless networks and cellular technology, reducing the impact of communication overhead on networks.

4.1 Introduction

Some of the applications of vehicular networks require a connection to the Internet through an AP that is on roadsides, like a cellular tower. The connection may lead to an overload of control messages and undergo an AP change, which could impact application performance. The simultaneous use of different interfaces can drastically improve the performance of applications. Assuming that a vehicle contains multiple network interfaces linked to different networking technologies, the vehicle can connect to different domains and access networks. Although these vehicles can connect to several network technologies simultaneously, modern vehicles are limited to choosing a standard interface for sending and receiving information. This limitation is related to the current management model of multiple interfaces, where

© Springer International Publishing AG, part of Springer Nature 2018   53
R. I. Meneguette et al., *Intelligent Transport System in Smart Cities*, Urban Computing, https://doi.org/10.1007/978-3-319-93332-0_4

the operating system accesses several interfaces [37]. Usually, operating systems employ user configuration files or are based on application type to select a default network interface to send and receive data [21].

To allow the use of more than one network interface at the same time, the Internet Engineering Task Force (IETF) has developed the technology of IP flow mobility, which can divide IP flows among multiple links according to application requirements and user preferences. Some groups of the IETF, such as the IETF mobility extensions for IPv6 (MEXT) [35] and IETF-based network mobility extensions (NETEXT) [3], have been working on the development and elaboration of a protocol that allows for the use of more than one interface concurrently. The MEXT has standardized a host-based IP flow mobility in Mobile IPv6, enabling flow bindings for mobile nodes (MNs) with multiple interfaces [35]. This method has an air resource waste problem, such as establishing IP-in-IP bidirectional tunnel over-the-air interface, exchanging mobility-related layer 3 (L3), and signaling messages via a wireless link [14]. To avoid overloading the wireless network, NETEXT has discussed the use of a network-based IP flow mobility in Proxy Mobile IPv6 (PMIPv6). This solution has a limitation in that the flow mobility of MNs should be initiated and controlled only by network-side entities [14].

Nowadays another way to manage communications between vehicles and a shoreline infrastructure is through architectures based on software-defined networking (SDN). SDN [22, 28] is an emerging network management paradigm that involves separating control decisions from the actual forwarding hardware in a move aiming to simplify the management of such networks and open them up to innovation [8]. This technology brings greater flexibility and programmability for the management not only of vehicle mobility but also services and applications for vehicular networks.

This chapter describes techniques and architectures that manage communications between APs and vehicles to allow heterogeneous communication between several network technologies, such as wireless networks and cellular technology, thereby reducing the impact of this communication on networks. The rest of this chapter is organized as follows. Section 4.2 describes the concept of vehicular-to-infrastructure (V2I) communication. Section 4.2.2 introduces the basic SDN architecture and the concepts that involve this architecture and discusses the main challenges and issues for potential future studies. Section 4.2.1 presents the mobility manager methods, protocols, and techniques that can be used to address the mobility manager; the section also discusses the main challenges and issues for future studies. Finally, Sect. 4.3 briefly summarizes the chapter.

4.2 Vehicle-to-Infrastructure Communication Concepts

The aim of V2I communication is to carry out communication between vehicles and a shoreline infrastructure, which can be cellular or wireless antennae. This communication seeks to provide connectivity to the Internet and enable services

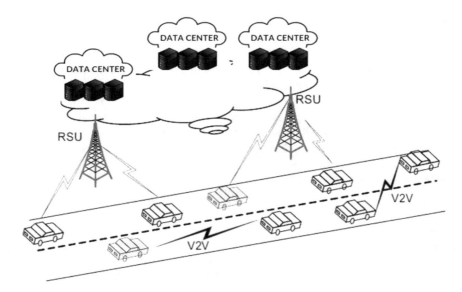

Fig. 4.1 V2I communication

and applications from data centers, the cloud, and other sources to vehicles [25]. Therefore, to establish such communication, a set of mechanisms must be designed to manage the mobility of vehicles, such as the exchange of vehicles from one AP to another without the user noticing the change. Also, the communication must deal with data flow and the management of data streams transmitted through the network. Figure 4.1 provides a general illustration of the described existing V2I communication scenarios.

What follows is a description of the mechanisms and technologies that assist in the management of mobility and control of traffic between roadside units (RSUs) and vehicles that travel in urban environments.

4.2.1 Mobility Management

Mobility management has two main components [2]: location management and handoff management. Location management allows a system to track the location of MNs among different APs where the nodes have been connected along their path. Handoff management enables mobile devices to switch networks while keeping the connection active.

In next-generation systems, two types of roaming exist for mobile devices: intrasystem (intradomain) and intersystem (interdomain). Intrasystem roaming happens in the movement of devices between different cells of the same system. The management techniques for intrasystem mobility are based on the same protocols and network interfaces. Intersystem roaming occurs in the movement of devices between different backbones, protocols, and technologies. Consequently, the condition of having intra- or intersystem roaming characterizes handoff and localization, meaning roaming can classify the type of mobility management in intra- or inter-handoff management and intra- or inter-system localization management [1].

Due to the heterogeneity of the protocols and technologies involved, the handoff of intersystem management presents a level of complexity that is much higher than intrasystem management. Several works in the literature proposed by researchers advocate implementation at different layers of the TCP/IP protocol stack. The possible alternatives are implementations at application layers, networks, links, and cross layers [1, 32].

4.2.1.1   Handoff

When a vehicle connected to an AP moves away from the AP coverage area, the signal level of the device undergoes degradation. When approaching another AP with a stronger signal level, a mechanism in the network is required to maintain the state of connection of the device, transferring responsibility for the communication to the new AP. This mechanism that transfers the communication of a device from one AP to another is known as handoff.

Also, an agent located on the user's device can decide to perform a handoff based on well-defined policies, such as bandwidth, cost, security, network coverage, quality of service (QoS), or even user preferences [26].

There are three types of handoff. Handoffs that occur between APs to the same technology are called horizontal handoffs. Handoffs that occur between APs belonging to different networks, such as Wi-Fi for 3G, are called vertical handoffs. Thus, a vertical handoff allows the transfer between heterogeneous cells of access networks that differ in many respects, such as bandwidth and signal frequency. These particular features of each network implement vertical handoffs in a very complex manner compared to horizontal handoffs, but standards exist to aid in their implementation, such as IEEE 802.21.

The aim of harnessing network resources of different technologies at the same time motivates diagonal handoffs that, instead of changing the link of a network connection, use two different network interfaces to communicate. This particular handoff causes a greater flow of data; however, it offers a difficulty in its implementation that is higher than in a vertical handoff.

Handoff decision metrics are used as a yardstick to determine when a handoff is required. Traditional handoffs were only based on radio signal quality and channel availability. In the new generations of heterogeneous wireless networks, new handoff metrics are required to allow high user mobility and to minimize handoff delay. In [27] some handoff decision metrics are proposed:

- **Type of Service**. Different types of service require different types of reliability, delay, and rate of transmission.

- **Cost**. Cost is an important factor for users. Because different networks may have different charging strategies, cost-based network choice affects user choice in handoffs.
- **Network Conditions**. Parameters related to network status, such as traffic, bandwidth availability, delay, and congestion (loss of packets), need to be considered for efficient network usage. The use of information related to the state of a network to choose the handoff can be useful for load balancing between different networks, allowing for reduced congestion.
- **System Performance**. To ensure high system performance, a variety of parameters can be employed in the handoff decision, such as channel propagation characteristics, path loss, signal-to-noise ratio, and error of bit transmission. In addition, battery charging can be a major factor for some users. When the battery level is minimal, a user can choose to do a handoff based on the battery consumption of the network, for example, for a Bluetooth network.
- **Mobile Device Conditions**. Vehicle features include dynamic factors, such as speed, type of movement, location, and movement history.
- **User Preferences**. User preferences can be used to submit special requests to the network.

4.2.1.2 Proxy Mobile IPv6

Proxy Mobile IPv6 (PMIPv6), as specified in [11], provides a network-based mobility manager for connecting hosts to a PMIPv6 domain. PMIPv6 introduces two new functional entities: the Local Mobility Anchor (LMA) and the Mobile Access Gateway (MAG). MAG is the first layer that detects a MN associated with this node and offering IP connectivity. The LMA is the entity that assigns one or more home network prefixes (HNPs) to the MN.

The fundamental basis of PMIPv6 is the MIPv6, extending MIPv6 through the addition concepts like the functionality of the home agent (HA). The LMA and MAG establish a bidirectional tunnel for routing all data traffic belonging to MNs. Mobility management supports freedom of movement within the PMIPv6 domain, meaning a mobile host can move freely within the PMIPv6 domain without changing its IP address [4].

Figure 4.2 shows a simple topology of the PMIPv6 protocol. This topology has a MN, a MAG connected to an AP, and a LMA that is connected to the corresponding node (CN). The CN can be any node on the Internet.

By default, the entire decision to move from one AP to another is made by the LMA, which manages the addresses of the MNs connected to its domain. The MAG registers a new user on the network, so the LMA can be aware that a particular node is connected to some MAG managed by it.

When a vehicle wants to enter a network, the source MAG senses the MN attached event. The source MAG uses the acquired MN identifier to send a Proxy Binding Update (PBU) to the LMA for the registration process. After the LMA receives the PBU message, it checks the ID of the vehicle in its Binding Catch

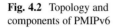

Fig. 4.2 Topology and
components of PMIPv6

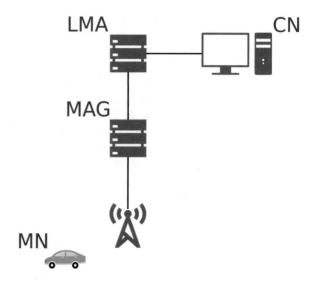

Entry (BCE). If the ID does not have an entry in the BCE, it is added. Then the
LMA provides the HNP of the MN to the source MAG by sending a Proxy Binding
Acknowledge (PBA) back to the source MAG. The LMA configures the IP tunneling
on its side at the same time. When the source MAG receives the PBA from the
LMA, it establishes a tunnel on its side. Then the source MAG advertises the router
advertisement (RA) message in the access link. It provides a HNP for the vehicle.
If the vehicle does not receive the RA, it sends a router solicitation (RS) message to
get the RA.

When a vehicle roams to another region in the localized network, it detaches
from the source MAG. The source MAG senses this event and sends a PBU for
a deregistration procedure to the LMA. The LMA receives the PBU message and
starts the BCEDelete timer to delete the entry of the MN in the BCE. Then a PBA
message is received from the LMA to the source MAG. When the target MAG
senses the vehicle attached event, it sends a PBU message to the LMA. The LMA
adds the new vehicle entry in its BCE, configures the IP tunnel, and sends the PBA
message to the target MAG. Then a tunnel between the target MAG and the LMA
is established. The target MAG advertises the HNP to the vehicle by sending a RA
message. Figure 4.3 describes the mobility management process using PMIPv6.

4.2.1.3 IEEE 802.21

IEEE 802.21 [10] is an IEEE specification effort that aims to allow transfers and
interoperability between heterogeneous networks, including 802 standards and non-
802 networks. One of the main ideas of IEEE 802.21 is to provide a common
interface for managing events and control messages exchanged between devices
on networks that have different technologies.

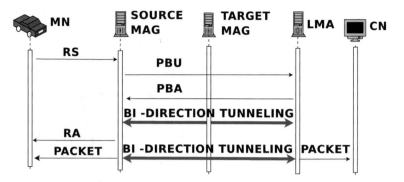

Fig. 4.3 Mobility management process using PMIPv6

The goal of IEEE 802.21 is to improve and facilitate the use of MNs, providing uninterrupted channel transmission across heterogeneous networks. To this end, delivery procedures may use the information collected from mobile terminals and the network infrastructure. At the same time, several factors can determine the distribution decision: service continuity, class of applications, QoS, negotiation of QoS, security, and so on.

The most important tasks of IEEE 802.21 are the discovery of new networks in the environment and selection of the most appropriate network for a given need [19]. Network discovery and selection are facilitated by network information exchange, which helps a mobile device determine which networks are active in its vicinity, allowing the mobile terminal to connect to the most appropriate network based on its handoff policies. However, the realization of this new connection presents a significant limitation, the disconnection time of the old base station, indicating that the execution of make-before-break is slow [30].

The core of 802.21 is the Media Independent Handover Function (MIHF). The MIHF must be implemented on every IEEE 802.21-compliant device (both hardware and software). This function is responsible for communicating with different terminals, networks, and remote MIHFs, as well as providing information services to the upper layers. Figure 4.4 illustrates the IEEE 802.21 service layer and its location in the TCP/IP protocol stack.

The MIHF defines three different services: Media Independent Event Service (MIES), Media Independent Command Service (MICS), and Media Independent Information Service (MIIS) [13].

MIES provides event classification, event filtering, and event reporting that correspond to the dynamic changes that occur in the link about the feature, state, and quality of the network link. The MIHF must register at the binding layer to receive binding events, while the upper layers interested in MIH events must register with the MIHF to receive those events. Events can be generated by the local stack or the remote stack of the Point of Access (PoA) that is acting as a point of service (PoS). MIH events and link events are divided into six categories: administrative, state change, link parameter, predictive, synchronous link, and link transmission.

Fig. 4.4 MIH services [9]

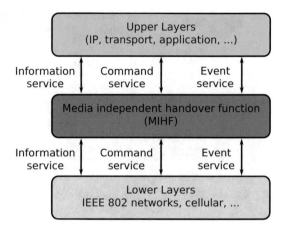

MICS allows MIH users to manage and control link characteristics relevant to handoff and mobility. The MIH commands originate in the upper layers of the MIHF. In the scope of this function, these commands become a remote MIH command for a remote stack and go to the lower layers as link commands of the MIHF. Link commands are specific to the access network in use and are only local.

MIIS confers the ability to obtain information required for handoffs, such as neighborhood maps, link layer information, and service availability. Briefly, this service provides a two-way road for all communication layers to share information elements (IE) to aid in handoff decision making.

These IEs are split into five groups: general information, such as area operators; access network, such as cost, security, and QoS; AP information, such as location, data rate, and channels; higher layer services, such as subnet information; and other information, such as vendor-specific information.

4.2.1.4 Proxy Mobile IP with IEEE 802.21 and Other Strategies

In the literature, some works have initiated the PMIP with IEEE 802.21 with the objective of offering heterogeneous communication between vehicles and RSUs. These proposals were related to mechanisms that, in some sense, enhance handover performance by enabling the simultaneous use of multiple interfaces during flow mobility.

The design of a flow mobility support approach allowed the updating and full coverage in PMIPv6 [7]. The approach is based on a virtual interface in a mobile network. A virtual interface makes all physical interfaces hidden from the network layer and above. Flow Interface Manager is placed at the virtual interface, and Flow Binding Manager in the LMA is paired with Flow Interface Manager. These elements manage the flow bindings and are used to select the proper access technology to send packets. The flow mobility procedure begins with three different triggering cases, which are caused by a new connection from the MN, by the LMA's decision, or by request from the MN.

Another work focused on the design and implementation of flow mobility extensions for PMIPv6 [24]. To do this, PMIPv6 was extended to support dynamic IP flow mobility management across access wireless networks according to operator policies. Considering energy consumption as a critical aspect for handheld devices and smartphones, the researchers assessed the feasibility of the proposed solution and provided an experimental analysis, showing the cost associated with energy consumption of simultaneous packet transmission/reception using multiple network interfaces. In this approach, the network, in particular the mobility anchor, is the decision control entity.

Another handover mechanism is aimed at allowing streaming over IP [14]. The mechanism is optimized for packet traffic and is based on network-based mobility management. The proposed mechanism uses the fast handover protocol PMIPv6 (FPMIPv6). Since this protocol does not support flow management, the handover approach required the definition of new mobility headers; the handover initiation for flow mobility (HIF) sends information from a MAG to other MNs. This handover scheme also incorporates another message to acknowledge that the handover is flow mobility (HAF), which is an extension of the handover acknowledgment message (HACK) responsible for sending commands to the MAG. The HACK message is defined in the FPMIPv6 protocol. These headers are an extension of the Handover Initiate (HI), which is responsible for the mobility management in the FPMIPv6 protocol. This extension was carried out to attain improved efficiency in the flow of carrier mobility in FPMIPv6. In addition, a new mobility option allows for the transmission of information about the communication interface, called the *interface-status-and-action* (ISA) option, which indicates the MN status, as well as the expected action of the MN's network interface.

A new mechanism for selective IP traffic offload (SIPTO) considers vehicular communication networks [21]. This mechanism provides support for offload data, seamless transfer, and IP flow mobility to mobile devices equipped with multiple interfaces. The authors created a mechanism called Multilink Striping Management (MSM), which allows data transfer flow and mobility between different access network technologies. Reports about link quality and network status, such as the network core and access, are used as triggers for the MSM. These triggers support the decision on whether there is a change in flow, either a data offload or handover, needed to avoid session interruptions. The Media Independent Handover (MIH) services are used to trigger the need for a change of flow offload data or handover. Through the use of primitives, MIH, IP flow mobility, handover, and data offload are performed smoothly, allowing better use of network resources while enhancing network capacity.

The Seamless Flow Mobility Management Architecture (SFMMA) consists of an architecture that serves as a common infrastructure to seamlessly enable multiaccess technology in wireless networks [25]. SFMMA works with WiMax and LTE technologies, as well as technologies for wireless carrier networks, providing a continuous and transparent connection to vehicular applications. The purpose of this architecture is to maximize network traffic while maintaining the minimum requirements of vehicular applications, such as packet loss, throughput, and delay.

Table 4.1 Works that deal with resource manager base on infrastructure

Work	Protocol	Auxiliary	Decision	Technology	State
Choi [7]	PMIPv6	HUR, HUA, Flow mobility messages	LMA, MN	Wlan, WiMAX, PPP (3G)	No
Melia [24]	PMIPv6	–	LMA	Wi-Fi, 3G	No
Kim [14]	PMIPv6	HIF, HAF, ISA messages	MN	Wi-Fi, 3G	No
Makaya [21]	MSM	MIHF	MN	Wi-Fi, 3G	Yes
Meneguette [25]	PMIPv6	MIHF	MN, MAG, LMA	LTE, 802.11p	Yes

HUR HNP Update Request, *HUA* HNP Update Acknowledge

Thus, a stream manager was created based on the application class of the vehicle networks and state of each active network in the environment. However, this proposal presents a high number of control messages to establish the return flow between interfaces, which is due to the use of the 802.21 protocol for performing the change of flow. For instance, for a change of flow initiated by a MN, at least 13 control messages are required, which can leave management slow and possibly generate unstable mobility.

Table 4.1 summarizes the characteristics of those works that address the proposed flow mobility management: (1) the technology used for mobility management (protocol); (2) the use of other protocol or messaging auxiliary (auxiliary); (3) the device used to initialize or to make decisions on flow changes (decision); (4) which network technology it has been tested into (technology); and (5) whether it takes into account the state of the network and its flows (state).

Although these works present efficient solutions to managing the mobility of a vehicle, all of them introduce a high number of control messages due to the features of the 802.21 protocol. Also, the decision-making mechanism to switch from one AP to another needs to be simple and optimized to make a quick choice about which RSU a vehicle can connect to.

4.2.1.5   Discussion and Challenges Encountered

It is necessary to emphasize the relevance of the use of the 802.21 protocol, which is a standard established by the IEEE for the assistance of mobility management in heterogeneous networks. Unlike proprietary or cross-layer protocols, this protocol is used for any network technology and not restricted to a single technology. The 802.21 protocol plays an important role because, in addition to being a generic protocol capable of serving any current network technology, it allows the capture of network states through its functions and messages. However, the protocol performs no practical management of mobility, meaning that it does not deal with addressing and routing information flow. This condition consequently requires that the PMIPv6 protocol manage the addresses and prefixes of each vehicle. Unlike the presented

MSM, the PMIPv6 is an extension of the MIPv6 protocol. Thus, the PMIPv6 has standardized and well-known functions, facilitating future interoperability among various flow mobility management protocols.

Therefore, one of the great challenges is to determine the application of such protocols without the use of control messages of both 802.21 and PMIPv6 protocols, avoiding the overload of the network. By doing so, a more concise information exchange, not only between vehicles but also between vehicles and the RSU, is implemented, consequently introducing faster decision making and a change in APs. Although the PMIPv6 protocol deals with the handling and addressing of vehicles, it establishes no policy that would define the change between APs. Hence, identifying and developing protocols for fast and efficient AP change is extremely challenging. The speed of vehicles, road conditions, and the service being offered significantly affect the handoff when not only attempting to attend to the needs of the vehicular network but also maintaining the quality of user experience.

4.2.2 Software-Defined Networking

SDN is an emerging technology that is manageable, dynamic, adaptable, and cost-effective. SDN can provide flexibility, programmability, and centralized control using various techniques, such as packet routing, wireless resource optimization, interference avoidance, and channel allocation. SDN allows forwarding in multi-hop, multipath scenarios, as well as network heterogeneity and efficient mobility management [33].

SDN consists of network management, which separates the data plane, where the forwarding of packets on the network interface toward the intended destination is performed, from the control plane, where the logical procedures are executed and all decisions are taken [5]. Thus, SDN can bring flexibility and programmability to networks, opening them up to innovation. Figure 4.5 illustrates a simplified view of the SDN architecture.

In practice, network elements, such as switches, follow a set of rules and policies defined by a logically centralized controller, the SDN element, which contains the actual network intelligence. Therefore, the main element of the SDN is the controller that communicates with the network switches that forward packets according to the controller-installed rules. Furthermore, the controller communicates with the network applications via a northbound API and translates their requirements into appropriate network decisions. The northbound API serves to provide a programming abstraction to the upper layers [16]; so far, there is no standard northbound API. The southbound API is used to enable communication between the data plane and the control plane. One of the most widely used southbound API protocols in SDN networks is Openflow [23].

OpenFlow is the first standard communication interface defined between the control and forwarding layers of an SDN architecture that consists of a set of specifications maintained by the Open Networking Forum (ONF). Furthermore, OpenFlow is an open standard that enables researchers to run experimental protocols

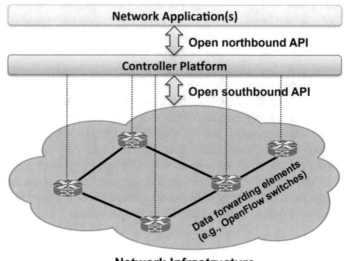

Fig. 4.5 Simplified SDN architecture [16]

in campus networks. The standard is added as a feature to commercial Ethernet switches, routers, and wireless APs and provides a standardized hook to allow researchers to run experiments, without requiring vendors to expose the internal workings of their network devices. Therefore, OpenFlow allows direct access to and manipulation of the forwarding plane of network devices, such as switches and routers, both physical and virtual.

In its specification, OpenFlow is defined as an abstract packet-processing machine, called a switch, as described in Fig. 4.6. The switch processes packets using a combination of packet contents and switch configuration states. Moreover, an OpenFlow Logical Switch consists of one or more flow tables, a stage of the pipeline that contains flow entries, and a group table, a list of action buckets and some means of choosing one or more of those buckets to apply on a per-packet basis. The switch performs packet lookups and forwardings on one or more OpenFlow channels, which are the interface between an OpenFlow switch and an OpenFlow controller used by the controller to manage the switch.

Each flow table in the switch contains a set of flow entries; each flow entry consists of match fields, counters, and a set of instructions to apply to matching packets. Through this information, the controller can add, update, and delete flow entries in flow tables, both reactively, in response to packets, and proactively.

With OpenFlow, the data plane elements become devices that just forward packets according to rules installed by the controller [20]. The general flow of a packet arriving at an OpenFlow switch can be described as follows:

- The packet is matched against the existing rules. Different versions of the Open-Flow protocols consider different packet information during a match, but some

Fig. 4.6 Idealized OpenFlow switch [29]

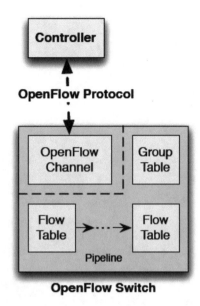

examples of information used in this match are the source and destination MAC address, the VLAN identification, and the source and destination IP addresses;

• If a packet matches an existing rule, perform the associated action. Examples of actions include dropping the packet, forwarding the packet to a particular port, or sending the packet to the controller;

• If no rule matches, the packet is sent to the controller, which then decides what to do with it and installs a new rule in the OpenFlow switch. The next time a packet of this flow arrives at the switch, it matches an existing rule, so it does not need to send the packet to the controller. This procedure works much like a cache, in which the packet is sent to the controller in a cache-miss event. In a future event of packet arrival, the switch knows what to do with this kind of packet.

Therefore, the switch communicates with the controller, and the controller manages the switch via the OpenFlow switch protocol. Thus, the OpenFlow can be defined for manipulating the switch's configuration state or receiving given switch events.

4.2.2.1 Software-Defined Networking with Vehicular Network

Several architectures using SDN already exist that aim to perform the control of communication not only between the infrastructure and the Internet but also between infrastructure and vehicles. These architectures are based on the abstraction proposed by the ONF [15]. These architectures introduce new elements and mechanisms in the SDN controller proposed by the ONF, aiming to enhance the networking performance.

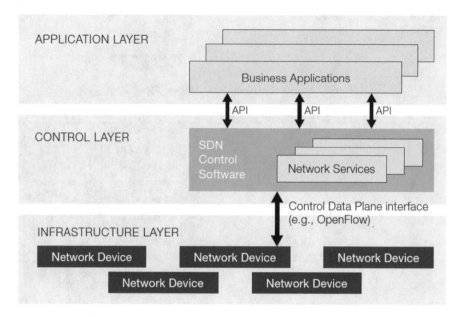

Fig. 4.7 ONF/SDN architecture [15]

The abstraction proposed by the ONF splits into a series of layers. (1) The application layer consists of the end-user business applications that consume the SDN communication services. (2) The control layer consolidates the control functionality that supervises the network forwarding behavior through an open interface. (3) The infrastructure layer consists of the network elements and devices that provide packet switching and forwarding. Figure 4.7 depicts the architecture in general terms.

4.2.2.2 An Overview of Smart City Architecture Based on SDN Elements

Vehicular networks can be used to assist in the fight against the ills of big cities, such as congestion, an inefficient public transport system, and a precarious control system. A central control system would be based on software-defined networks, in which the system monitors and controls not only the data flow of the network but also the traffic of vehicles on streets.

The main objective of the intelligent transport system (ITS) architecture is to provide QoS in the transfer of information between vehicles and the vehicular road infrastructure. The exchange can receive information about the state of the network, make inferences, and take appropriate actions, such as releasing a particular traffic light for a longer time owing to the high congestion of tracks. Thus, it can lead to reductions in congestion in a particular place and, consequently, emissions of CO_2, average travel time, and fuel consumption.

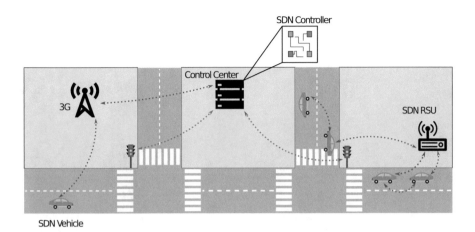

Fig. 4.8 Communication between components

The central concept of SDN is the separation between the control plane and the data plane. The latter is used for routing data while the former is used to control network traffic. Several works have already attempted to develop an SDN architecture for the development of urban ITSs [8, 17, 38]. Figure 4.8 describes a general abstraction of an SDN architecture for an ITS. Such architectures are usually implemented using tools. Ryu and OpenvSwitch have been used for the development of controllers that monitor and control transportation on the roads of a large city through a vehicular network, with the objective of reducing congestion, informing drivers about road events, and providing new routes, for instance. The architecture consists of the following elements:

- **SDN Controller**. This is the logical intelligence center of a VANET-based SDN system. The SDN controller controls the behavior of the systemwide network.
- **SDN Vehicles**. These are elements of the data plane that are controllable by the SDN controller. SDN vehicles receive a control message from the SDN controller to perform actions through OpenvSwitch.
- **RSU SDN**. This refers to fixed data planes that are controllable by the SDN controller. They are the infrastructure RSUs that are deployed along road segments.

Figure 4.8 displays the communication between components of the proposed SDN-based architecture. The control mode includes all operating modes of a system in which the SDN controller controls any element, in connection with the APs, the connection between APs and vehicles (RSU road infrastructure), as well as the connection among the vehicles themselves. The SDN driver does not have complete control but instead can delegate control over packet-processing details to local agents. Therefore, traffic control is switched among all SDN elements. Thus, the controller only instructs SDN vehicles and SDN RSUs to execute a specific routing protocol with certain parameters.

Fig. 4.9 Centralized SDN
approach

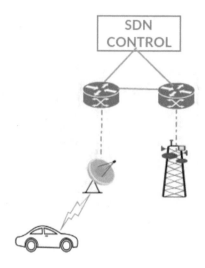

4.2.2.3   SDN as Manager of Vehicles Communication

When we consider the SDN architecture as a structure that manages communication among vehicles, it enables an infrastructure that manages the mobility of vehicles between a network technology and communication bursts. This architecture is expected to provide greater dynamism and control of mobility because in SDN the IP header of packets is no longer used directly for packet routing [18] but in the packet data stream. These fluctuations are identified by the message fields of the packages, making it flexible and easy to communicate with different network technologies.

Mobility management using SDN can be divided into three parts [18]:

- **Centralized SDN**. The SDN controller manages all elements of the network. In other words, the controller coordinates all SDN switches, as depicted in Fig. 4.9. Therefore, the controller has a global view of the network and can make the best decision regarding the exchange of one AP to another and load balancing in the network, among other decisions. However, this strategy requires a good quality of communication between switches and the controller, and it must treat scalability when increasing the number of elements in the network.
- **Semicentralized SDN**. In this approach, there is not a central controller, but a set of controllers that can be geographically distributed or deal with different domains, as shown in Fig. 4.10. Therefore, each controller is responsible for one set of switches and must deal with communication between other controllers so that it is possible to switch from one AP to another when vehicles are moving. Owing to this communication between controllers, the number of packets in the network is larger so that the exchange of APs is enabled by different controllers.
- **Hierarchical SDN**. This approach is an extension of the semicentralized one; however, there is no longer direct communication between the various con-

Fig. 4.10 Semicentralized approach

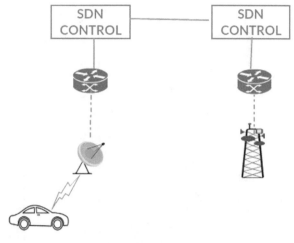

Fig. 4.11 Hierarchical approach

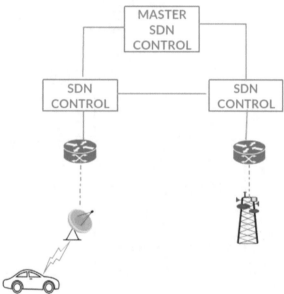

trollers. In a hierarchical approach, a master controller must manage the other controllers, thereby creating a hierarchy of controllers, as shown in Figs. 4.9 and 4.11. This master controller manages the subdomains controlled by the controllers under its domain. Therefore, this approach takes advantage of the centralized approach, in which the controller has a global network neighbor by communicating with the controllers below it.

Regardless of how mobility management is handled, SDN provides more efficient use of a network by reducing the number of control messages needed to perform AP exchange. For example, we assume users are using a set of applications

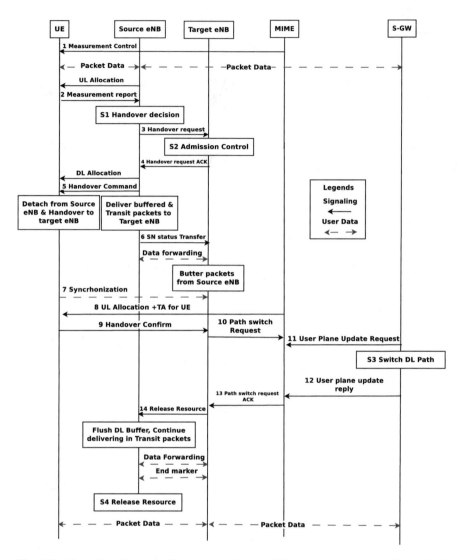

Fig. 4.12 Abstraction of message flows generated by mobility management system with standard LTE [18]

on their smartphones. These smartphones are connected to a cell phone tower. However, since these users are on the move, they need to change APs to continue using the services, considering that such APs and a telephony provider use LTE technology to provide access to data. If the provider employs all the infrastructure and functionality of the LTE protocol, the system generates a set of 20 control messages to perform this AP exchange. However, if the system uses SDN, this number is reduced to 14 messages for the same hypothetical scenario. Figures 4.12 and 4.13 show an abstraction of the message flows generated by the mobility

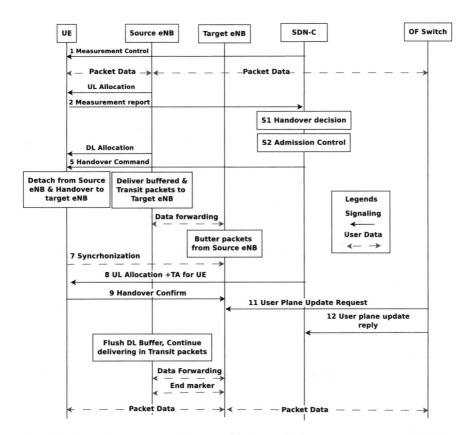

Fig. 4.13 Abstraction of message flows generated by mobility management system with SDN-supported LTE [18]

management system for performing switching from the current antenna, source eNB, to the next antenna, target eNB, considering both a solution with and without SDN [18].

The reduction of messages is possible because SDN incorporates some 802.21 protocol components, as described earlier, that allow better management of network information. In addition, SDN makes it possible to add other protocols such as PMIPv6 to aggregate its operation to bring better management of data flows in the network or other functionality. However, this inclusion can generate an ambiguity in the functions of the SDN with the added protocol, as is described in Fig. 4.14. Therefore, the adequacy of the combined protocol is necessary to take advantage of this integration, as depicted in Fig. 4.15.

In the literature, few studies use this advantage of SDN for the management of vehicular network mobility. Thus, we describe mobility management works that consider applications in a wireless network as in a vehicular network.

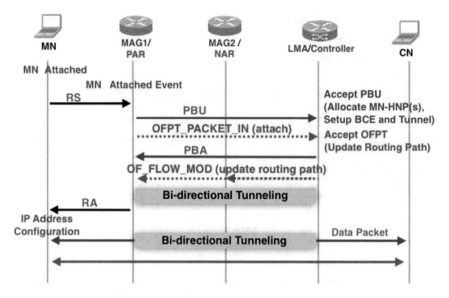

Fig. 4.14 Redundancy of PMIPv6 and SDN signaling [34]

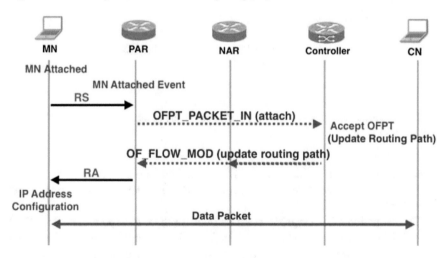

Fig. 4.15 Fixed redundancy of PMIPv6 and SDN signaling [34]

A proactive flow management approach enables an SDN controller to set up flow entries on individually chosen target switches before a packet-in event is triggered due to handover or new network selection in an SDNized wireless network [12]. For this, the authors used a learning component that could predict the next point of attachment for mobile hosts. This learning component is implemented in the SDN control to manage the mobility of users proactively. The approach also uses OpenFlow as the standard southbound protocol to collect the required parameter values from core network switches. The controller obtains required parameter values from the core network and last mile entities to compute user satisfaction (QoE) for the offered network services and application type. Thus, the proactive learning algorithm identifies the potential next point of attachment (PoA) and the optimal path toward a new PoA, with corresponding flow rules installed on the switches by the controller.

Mobility SDN (M-SDN) consists of a mobility management scheme for SDN-based enterprise networks that reduces the traffic pause time caused by a host-initiated layer-2 handover [6]. M-SDN performs handover preparation in parallel with the layer-2 handover that involves N-casting of active flows to every potential handover target. Handover preparation is enabled by effective address resolution and location tracking. Thus, SDN demands neither host modification nor IP tunneling; it reduces the traffic pause time caused by a host-initiated layer-2 handover using handover preparation that projects an imminent handover and performs N-casting to potential handover targets in parallel with the layer-2 handover. M-SDN designates a location server together with a mobility application on the controller to keep IP-MAC addressing binding, topology information, and device location information to carry out handover preparation, such as handover target projection and N-casting. This approach can deal with vertical handover and application layer session continuity for service continuity.

An SDN-based architecture has been proposed to achieve the seamless convergence of LTE and wireless networks [36]. For this, the approach incorporates a virtual middle box in User Equipment (UE), which is responsible for transmitting control messages to the network controller and act in accordance with corresponding commands. The middle box consists of three parts: Agent, Data Forward, and network interfaces. The Agent is responsible for reporting UE status and exchanging control signaling with a controller. The data forward module routes packets to different interfaces according to rules from the controller. The network interfaces consist of an LTE interface, WLAN interface, and a virtual interface. When UE connects to the network, either through LTE or WLAN, the virtual interface retrieves an IP address. This IP address does not change until UE leaves the network or becomes idle. As the IP address of the virtual interface remains unchanged, services on the UE can use this interface to set connections to the remote server. Thus, when a handover is triggered, the controller tells the middle box to connect to a WLAN AP and deliver new flow table to forwarding devices in the core network to copy packets to the WLAN network.

A novel SDN-based architecture has been designed to make use of Distributed Mobility Management (DMM) concepts to deploy fast, flexible, reliable, and scalable mobility management mechanisms at both local and regional levels [31]. The proposed approach relies on two main entities, the local controller (LC) and the regional controller (RC), and provides mobility at two differentiated levels. To achieve this mobility, the architecture contains mechanisms that enable fast layer-2 mobility within a domain, the so-called district. A district is an isolated single-technology domain, similar to the localized mobility domains of PMIPv6. A district is composed of a dense deployment of APs connected by a switched network of

SDN-enabled interconnection nodes (OpenFlow switches). A district includes at least one gateway (DMM-GW) that connects the district to the Internet and plays a central role in the interdistrict mobility solution. The approach also used the SDN to deal with intradistrict mobility.

4.2.2.4 Discussions and Challenges Encountered

A summary of features and mechanisms used in the works presented in this chapter is given in Table 4.2. A more detailed description of such aspects is presented as follows.

It is worth noting the benefits of using SDN: a reduction in the number of control messages in a network and the ease of performing vehicle mobility management. In addition, SDN facilitates communication between different network technologies, providing an abstraction between these technologies through the controller and its switch. Because SDN can integrate with other protocols, it allows greater flexibility and compatibility with other protocols already well known in wireless networks, such as 802.21 and PMIPv6. SDN also enables path management to be optimized based on individual service needs and not bound by the routing configuration. Path management is especially important in the mobile environment where end users are constantly changing their location, bandwidth demands vary widely depending on the type of content being sent, and basic wireless coverage is not uniform. Furthermore, the flow paradigm in SDN is particularly well suited to provide end-to-end communications across multiple distinct technologies. Flows can have granular policies for adequate traffic isolation, service chaining, and QoS management.

Although SDN can bring many advantages in the management of vehicular mobility, there are still gaps that need to be taken into account when projecting mobility management mechanisms for vehicular networks. As we can see, few works have determined the time of connectivity between vehicles with the base station, which is the time of connection between the MN and the AP. In addition, it is also interesting to consider the speed and direction of a vehicle so that the controller can predict the next best AP for the vehicle to connect to. Therefore, there is still a lack of policy on detention between APs, considering all the peculiar characteristics of vehicular networks. Another important point is the cost of implementing such systems, as well as the security of data transfer between vehicles and the MSW.

Table 4.2 Works that deal with resource manager based on infrastructure

Work	Contribution	Disadvantage
Khan et al. [12]	Learning component that can predict next point of attachment	Complexity
Chen et al. [6]	Low-latency handover	Complexity
Wang et al. [36]	Virtual middle box in UE	Cost and complexity
Sanchez et al. [31]	Distributed Mobility Management (DMM) paradigm	Complexity

4.3 Final Discussion

In this chapter, we have introduced the concept of V2I communication. We described the management of mobility in vehicular networks showing the problems of some of the traditional techniques already known in wireless networks but applied in vehicular networks. These issues include management of some control messages generated by conventional protocols, as well as the use of access-point-switching decision models. We also present a new technology to manage the communication between vehicles and the RSU known as software-defined networking and demonstrated the benefits of using such technology in performing mobility management. We also discuss the challenges associated with such technology. Then we listed and explained the state-of-the-art techniques for mobility management. Finally, we discussed the significant challenges in the field and research opportunities.

References

1. Akan O, Akyildiz I (2004) ATL: an adaptive transport layer suite for next-generation wireless internet. IEEE J Sel Areas Commun 22(5):802–817
2. Akyildiz I, Xie J, Mohanty S (2004) A survey of mobility management in next-generation all-ip-based wireless systems. IEEE Wirel Commun 11(4):16–28
3. Bernardos CJ (2012) Proxy mobile IPv6 extensions to support flow mobility. draft-ietf-netext-pmipv6-flowmob-03
4. Bernardos CJ, Calderon M, Soto I (2012) PMIPv6 and network mobility problem statement. draft-bernardos-netext-pmipv6-nemo-ps-02
5. Bizanis N, Kuipers FA (2016) SDN and virtualization solutions for the internet of things: a survey. IEEE Access 4:5591–5606
6. Chen C, Lin YT, Yen LH, Chan MC, Tseng CC (2016) Mobility management for low-latency handover in SDN-based enterprise networks. In: 2016 IEEE wireless communications and networking conference, pp 1–6
7. Choi HY, Min SG, Han YH (2011) PMIPv6-based flow mobility simulation in NS-3. In: 2011 Fifth international conference on Innovative Mobile and Internet Services in ubiquitous computing (IMIS), pp 475 –480
8. Correia S, Boukerche A, Meneguette RI (2017) An architecture for hierarchical software-defined vehicular networks. IEEE Commun Mag 55(7):80–86
9. Eastwood L, Migaldi S, Xie Q, Gupta V (2008) Mobility using IEEE 802.21 in a heterogeneous IEEE 802.16/802.11-based, IMT-advanced (4G) network. IEEE Wirel Commun 15(2):26–34
10. Fernandes S, Karmouch A (2013) Design and analysis of an IEEE 802.21-based mobility management architecture: a context-aware approach. Wirel Netw 19(2):187–205
11. Gundavelli S, Leung K, Devarapalli V, Chowdhury K, Patil B (2008) Proxy mobile IPv6. http://tools.ietf.org/html/rfc5213
12. Khan MA, Dang XT, Peters S (2016) Preemptive flow management in future SDNized wireless networks. In: 2016 IEEE 12th international conference on wireless and mobile computing, networking and communications (WiMob), pp 1–8
13. Khattab O, Alani O (2013) Survey on Media Independent Handover (MIH) approaches in heterogeneous wireless networks. In: IEEE 19th European wireless 2013 (EW 2013), pp 1–5
14. Kim J, Morioka Y, Hagiwara J (2012) An optimized seamless ip flow mobility management architecture for traffic offloading. In: Network Operations and Management Symposium (NOMS), 2012. IEEE, Piscataway, pp 229–236

15. Kolias C, Ahlawat S, Ashton C et al (2013) Openflow-enabled mobile and wireless networks. White Paper
16. Kreutz D, Ramos FM, Verissimo PE, Rothenberg CE, Azodolmolky S, Uhlig S (2015) Software-defined networking: a comprehensive survey. Proc IEEE 103(1):14–76
17. Ku I, Lu Y, Gerla M, Ongaro F, Gomes R, Cerqueira E (2014) Towards software-defined VANET: architecture and services. In: 2014 13th annual Mediterranean ad hoc networking workshop (MED-HOC-NET), pp 103–110
18. Kuklinski S, Li Y, Dinh KT (2014) Handover management in SDN-based mobile networks. In: 2014 IEEE Globecom Workshops (GC Wkshps), pp 194–200
19. Lampropoulos G, Salkintzis A, Passas N (2008) Media-independent handover for seamless service provision in heterogeneous networks. IEEE Commun Mag 46(1):64–71
20. Lara A, Kolasani A, Ramamurthy B (2014) Network innovation using openflow: a survey. IEEE Commun Surv Tutorials 16(1):493–512
21. Makaya C, Das S, Lin F (2012) Seamless data offload and flow mobility in vehicular communications networks. In: Wireless Communications and Networking Conference Workshops (WCNCW). IEEE, Piscataway, pp 338–343
22. McKeown N (2011) How SDN will shape networking
23. McKeown N, Anderson T, Balakrishnan H, Parulkar G, Peterson L, Rexford J, Shenker S, Turner J (2008) Openflow: enabling innovation in campus networks. ACM SIGCOMM Comput Commun Rev 38(2):69–74
24. Melia T, Bernardos C, de la Oliva A, Giust F, Calderon M (2011) Ip flow mobility in PMIPv6 based networks: solution design and experimental evaluation. Wirel Pers Commun 61:603–627
25. Meneguette RI, Bittencourt LF, Madeira ERM (2013) A seamless flow mobility management architecture for vehicular communication networks. J Commun Netw 15(2):207–216
26. Márquez-Barja J, Calafate CT, Cano JC, Manzoni P (2011) An overview of vertical handover techniques: algorithms, protocols and tools. Comput Commun 34(8):985–997
27. Nasser N, Hasswa A, Hassanein H (2006) Handoffs in fourth generation heterogeneous networks. IEEE Commun Mag 44(10):96–103
28. Nunes BAA, Mendonca M, Nguyen XN, Obraczka K, Turletti T (2014) A survey of software-defined networking: past, present, and future of programmable networks. IEEE Commun Surv Tutorials 16(3):1617–1634
29. Pfaff B, Lantz B, Heller B et al (2012) Openflow switch specification, version 1.3. 0. Open Networking Foundation, Menlo Park
30. Qureshi R, Dadej A, Fu Q (2007) Issues in 802.21 mobile node controlled handovers. In: Australasian telecommunication networks and applications conference, 2007, ATNAC 2007, pp 53–57
31. Sanchez MI, de la Oliva A, Mancuso V (2016) Experimental evaluation of an SDN-based distributed mobility management solution. In: Proceedings of the workshop on mobility in the evolving internet architecture. ACM, New York, pp 31–36
32. Siddiqui F, Zeadally S (2006) Mobility management across hybrid wireless networks: trends and challenges. Comput Commun 29(9):1363–1385
33. Soua R, Kalogeiton E, Manzo G, Duarte JM, Palattella MR, Di Maio A, Braun T, Engel T, Villas LA, Rizzo GA (2017) SDN coordination for CCN and FC content dissemination in VANETs. Springer, Cham, pp 221–233
34. Tantayakul K, Dhaou R, Paillassa B (2016) Impact of SDN on mobility management. In: 2016 IEEE 30th international conference on advanced information networking and applications, pp 260–265
35. Tsirtsis G, Soliman H, Montavont N, Giaretta G, Kuladinithi K (2011) Flow bindings in mobile IPv6 and network mobility (NEMO) basic support. IETF, Fremont; RFC 6089
36. Wang L, Lu Z, Wen X, Cao G, Xia X, Ma L (2016) An SDN-based seamless convergence approach of WLAN and LTE networks. In: 2016 IEEE information technology, networking, electronic and automation control conference, pp 944–947
37. Wasserman M, Seite P (2011) Current practices for multiple-interface hosts. IETF, Fremont; RFC 6419

38. Yap KK, Huang TY, Kobayashi M, Yiakoumis Y, McKeown N, Katti S, Parulkar G (2012) Making use of all the networks around us: a case study in android. In: Proceedings of the 2012 ACM SIGCOMM workshop on cellular networks: operations, challenges, and future design. ACM, New York, pp 19–24

Chapter 5
Vehicle-to-Vehicle Communication

Abstract Intervehicle communication has spurred an increase in the application of intelligent transportation systems. The related services and applications use vehicles to sense a particular region of a city or even monitor traffic conditions in a given urban area. These applications use the communication between vehicles to disseminate information and propagate data quickly and efficiently. Thus, the dissemination of data in a vehicle network becomes an important tool because certain regional content or information may be relevant to a certain set of vehicles. However, due to variations in road density, the high mobility of vehicles, the short time of vehicle residence, and frequent changes in network topology, the development of an efficient routing or data dissemination protocol for this type of network poses a challenge. This chapter describes techniques and a protocol that can be used to perform data dissemination and transmit a data route in a vehicular network to allow that information to reach its destination.

5.1 Introduction

Currently, new applications and services are emerging for intelligent transportation systems (ITSs). The main functions of these services and applications comprise sensing urban environments. Examples of such applications include traffic control, monitoring of road conditions, and applications that help drivers to obtain relevant information about traffic conditions and enable drivers to take some sort of action, such as changing routes to avoid a congested region [13, 44]. These services and applications require routing protocols so that the information captured by vehicles can be disseminated in networks. Thus, dissemination is a vital function in this type of network, because a message may be of great interest to vehicles in a given region [28]. For example, warnings to avoid collisions and post-crashes require efficient and reliable data dissemination. Communication among vehicles is particularly needed when the distances between sending and receiving vehicles are greater than the radius of communication.

However, vehicular ad hoc networks (VANETs) face some challenges regarding data dissemination owing to variations in vehicle density and frequent changes in

© Springer International Publishing AG, part of Springer Nature 2018
R. I. Meneguette et al., *Intelligent Transport System in Smart Cities*, Urban Computing, https://doi.org/10.1007/978-3-319-93332-0_5

network topology induced by high vehicle mobility and short-range communications [41]. These challenges limit the use of existing data dissemination protocols
for mobile networks [10]. Therefore, new protocols must be designed, taking into
account the intrinsic characteristics of vehicular networks.

Protocols for data dissemination in VANETs should consider two key issues.
The first, known as a broadcast storm, occurs when multiple vehicles try to
broadcast simultaneously. These storms cause high data traffic, network congestion,
packet collisions, and even service interruption at the media access control (MAC)
layer [29]. The second, known as a network disconnection, occurs when the number
of vehicles in an area of interest (AOI) is not sufficient to perform the dissemination
of data between groups of vehicles close to one another [2]. In this scenario,
if the vehicle is not aware that the network is disconnected when it receives a
new message, it simply retransmits the message in broadcast and discards the
message in sequence. Since there is no other vehicle within the transmitting area
of the sending vehicle to receive the message, it is simply lost. The problem of
network disconnections is very common in a VANET because of the sparse and
random distribution among vehicles. Such a problem poses major challenges for the
dissemination of data since messages cannot be easily forwarded between partitions.

This chapter describes techniques and protocols that perform routing and data
dissemination among vehicles so that the information is propagated in a vehicular
network. The rest of this chapter is organized as follows. Section 5.2 describes the
concept of vehicle-to-vehicle (V2V) communication. Section 5.3 discusses some
techniques that use the data dissemination protocol and routing protocols. Finally,
Sect. 5.5 briefly summarizes the chapter.

5.2 Vehicle-to-Vehicle Communication Concepts

The aim of V2V communication is communication among vehicles. This communication enables collaboration and coordination between vehicles, allowing for the
dissemination of information without the need for any infrastructure. Due to the
unique characteristics of vehicular networks, that is, their high mobility and low
communication time, it becomes a challenge to develop communication protocols
and efficient data dissemination without impacting the performance of the networks.
Figure 5.1 provides a general illustration of the described V2V communication
scenarios.

Owing to the features of vehicular networks, as well as the need not to
overload networks with retransmission messages and many control messages in the
network, the protocols for routing and data dissemination must deal with several
challenges:

- **Broadcast Storm**. The flooding of messages in a network is caused by the
  sending of messages by several vehicles simultaneously.

Fig. 5.1 V2V
communication

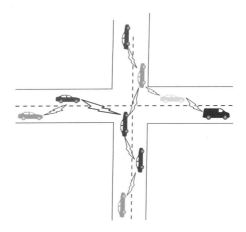

- **Network Disconnection**. The movement of vehicles and the communication radius leads to network fragmentation, and a vehicle cannot directly forward data to other vehicles.

To deal with these challenges, some techniques consider the position of vehicles, the area of communication, time of communication, and other aspects. What follows is a description of the techniques used to handle broadcast storms and network disconnections.

5.2.1 Technique for Dealing with Network Disconnection

The most widely used technique for dealing with network partition is known as store-carry-forward. This mechanism allows a vehicle that is routing data to store the information if it finds fragmentation in the network; the data are not discarded. Figure 5.2 depicts three network fragments. For the development of this mechanism, we can use some strategies like timing and control messages that are used for the detection and management of network fragmentation.

In timing, vehicles are not aware that there is fragmentation in the network, making it difficult to detect this disconnection. For the data to not be lost due to this fragmentation, the vehicle attempts to forward that message in the network from time to time. However, this mechanism may bring a substantial overhead to the network. One solution to decrease the number of messages in the network is to count the number of attempts that are made and to establish some valid attempts. Thus, the communication is less costly by reducing the number of messages in the network; however, there is no precise value for limiting the number of transmission attempts; the value is an trade-off between making routing possible without data being lost and avoiding to generate unnecessary data in the network.

Fig. 5.2 Example of
networking fragments in
urban environments

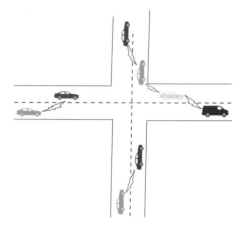

When we consider the use of control messages, that is, the use of beacon message
that can be sent every 1 s by vehicles to inform about their position, direction,
and speed, among other information [17], this message is often used to detect the
presence of a nearby vehicle. Thus, if a vehicle receives a control message, it knows
there are vehicles nearby. Because such information is sent within a fixed period of
time, the vehicle can be considered inexistent with the failure to receive this type of
message for a long period, possibly as a result of a disconnection or fragmentation
in the network.

In addition to assisting in detecting network fragmentation, these messages can
be used in the store-care-forward mechanism to inform the vehicle of the appearance
of a new connection and allow the vehicle to forward the data to the destination.
Thus, when a vehicle receives this control message, it knows that there are vehicles
nearby that can further disseminate the information. Therefore, the control message
becomes an information mechanism for store-care-forward mechanisms so that it
can repropagate its information to other vehicles.

Finally, using the store-care-forward mechanism embedded in routing protocols
and data dissemination protocols, it is possible to reduce congestion generated by
the disconnection of a vehicle due to its high mobility and low connection time
between vehicles.

5.2.2   Technique for Dealing with a Broadcast Storm

The exchange of messages for the dissemination and routing of data consists of
another major challenge in Vehicular Networks. In other words, control messages
are needed to properly convey correct information to recipients, but they most likely
lead the network to overburden when they transmitted in a mesh fashion.

To reduce the number of messages required for to route and disseminate given
data, a vehicle selection mechanism is used to retransmit the information. The

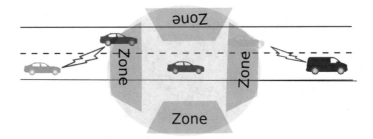

Fig. 5.3 Example of an transmission zone to cope with network fragmentation

selection of these vehicles usually relies on the communication envelope area of the vehicle that transmits or routes the data, location, and direction of all vehicles within the communication area of the transmitter.

The choice of vehicle for routing the data can be based on both the transmitter of the information and the vehicles near it. The choice of which vehicle to use to route information depends on the strategy applied by the routing protocol. Both forms of routing selection may use location and direction information.

One of the techniques used is the division of the communication coverage area into transmission regions, called retransmission zones [49]. Thus, vehicles within that transmission zone are more likely to retransmit the information than vehicles outside that retransmission area. This technique is often used in urban environments, where it suffers a change of density in its pathways, having good performance both in a dense environment with many vehicles and in a sparse environment with few vehicles. Figure 5.3 illustrates the transmission range of the transmitter in retransmission zones; the vehicles within that zone become the data relays.

When we consider the location and direction of vehicles, the position of the transmitter is almost always used as reference to determine distances between vehicles. The vehicle nearest, farthest, or at an intermediate distance to the transmitter can relay the information. These methods use a beacon to trap vehicles to calculate their distances and decide which one will carry out the retransmission. Such decoding can start from the transmitter, that is, the transmitter calculates the distance towards all its neighbors; after it calculates and verifies who is the farthest, the transmitter later forwards the information to a vehicle farther away. Other variations of this type of strategy use vehicles that are closer and at a medium distance. The decoder can be in charge of the relay's neighboring nodes. The transmitter sends the data to all its neighbors and the neighboring vehicles that calculate the distance between it and the transmitter to decide whether or not it will carry out the retransmission of the information. Figure 5.4 describes this technique, treating the green vehicle as the transmitter and the red vehicles as the vehicles that perform the retransmission due to the distance between them and the transmitter. To assist in this technique, vehicle steering is used to increase the efficiency of the mechanism. However, these techniques do not perform well in low-density urban environments due to the high

Fig. 5.4 Example of routing, store-carry-forward, based on location and direction in Vehicular Networks. Green vehicle is the original transmitter, red vehicles are relay nodes, and yellow vehicles the destination node

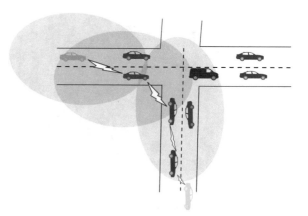

fragmentation rates, and a store-care-forward mechanism is required to increase their efficiency.

The location is just another parameter widely used by routing protocols. These protocols always select vehicles that are closest to the destination for information relay within the coverage area of the transmitter. Like the previous technique, this technique is not recommended for low-density environments, requiring a store-care-forward mechanism or other vehicle search engine to increase the performance of the mechanism.

Another technique used to select the retransmitters is the amount of neighbors a vehicle can have. The transmitter sends the data to be retransmitted to the vehicle that has a larger number of neighbors, so it increases the likelihood that the information will arrive at its intended destination.

These techniques use a beacon as a support mechanism for the abstraction of location information, speed, and direction. With this information, the vehicle can calculate the number of neighboring vehicles, the distance between vehicles, and the time of connectivity between them. All this information is used by the selection and retransmission techniques, which we have described previously.

Protocols use the techniques described in the following sections to perform data routing and dissemination efficiently without overloading the network with unnecessary information or with a lot of control messages. In the next section, the main routing and data dissemination protocols for vehicular networks are described.

5.3 Routing and Data Dissemination Protocols

Currently, several communication protocols support applications and services for vehicular networks. These protocols aim at minimizing delay, packet loss, and control messages and seek to maximize network throughput.

There are various ways to classify the routing and data dissemination protocols in vehicular networks [5, 8, 17]. However, we adopt the following classification: ad hoc, based on geographic positioning, cluster-based, geo-cast, multicast, and broadcast.

5.3.1 Ad Hoc Routing

This class of protocols is based on the network topology, which is determined by the distribution of vehicles in the network, as well as the information about the existing links among vehicles.

This class of routing protocols can be subdivided into three subclasses:

- **Proactive**. Information is stored in each form vehicle of a table. The table is shared by all vehicles, and to keep the information in this table consistent, updated data are sent over the network if any value in that table is changed. Thus, these updates consume a portion of the network bandwidth. Also, these protocols may be inefficient in a high-mobility scenario because of the number of update messages resulting from the frequent changes to network topology. Examples of this type of protocol category include the Optimized Link-State Routing (OLSR) protocol [14], Wireless Routing Protocol [31], and the Topology Dissemination Based on Reverse-Path Forwarding (TBRPF) protocol [36].

- **Reactive**. Vehicles do not have a routing table, so a route must be found when there is a message request. The protocol creates routes only when the source wants to send data to any destination. When the source-destination route is found, the source then starts to use it for a period. These reactive protocols use a mechanism and flood to establish a route, which can generate substantial overhead due to the broadcast storm and the number of routes that can be generated by the vehicles involved. Examples of this type of protocol category include Proactive Ad hoc On-Demand Distance Vector (Pro-AODV) routing [32], Dynamic Source Routing (DSR) [15], and AODV + Preferred Group Broadcasting (PGB) [34].

- **Hybrid protocol**. This is a combination of a reactive protocol with a proactive one to reduce the amount of messages caused by both protocols and to reduce the network delay caused by the creation of routes by the reactive protocol, bringing greater efficiency to the routing protocols. For this purpose, these protocols divide vehicles into different zones to improve the time of discovery and maintenance of routes. Like the other protocol categories, this category was not developed for scenarios with high vehicle mobility or with a highly dynamic network topology. Consequently, their performance is not relevant for vehicular networks. An example of such a protocol is a hybrid ad hoc routing protocol (HARP) [43].

The ad hoc protocols most geared toward wireless networks were inherited by the network carriers at the outset. However, because of the different characteristics of the two networks, these protocols did not show good performance, as revealed in the studies by [33, 39]. These studies showed that most ad hoc protocols, such as AODV and DSR, suffer from the natural dynamism of node mobility since they tend to have low communication throughput. In the work of Wang and colleagues [21], the AODV protocol was evaluated in a real experiment with six vehicles in which each vehicle had an IBM A-model laptop with an IEEE 802.11b NIC PCMCIA card. It was shown that the AODV protocol was unable to quickly find, maintain, and update long-distance routes in a vehicular network. There is large packet loss due to excessive routing error, making it difficult to establish a TCP connection. Therefore, some changes are made in the existing ad hoc protocol so that it can handle high mobility with highly dynamic topology. In what follows we describe some ad hoc routing protocols.

One of the well-known protocols in wireless networks is the OLSR protocol [14]. It is proactive, meaning it periodically exchanges information about the network with the nodes to constantly update its routing tables. This is a protocol based on link states. Its main function is to limit the number of network nodes that forward link states to eliminate redundant messages. For this, a technique called multipoint relay (MPR) is used.

The OLSR limits the number of vehicles that relay information. This approach works as follows. Among the vehicles in a network are some called MPRs. The choice of each MPR is made by a consensus among its one-hop neighboring nodes. Thus, when information needs to be updated on the network, packets sent by a vehicle reach all its neighbors; however, only the MPRs are able to relay the information later. This process repeats itself with the next nodes receiving the packets. In this way, each vehicle only receives the information once; no vehicle receives the packages more than once. The OLSR protocol is a more organized and efficient way to manage control packet traffic between two vehicles; it always looks for the shortest route. These mechanisms maintain in each vehicle an updated route table. However, for this, a large number of control messages are generated in the network.

The TBRPF protocol [36] is a proactive protocol based on link-state routing intended for an ad hoc wireless network. Each vehicle that uses this protocol calculates a source tree based on information from the partial network topology stored in the topology table. This source tree provides the shortest path for all reachable vehicles, so TBRPF uses a modification of the Dijkstra algorithm. To minimize the number of messages in the network, each vehicle sends only from its source tree to its neighbor.

Therefore TBRPF sends periodic messages about different updates to keep all neighbors informed about part of their source tree. Also, in this protocol, the function of neighbor discovery is performed by Hello messages that only report path state changes. These messages are much smaller than those of other link-state routing protocols such as Open Shortest Path First [30]. This protocol has a relevant amount of messages to keep the source tree up to date.

Namboodiri et al. [33] considered the routing of a vehicle with a gateway. The scenario of a highway was used in the simulation, in addition to information about the nodes, like speed and location, to predict the lifetime of the link. The strategy for reducing the effect of frequent interruption of routes was the development of protocols based on the prediction. One of the protocols was the PRAODV, which constructs a new alternative route before the estimated useful life of the link. PRAODV-M, on the other hand, chooses the path that has a longer predicted useful life among multiple route options, instead of selecting the shortest path in AODV and PRAODV. The simulations revealed a small improvement in package delivery rate, but the method depends on the accuracy of the forecasting method.

PGB [34] is a routing protocol that aims to reduce network overhead caused by the AODV protocol route discovery mechanism. For this purpose, this protocol uses vehicles that are traveling as wireless hosts. Also, PGB uses signal strength to determine which vehicles will forward information. Only one vehicle from the selected group will perform the retransmission.

This protocol has some limitations, like taking more time for path detection due to group creation and relay selection. A packet may be dropped due to a lack of a vehicle in the relay group. To reduce this problem, the authors developed packet replication [34], which determines that two retransmission group nodes can retransmit simultaneously, thereby generating the same overhead caused by the DSR protocol [15].

Harp [43] represents a combination of reactive and proactive zone-based mechanisms. HARP is divided into two levels, intrazone and interzone, depending on the location of a vehicle. Intrazone routing uses a proactive mechanism, and interzone routing uses a reactive mechanism. In this protocol, each vehicle retains only information about vehicles that are in the same zone or its neighboring zones.

HARP uses distributed dynamic routing (DDR) [35] to create zones and to aid in the proactive process, in other words, it manages network topology. HARP also has a mechanism for discovering and maintaining paths to satisfy application requirements. For path generation and selection, the HARP is based on [46], in which are differentiated vehicles at various levels depending on the zone they belong to, thereby reducing both the bandwidth used and the amount of energy consumed to carry the information forward.

5.3.2 Geographic Positioning Protocol

Positioning-based routing uses geographic information obtained from city maps, traffic patterns, or vehicle onboard navigation systems. Thus, vehicles know their location and their neighboring vehicles through this location information. Vehicles can make use of positioning information to decide on the time for forwarding information. According to Li and Wang, this routing model was identified as the most promising routing paradigm for VANETs.

This category of routing protocol may or may not use a store-carry-forward mechanism to deal with more scattered urban environments, such as environments in which there is highly frequent disconnections in the network. Also, position-based

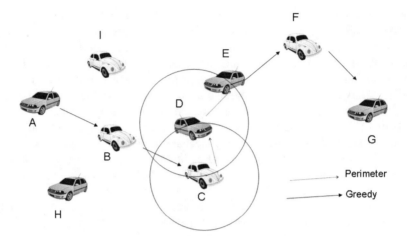

Fig. 5.5 Operation of GPSR protocol

protocols can be used as beacons to aid in capturing location, direction, and speed information.

Protocols based on geographic positioning, placed within a city, face great challenges since vehicles have an unequal distribution; there is a greater concentration of vehicles on one road than on others. Also, their mobility is restricted by road patterns and obstacles encountered such as buildings and can lead to disconnection from the network. Some routing protocols that use vehicle positioning are described in what follows.

The Greedy Perimeter Stateless Routing (GPSR) protocol [16] is one of the best-known position-based protocols in the literature. The GPSR protocol understands that the source node knows the location of the destination. Also, each node has current information about the position of its neighbors (obtained through a beaconing procedure). All packages include the location of the destination. Thus, when a node receives a packet, it can make the best decision by transmitting the packet until it reaches its destination. This protocol uses two methods of transmitting data (Fig. 5.5):

- **Greedy**. The origin node always seeks to choose the node closest to the destination at the limit of cells in reach, without considering the next jumps in the communication. For this purpose, the protocol does not use the positioning information of immediate neighboring nodes.
- **Perimeter**. If no neighboring node is close to the receiver, the GPSR activates perimeter routing mode, which performs routing through neighbors closer to the receiver. If no nodes are very close, the node sends the message to the node that is far from the destination node until another node is found that is near the destination node, returning to greedy mode.

Figure 5.5 shows the operation of the GPSR protocol. In this example, vehicle, or node, A wants to send data to node G. Node A sends the packets to node B, which is the nearest neighbor of G, the same as with node B. Vehicle C, upon receiving the packet, verifies that none of its neighbors, which are vehicles within the circle with its center in C, is closer to G than itself. Thus, node C activates perimeter mode (dashed arrow) and sends the data to D, the same way D uses perimeter mode to send data to E. In turn, D finds a node closer to G than node C, and the packet is again sent through the greedy strategy to node G.

This protocol does not perform well in urban environments because the greedy routing engine may fail due to a lack of nearby vehicles. If the greedy mechanism fails, the GPSR protocol uses the recovery mode that uses an extended path to reach the destination, which increases the delay in sending information. Due to the nature of the stateless GPSR, modified versions of the protocol have been proposed for vehicular networks [42]. Some researchers use the digital map in the navigation system to calculate a route from source to destination [20, 24].

Lochert et al. [24] proposed a routing protocol known as Geographic Source Routing (GSR), which is aided by a city street map. The GSR uses a reactive location service to reach the destination. The algorithm needs to know the city's global topology, which is provided by a static map of the streets. Given this information, the sender determines the junctions that the packet has to traverse, for which it is using the Dijkstra shortest path algorithm. Transmission between junctions is done through a positioning model, which combines geographical routing with a knowledge of the topology of the city streets given by the static map. The results of the simulation showed that the GSR has a better average message delivery rate, lower total bandwidth consumption, and a latency similar to that of the AOVD and DSR protocols.

Lochert et al. [25] proposed a modification of the GPSR protocol, the Greedy Perimeter Coordinator Routing (GPCR) protocol, where no route or map availability source is used. It uses the fact that nodes in a junction between streets follow a natural planar graph. These junctions are the only places where one decides to whom a message is transmitted so that it can reach its recipient. Instead of crossing those junctions and going to the node closest to the recipient, messages are sent to the node, called the coordinator, which is a junction. Figure 5.6a illustrates this strategy. If we were working with a greedy algorithm, node S would have sent the message to node N1; however, with the model used in this work, node S sends the message to node C1.

In addition to using this restriction in the greedy algorithm, this solution also uses a repair strategy to get out of the local minimum. In cases where a node has no neighbors closer to the destination, this repair strategy decides, at each junction, which would be the next street that the packet could be transmitted (right-hand rule) and applies greedy routing, between junctions, to find the next junction between the streets. Figure 5.6b demonstrates an example using the right-hand rule to decide which street the package can continue to use the repair strategy on. The simulation was performed in NS-2 with the topology of the city of Berlin, Germany, showing

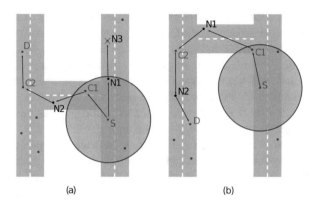

(a)   (b)

Fig. 5.6 GPCR protocol strategies [25]. (**a**) Restricted greedy. (**b**) Right-hand rule

that the GPCR has a higher delivery rate than GPSR, however with a higher hopping average and an increase in packet delivery time.

Liu et al. [23] proposed a new protocol based on geographic positioning called A-STAR (Anchor-based Street and Traffic-Aware Routing). This solution uses street maps to calculate junction sequences, here called anchors, through which the packet must pass to be delivered to its intended recipient. Unlike GSR, this solution calculates anchors according to car traffic conditions using statistical maps (counting the number of bus routes in the city to identify the most connected anchors) and dynamic maps (dynamic monitoring of the latest traffic conditions) to identify the route that the packet travels to reach its intended recipient. Another difference is the local recovery strategy. To prevent other packets from passing through empty areas, the route by which the local minimum occurred is temporarily marked as "out of service." Streets that are out of service are not used as anchors. These roads are computed only after certain time t when they go into an "operational" state. This solution showed better performance compared to the GSR and GPSR because they can choose the path with better connectivity for packet delivery.

The Grid-Based Predictive Geographical Routing (GPGR) protocol [4] is a grid-based predictive geographical routing protocol. GPGR uses map information to create a road grid, as well as predict the movement of vehicles along that road grid. GPGR uses vehicle mobility information, such as its position, direction, and velocity in the grid sequence, to assist in routing information from the network.

Therefore, GPGR employs map information to abstract the topology of streets and roads. This road topology is used to route messages between vehicles. The approach assumes that vehicles have a GPS that provides their location and a digital map that provides road information.

GPGR partitions a map into a two-dimensional logical grid. Grids are numbered (x, y) in which x and y are Cartesian coordinates, and each grid is a sequence area of size $d \times d$, as shown in Fig. 5.7. Given the location of the vehicle, it is possible to define its position on the grid. Each vehicle has a radio range r, and each grid has a size, which is defined as $d = r/2\sqrt{2}$. Thus, a vehicle located somewhere on

Fig. 5.7 Side length of grids
d is determined by
$d = r/2\sqrt{2}$, where each
vehicle has a radio range of
r [4]

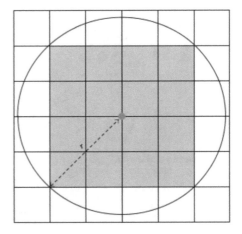

the grid is capable of transmitting data to any vehicle in its eight neighboring grids. Therefore, this protocol can reduce local maxima and link failure by choosing the retransmitter vehicle, which is based on road topology.

The vehicle-assisted data delivery (VADD) protocol [52] is based on carrying and forward [48] in which the vehicle retains a message when a route does not exist and retransmits the message to a new moving vehicle into its vicinity. VADD uses a mechanism of predictable mobility in a vehicular network, where it is limited by road layout and traffic pattern.

To route, the VADD protocol follows some principles such as the following [52]:

- Whenever possible, carry out transmission through wireless channels.
- The street chosen has the highest speed.
- The selection of paths is to be continuously executed through a packet-forwarding process.

Thus, a vehicle at an intersection of tracks may skew, and then the next path will be followed with negligible packet delivery delay. A walk is simply a division of roads of an intersection. The best packet route is chosen among three packet modes (intersection, straightway, and destination), based on the location of the packet carrier, as seen in Fig. 5.8. By switching between these packet modes, the packet carrier takes the best packet-forwarding path. The intersection module is the most crucial and complicated module since vehicles have more choices at an intersection.

The Contention-based Forwarding (CBF) [12] protocol is a routing protocol that does not use control messages as an aid in abstracting information from neighboring vehicles. Thus, this routing protocol reduces the number of messages sent in the network, as well as the bandwidth used. CBF uses direct communication between neighbors and selects only one vehicle to route the message. This selection is based on the distributed timer-based contention process. This process uses the distance

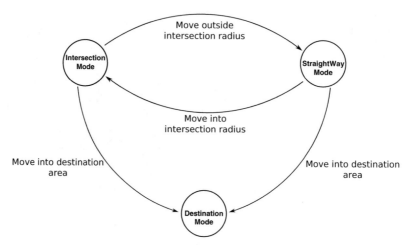

Fig. 5.8 Transition modes in VADD [52]

between the receiver and the vehicle that has just received the call; whichever has the smallest distance with the least hops is selected to retransmit.

By not using beacons, this protocol makes better use of its bandwidth. Also, it avoids an overload of control messages, reducing the number of message collections. Although this protocol performs well in a highway environment, in urban environments a high frequency of local maximum can occur with respect to the distance between vehicles, making it difficult to create a route.

The Hybrid Geographic and delay-tolerant networking (GeoDTN) routing + Nav protocol [9] is the junction of non-DTN and DTN routing protocols. Like the GPSR, it uses a greedy mode, perimeter mode, and a DTN module. Thus, the protocol can modify its operation mode from non-DTN mode to DTN mode according to the number of jumps in a packet, the quality of delivery of the message and the direction of the neighboring vehicles of the recipient. The DTN module has a store-carry-forward function because it can deliver information even when the network is partitioned. Thus, this module is triggered when the recovery mode fails since there are no vehicles to retransmit.

The quality of delivery of information is obtained through the virtual navigation interface (VNI) that uses information from other devices such as navigation system and event data recorder (EDR), among other devices. These providers supply information relevant to the protocol to determine the route that particular information follows. The results showed that this protocol had better performance than GPSR and GPCR due to the store-carry-forward mechanism.

Fig. 5.9 Cluster routing model [21]

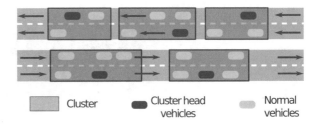

☐ Cluster   ● Cluster head vehicles   ● Normal vehicles

5.3.3 Cluster Protocol

In cluster-based routing, a virtual network infrastructure is created between vehicles through a cluster that provides greater scalability. Figure 5.9 illustrates cluster-based routing in VANETs. Each cluster can have a cluster head, which is responsible for intra- and intercluster coordination in the Network, and has a management function. Nodes within a cluster communicate through direct connections. Intercluster communication is performed through cluster heads, which are able to select vehicles to perform the functions of gateways and execute communication between the clusters. These protocols were considered adequate for networks since the vehicles are on a highway and can naturally form a cluster [42].

However, the selection of cluster heads and cluster gateways comprehends one the great challenges of this category of routing protocols. Due to the high mobility of vehicles, the exchange of the cluster head in an urban setting could be very high, requiring greater processing time for the selection of these vehicles. Also, the formation and maintenance of these clusters may require a lot of control messages [21]. Below are some cluster-based routing protocols.

Santos et al. [39] presented a locally based reactive routing algorithm that serves as the basis for a cluster to perform flooding in VANETs, called LORA_CBF. Each node can be a cluster head, gateway, or member of a cluster. Each cluster has exactly one cluster head. If a node is connected to more than one cluster, it is called a gateway. The cluster head holds information about its members and gateways. Packets are transmitted from a source to a recipient by a routing protocol similar to a greedy one. If the destination location is not available, the source sends the location request (LREQ) packets. This process is similar to the discovery phase of the AODV route, but only the cluster head and the gateways release LREQ and LREP (location response) messages. Figure 5.10 illustrates the structure developed by Santos and his collaborators. For performance abstraction, a comparison was made between the AODV and DSR protocols and the LORA_CBF in an urban setting and on a motorway. The results showed that the mobility of the network, as well as its size, had a more significant impact on the AODV and DSR protocols than on the LORA_CBF [39].

The Moving Zone-Based (MoZo) routing protocol [22] consists of several mobile zones that are formed by the vehicle mobility pattern. For each zone, a captain is elected and is responsible for managing the information that is traveling in its

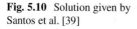

Fig. 5.10 Solution given by
Santos et al. [39]

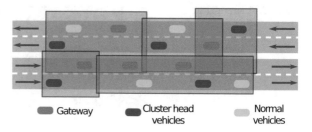

zone, collecting details about the vehicles members of the zone. This mobile zone is
established when a vehicle initiates the protocol. It initially starts the joining process
to check for possible mobile zones near it or to form its own mobile zone. The zone
setting is based on the similarity of vehicle movements. The captain of each zone
maintains a moving object index that manages up-to-date information about all its
member vehicles.

The Multihoming Clustering Algorithm for Vehicular Ad Hoc Networks (MCA-
VANET) [50] was proposed by Vodopivec et al. With this protocol, unlike conventional clustering methods, instead of vehicles starting with an unknown state
and subsequently creating or participating in some cluster, the authors assume that
vehicles are the head of their clusters and subsequently decide whether they will join
another cluster, becoming a member or allowing other vehicles to become members
of that cluster. The decision is based on an 8-bit counter stored in each vehicle. The
counter is incremented for each Hello message received from a neighbor, which is
a beacon control message sent periodically and halved each time a period expires
without receipt of a control message. Thus, vehicles decide the eligibility of their
neighbors to be cluster heads independently of other nodes. This process does not
require GPS data, which may be imprecise in urban areas, but rather estimates the
proximity of the connectivity. Also, vehicles can have access to multiple cluster
heads as a form of route redundancy.

5.3.4 Broadcast Protocol

Broadcast routing has several purposes in a VANET, such as the dissemination of
traffic conditions on a given street and reporting on weather conditions, advertisements, and road accidents, among others.

The easiest way to implement broadcast routing is by using flooding, causing
each vehicle to relay messages to all its neighbors except the vehicle that sent
the message. Flooding ensures that the message is delivered to all participating
vehicles on the network. This strategy performs well for a limited number of
nodes in a network and is easily implemented. However, when the number of
nodes increases, performance drops, as there may be a significant increase in their
bandwidth, overloading the network. Therefore, in this category of routing protocol,

it is necessary to perform broadcast storm management to prevent the network from overloading with unnecessary messages. Some of these protocols are described in what follows.

Durresi et al. [11] presented an emergency broadcast protocol, BROADCOMM, based on a hierarchical structure for a network developed on a motorway. In BROADCOMM, the virtual highway is divided into cells whose movement resembles that of vehicles. The nodes on a motorway are divided into two hierarchical levels: the first level includes all nodes in a cell, while the second level is represented by reflecting cells, which are nodes that are usually close to the geographical center of cells. Reflector cells behave as a base station (cluster head), in a given time interval, that deals with emergency messages coming from members of the same cell or nearby members of neighboring cells. Also, reflector cells serve as intermediate nodes in the routing of transmitted emergency messages from neighboring reflecting cells. This protocol performs similarly to the routing protocol based on flooding. However, it is simpler and only works with networks created on a highway.

The urban multi-hop broadcast (UMB) protocol [19] was developed to overcome interference, packet collisions, and hidden node problems during multihop broadcast messages. In UMB, the source node tries to select the farthest node by directing the broadcast and causing the packet to be recognized without any a priori information on the topology. Repeaters are installed at intersections to transmit packets to all segments of the road. The UMB protocol has a higher success rate, with a packet overhead in the network and dense vehicle traffic, greater than the 802.11 distance protocol and the 802.11 random protocol, which are adapted from the IEEE 802.11 standard to avoid collisions during packet forwarding.

PREDAT [29] is a routing protocol that seeks to reduce the number of retransmissions without compromising coverage. The proposed algorithm makes use of two mechanisms, the first one to avoid a broadcast storm and the second to maximize data dissemination capacity between network partitions at low cost, with a slight delay, and with high coverage. In the first mechanism, we define a region called a preference zone, a region that assigns a priority to vehicles to perform retransmission. Vehicles that are within that region have higher retransmission priority. The second mechanism is an autonomic technique that simulates the function of a store-carry-forward when there is partitioning in the network. For instance, a vehicle stores the data while its propagation efficiency is low or until the number of packet jumps is beyond a certain threshold. In addition to simulating a store-carry-forward, propagation efficiency assists in the decision to relay or not relay information. In what follows, we describe the characteristics of each mechanism.

The preference zone is intended to eliminate the broadcast storm problem because vehicles within the zone of preference transmit packets with the least delay and abort the transmissions of the same packet from other vehicles that are not in the zone of preference. Among vehicles in the preference zone, the one furthest from the transmitting vehicle first transmits and aborts the scheduled transmissions of neighboring vehicles. In case there are no vehicles in the zone of preference, the vehicle furthest from each quadrant retransmits the information. For the sake of simplicity, the shape of the communication area is considered circular, where the transmitting vehicle is in the center of the circle. The area of communication is decomposed into four quadrants, and in each quadrant, a subarea of the quadrant is defined as a zone of preference. Through the zones of preference, we can prevent the transmission of the same information from the vehicles that are close to each other and belong to different quadrants, thereby avoiding a situation where messages reach similar areas, which would be an unnecessary redundancy.

Although the zone-of-preference approach reduces communication issues and effects of a broadcast storm, the approach does not deal with the problem of partitions in a network. Thus, to solve this problem, we use an autonomic technique that calculates the probability that a vehicle will disseminate information. This decision is based on the current propagation efficiency of each vehicle (Eq. (5.1)) and the geographical location of the vehicles. Efficiency is the ratio between the number of data packets transmitted and the number of beacons received.

Propagation efficiency is used to control the transmission of each vehicle. Thus, if this efficiency is below an acceptable limit, a vehicle retransmits the data; however, if the efficiency is above the threshold, the vehicle does not transmit the data. Efficiency is calculated every round, meaning over time a given vehicle checks the efficiency of its data delivery.

$$\text{Propagation efficiency} = \text{Transmission/Beacons} \tag{5.1}$$

In addition to propagation efficiency, another factor that can influence the relaying of information is information lifetime. Based on this mechanism, a vehicle stores information until its efficiency exceeds a threshold or until one of the other parameters is reached, allowing for the delivery of the information, even in the presence of network partitioning.

Thus a vehicle wanting to propagate some data transmits the data packet to all neighboring vehicles. Upon receipt of the package, each vehicle checks if it is within the AOI. If this condition is not met, the vehicle discards the received packet. Otherwise, the vehicle calculates the wait time and schedules the retransmission of the packet. If the vehicle receives some package duplicated, then retransmission of the package is canceled.

Whenever possible, partitioning in the network is detected by a vehicle, which is indicated by the absence of beacons, and the vehicle waits to receive new beacons to continue the data dissemination process. For example, suppose the source vehicle (S) and another vehicle (A) belong to a partition (P1), and the remaining vehicles of the AOI are in a second partition of the network (P2). In this case, S and A, which is in P1, do not notice a partitioning in the network, because S receives beacons of A, and A receives beacons of S, so both S and A do not perceive any partition in the network. However, if S or A receives a beacon from a vehicle that was in the P2 partition, these vehicles resume the dissemination process and check whether they are capable of spreading data according to propagation efficiency. A threshold of propagation efficiency of less than 50% indicates that the vehicle is capable of spreading. Also, the vehicle that received the beacon also checks if the transmitting vehicle is within the AOI and if it has already received the information being disclosed. If the vehicle is within the AOI and has not yet received the information, the vehicle that has the information performs the disclosure. Otherwise, the information is not disseminated. The protocol uses the number of hops to limit the amount of dissemination of information.

Tonguz et al. [47] proposed the Distributed Vehicular Broadcast (DV-CAST) protocol, which aims to solve both problems (broadcast storm and network partitions). DV-CAST uses periodic beacons to create a local topology (one-hop neighbors), which is used to relay messages. DV-CAST performs data dissemination in both dense and sparse networks. For this, during the dissemination of data, if the connectivity degree of the local topology is high, the receiver applies the transmission suppression algorithm. Otherwise, it uses the store-carry-forward mechanism as a solution in a low-density region. However, in scenarios with high mobility, DV-CAST performance depends on the frequency of the beacon, whose ideal value is difficult to establish.

Schwartz et al. [40] proposed the Simple and Robust Dissemination (SRD) protocol, which is designed to operate in dense and sparse vehicular networks and represents an improvement over DV-CAST. Like DV-CAST, SRD relies solely on information from a local neighbor with a jump and employs no special infrastructure. Among the main improvements over DV-CAST is the proposal to optimize the technique of broadcast suppression. Vehicles have different priorities for retransmission, according to their direction of travel. SRD avoids the broadcast storm problem in dense networks and handles disconnected networks with the store-carry-forward communication model.

Hybrid data dissemination (HyDi) [26] was developed by Maia et al. It is a data dissemination protocol for road scenarios. HyDi uses the direction of vehicles' movement; the protocol also employs the direction in which vehicles' data need to follow, which is the direction of the dissemination of messages. In addition, this protocol handles broadcast storms when a network is well connected through a combination of sender- and receiver-based methods.

Using the sender-based mechanism, a vehicle selects a relay first. However, with the receiver-based mechanism, one of the vehicles that received the message is responsible for forwarding the message. The message is selected and sent later. If a vehicle cannot find other vehicles to deliver the message to, it implements transport techniques and forwarding by holding on to the message until a new connection is recognized as a vehicle that can return the message to its prerecognized route. Later, the vehicle transmits the message. The experimental results presented in [26] showed that HyDi has good performance, though it has not been tested in an urban environment.

5.3.5 Multicast Protocol

Multicast protocols have the objective of transmitting data to a group of vehicles; a single vehicle sends certain information to several vehicles. This category of protocols was also inherited from wired networks and wireless networks in which the topology is stable or has low variation compared to vehicular networks. Thus it is necessary to make adaptations in these protocols so that they can be executed efficiently in an urban environment, keeping the information of the links updated. However, vehicular networks can benefit from this type of protocol because its wireless nature allows for the sending of data by themselves received by several vehicles.

To establish a connection between the vehicle for sending data and the group of vehicles for receiving these data, these protocols may use a tree structure or a mesh, facilitating the management of the multicast group that would like to receive certain data.

Tree-based protocols create and maintain a shared tree of vehicles that receive certain information. This strategy performs poorly in urban environments with high vehicle mobility as a processing card, and a large number of control messages are generated to maintain and rebuild this tree [21].

The mesh-based protocol involves creating a mesh that contains all connected vehicles in a particular multicast group. Some multicast routing protocols are described in what follows.

MAODV [38] is an extension of the AODV protocol [37]. It maintains a shared tree for each multicast group. It uses broadcast to find a route, on demand, and build a routing tree. The first multicast group node becomes the group leader. The leader of the multicast group is responsible for maintaining the sequence number of the group and sending that number to all members. According to Fig. 5.11, a node that wants to join the multicast group sends a broadcast request (RREQ). This message is broadcast to all intermediate nodes until it finds a node in the tree. This node then sends a unicast request response (RREP) through the reverse path to the requesting node. The requesting node can receive more than one RREP message. It then selects the shortest (based on the number of jumps) and most current route (based on the sequence number) by sending a unicast activation message (MACT) through the chosen route. The entire intermediate node is a forwarding node.

The routing tables are updated with information showing that there is one more member of the multicast group and other routing nodes. In this way, there is only one path between any pair of nodes in the tree. When a fault occurs, a route discovery process must be carried out again. If a node wants to leave the multicast group, it may exit if it is a node that has no children. If it has children, it may leave the multicast group, but not the multicast tree because it must forward messages to its child nodes.

Multicast with Mechanisms of Ant Colony Optimization for VANET-based MAODV protocol (MAV-AODV) [45] is a protocol that uses the principles of MAODV [38] to do multicast routing in VANETs. The MAV-AODV protocol uses vehicular mobility information to attempt to provide multicast routing stability in VANETs. Also, MAV-AODV uses mechanisms to optimize the construction and maintenance of multicast trees. Protocol messages act as bioinspired agents (ants) when depositing pheromones to assess the attractiveness of each route.

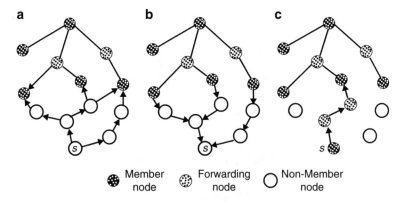

Fig. 5.11 MAODV join operation [41]

MAV-AODV uses beacons to abstract information regarding speed, direction, and positioning of vehicles. These beacons are dispatchers notifying others that a particular vehicle may know some other vehicles' neighborhood. When vehicles receive a link, it calculates the estimated time of the link between vehicles. After performing the calculation, the vehicles store this value in their routing table. Using vehicle mobility information, the MAV-AODV protocol defines the methods for requesting the route that forms the multicast tree.

For a route request, the protocol uses two main messages: route request message (AntRREQ-J) and reply message (Ant-RREP). The route request has the functionality of an ant, exploring the network paths in search of members who would like to join the multicast group. This message is sent via broadcast. Each Ant-RREP message consists of the number of hops to the destination node and the lifetime of the link. This link lifetime is calculated through the beacon message and is continuously updated.

As a response message, the MAV-AODV protocol uses the Ant-RREP, which also act as ants depositing their pheromones on the way back to the requesting vehicle after having found a member of the multicast tree. Therefore, when the vehicle receives an Ant-RREQ message, it may respond if it has a route to the multicast array and its registered sequence number is greater than or equal to the number contained in Ant-RREQ-J. The vehicle that responded to Ant-RREQ increases the number of jumps in the table.

Before generating a response message, the vehicle examines the lifetime and hop count. These values are used to calculate the pheromones on the traveled route. A pheromone can be defined as follows:

$$\text{Pheromone}(p) = \text{Lifetime}(p)/\text{HopCount}(p), \tag{5.2}$$

where p is the path (route) traveled by the Ant-RREQ.

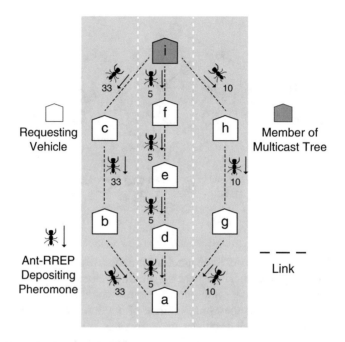

Fig. 5.12 Example of route reply [45]

This value is updated and placed in the Pheromone field in the reply message. After all calculations have been performed, the message is sent to the requester via unicast.

Figure 5.12 illustrates the path of RREPs (represented as ants) to the source node. RREP deposits the pheromone (p) value in the nested multicast routing tables (Pheromone field) all the way back to the source node.

When nodes, along with the path to the source node, receive an RREP for the first time, they add an entry to the node from which they received the RREP in the multicast routing table, thereby creating a routing path. However, even these intermediate nodes can receive more than one RREP for a given pair (source–destination). In this case, MAV-AODV analyzes some parameters to check whether the route of the RREP is valid and up to date. If it is, the MAV-AODV probabilistically chooses between the RREP that was already stored in the multicast routing table and the RREP that has just reached the intermediate node.

This process of probabilistic choice occurs through a roulette mechanism. Each RREP has a stored amount of pheromone. The RREP that was already in the multicast routing table (we will call this RREPolder RREP) has the amount of pheromone stored in that table itself, which we will call Pheromonetable. The RREP that has just arrived (let us call this RREP newer RREP) has the amount of pheromone stored in the message itself in the Pheromone field (called the Pheromonepacket).

The RREP that arrived later has a greater amount of pheromone and a greater probability of being chosen. If such an RREP is chosen, the multicast routing table must be updated, and this RREP continues to be routed to the source node. Otherwise, the routing table remains unchanged, and the RREP that arrived later is discarded.

Also, if more than one RREP arrives at the source node, this selection process is repeated for each new RREP that arrives until a time limit expires. After the time limit runs out, a route activation mechanism is triggered. After that, an activation message is sent through the chosen path by the chosen Ant-RREP. The route that has the highest probability of being chosen, the new route of the multicast tree, is $a - b - c - i$.

5.3.6 Geocast Protocol

Geocast routing is fundamentally a multicast routing protocol based on positioning that aims to deliver messages from one source vehicle to all other vehicles belonging to a specific geographical region (ZOR). Vehicles outside this region are not alerted, preventing the unnecessary sending of a message. However, the ZOR [51] can be defined as a geographic region where vehicles can receive data that are being sorted.

Geocast can be implemented with a multicast service simply by defining the multicast group as geographic regions. Most of the methods used for geocast routing are based on directed flooding, which attempts to limit the overhead of messages on the network by causing the flooding to occur only within a relevant region. This category of protocol routing does not perform well in low-density urban environments because it has a high level of network fragmentation. Some routing protocols are described in what follows.

UGAD [1] is a routing protocol that adapts a delay-based scheme for geocast and urban environments. Like the Mobicast protocol, vehicles also select a region of relevance they call the geocast region (GR). Also, the authors use a forwarding zone in which they are defined as the region that is closer to the GR than a sender.

Therefore, when the transmitter sends data, the vehicles that receive these data verify whether they are in the forwarding zone. If the vehicles are in the forwarding zone or the GR, they calculate the time for retransmission of the message and retransmit. If a vehicle receives duplicate packages, the vehicle cancels its retransmission.

The retransmission time can be calculated in two ways by greedy forwarding mode in which it seeks to maximize the propagation gain in each hop and minimize redundant rebroadcasting. For this, the vehicle calculates the back-off time based on the package received from another vehicle. This back-off time is defined as

$$T_{GF\_i} = T_{max\_R}(R - d_{i,j}/R) \tag{5.3}$$

where T_{max} is the maximum waiting time for receivers, R is the transmission range, which is common in each vehicle, and d is the distance between vehicles.

Fig. 5.13 Example of packet
forwarding in
intersection-based forwarding
mode [1]

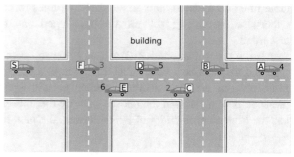

The other way to calculate is intersection-based forwarding (IF), which aims to
maximize the opportunities for vehicles to rebroadcast packets at intersections. For
this, vehicles that are at intersections are chosen to retransmit the data. The IF is
calculated based on the waiting time for the vehicle to receive data from another
vehicle. Thus the IF can be defined as

$$
T_{IF\_i} = \begin{cases} T_{\max\_i} \dfrac{R-d_{i,j}}{R} & \text{(intersection)} \\ T_{\max\_i} + T_{\max\_i} \dfrac{R-d_{i,j}}{R} & \text{(otherwise)} \end{cases}
\tag{5.4}
$$

where $T_{\max_i}$ is the maximum waiting time for vehicles at intersections, $T_{\max_R}$ is
the maximum waiting time for other vehicles on roads, R and d correspond to
that in Eq. (5.3). Vehicles at intersections have a greater preference for performing
retransmissions when compared with vehicles that are far from intersections.

Figure 5.13 describes the operation of the UGAD. When vehicle S wants to
transmit data, it propagates its information in the network. The vehicles that receive
the information calculate their waiting time. Vehicles A, B, and C that are at a
segment intersection have a shorter waiting time and, thus, a greater probability
of performing the retransmission. Also, the waiting time based on the distance
between vehicles and transmitter is calculated. The vehicle that has the shortest time
retransmits. In this case, vehicle B has forwards the data. The other vehicles cancel
their retransmissions because they have already received the data from vehicle B.

Mobicast [6] is a spatiotemporal multicast/geocast routing protocol that considers not only the time but also the space to perform its routing. The purpose
of this protocol is to transmit data from a source vehicle to all vehicles within a
relevant area (ZOR) at a given time t. ZOR is the elliptic area in which the data
to be transmitted are relevant; this area is divided into four quadrants, where each
quadrant is a subarea of relevance, and the transmitting vehicle is the center of these
quadrants, as shown in Fig. 5.14.

For messages to be propagated inside the ZOR within a time t in an efficient
manner, Mobicast has used a zone called a zone of forwarding (ZOF) that handles
network partitioning. ZOFs have varied formats and dimensions. Consequently,
errors may occur when delineating the areas of ZOFs. If the area is too large, some
vehicles forward packages unnecessarily. However, if the size of the area is too

Fig. 5.14 Example of relevant area [6]

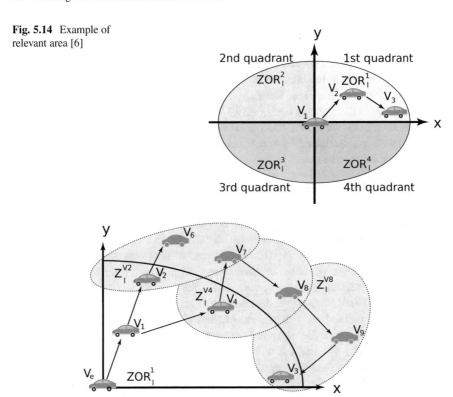

Fig. 5.15 Creation of routing zone [1]

small, the partitioning problem may still occur. As a predictor of ZOF size, the authors proposed a zone of approach (ZOA) which is an elliptical area in which vehicles that are the nearest to the message recipients are selected to retransmit the messages. Figure 5.15 describes the creation of a routing zone, in which vehicles V3 and V4 cannot find other vehicles in the ZOR, so Z1 and Z2 are created. Vehicle V8 also cannot find other vehicles in Z2 next to the vehicle that belongs to ZOR, so it starts a Z3. Thus, the ZOF is defined as follows:

$$ZOF = ZOR + Z1 + Z2 + Z3. \tag{5.5}$$

Therefore, the information is transmitted to all vehicles within a zone of interest. Although the Mobicast protocol deals with network fragmentation, the data are lost if no neighbor is found within the forwarding zone. To solve this problem, Lin et al. [7] proposed a store-carry-forward mechanism to allow messages to be lost during the propagation of information in the ZOR, increasing the information delivery capacity of the Mobicast protocol.

Maihöfer and Eberhardt [27] discuss the cache structure and how to select a neighborhood to handle high-speed situations in VANETs compared to regular geocast protocols. The main idea of a greedy geocast cache, within the ZOR protocol, is to add a small cache to the routing layer that holds those packets that a node cannot transmit because of its lack of neighbors. When a new node arrives, the message that is in the cache may be passed to that newly discovered node. The neighbor's distance knowledge strategy chooses the nearest destination on a radius r, instead of the last node of the transmission range, as in the greedy routing model. In a greedy model, the intermediate node always selects the next closest node to the nodes that are at the edge of the transmission range, and it retransmits the message so that the next node to be selected has a good chance of leaving the transmission range owing to the high mobility of the node. The results of a simulation show that the caching for messages that cannot be transmitted because of network fragmentation or lack of neighbors had a significant improvement in the delivery rate of messages in a geocast. The selection strategy of the neighbors resulted in a decrease in the load of messages in the network and a decrease in the delay in the delivery of information.

The robust vehicular routing (ROVER) protocol [18] was developed by Kihl et al. It is a reliable geographical multicast protocol in which only control messages are sent via broadcast in the network and other messages are sent individually by unicast. ROVER aims to send messages to all vehicles within a specific zone. Messages are defined by a triple A, M, and Z, which identify the application used, the message, and the ad zone identification. Thus, when a vehicle receives a message, it checks whether it is within the ZOR if the vehicle processes the image; otherwise, the message is discarded.

ROVER uses a reactive mechanism to search for a route within the ZOR. It generates a very large number of redundant messages in the network, creating a lot of congestion and, consequently, increasing message delays. To attempt to solve this problem, Bronsted and Kristensen [3] proposed an extension of the protocol where they used a two-zone dissemination protocol. In this mechanism, a hop count is used in a message to reduce redundant messages. Thus, if the hop count gets to zero, the message is removed.

5.4 Discussions and Challenges Encountered

An efficient protocol for routing and disseminating data in a vehicle network needs, in addition to considering the constraints of vehicular networks such as their low transmission time, a high speed of vehicles and a highly dynamic topology. Also, the requirements of a particular application must be taken into account. Therefore, the protocol has to deliver messages in a short period of time with little packet loss and without overloading the network with unnecessary control messages or duplicate messages.

Several works have sought to develop a protocol that deals with various traffic considerations, seeking greater message delivery, reducing interference and collisions between messages in the network. Furthermore, such a protocol would provide greater scalability in the delivery of messages, in other words, it would allow for delivery in a short time period. A summary of the features and mechanisms used in the works presented in this chapter is described in Table 5.1. The routing protocols were categorized based on their routing strategy.

On the basis of the work studied we can observe the ability of a protocol to abstract information from the network and neighborhood of vehicles to assist in the generation and maintenance of this information. This knowledge comes through control messages, as is the case with some broadcast protocols such as PREDAT and Hydi, as well as in cluster-based and positioning protocols. Such messages can be used to detect road conditions and check traffic density, as with A-STAR and VADD protocols. These protocols merge information from different sources by joining data collected through beacon messages with probabilistic and mathematical methods to try to classify traffic conditions. With this traffic density information, the protocols can adjust their parameters to better meet the needs of a certain application given present state of the network. Another way to optimize the delivery of information is through the knowledge of the topology of streets and roads. This knowledge is obtained through the digital map of the place. This approach is followed by GeoDTN + Nav, Lora CBF, and GPCR protocols, which use knowledge of a map for the generation of efficient paths for the delivery of information.

Looking at how protocols deal with network partitioning and fragmentation, it is possible to abstract two main strategies, store-carry-forward and mobility prediction. The store-carry-forward strategy, as previously described, is a storage mechanism that a vehicle uses when there is a disconnection in the network. The message is stored in the vehicle until the network is reconnected. Thus, avoiding a situation where the message is lost in the network for lack of a valid route, this strategy can be seen in the great majority of existing protocols such as PREDAT, MCA-VANET, GPCR, and others. However, this store-carry-forward method increases the end-to-end delay because of the time spent waiting for a new connection. Thus, it is necessary to reduce the waiting time, for example, by increasing transmission power in sparsely populated areas, thereby increasing the communication range.

Another strategy used involves trying to predict vehicle mobility. This mechanism analyzes the current position of a vehicle, its speed and direction, and its last known locations. With this information, the protocol uses probabilistic methods to try to predict the vehicle's next step. Thus, the protocol attempts to time the duration of a route to determine how a new route will begin based on the new positioning of the vehicle. Therefore, new routing protocols can take advantage of driver behavior to increase the efficiency of route generation and maintenance.

Although existing routing protocols and methods try to cope with vehicular network limitations, some challenges remain, for example, concerning the heterogeneous use of these protocols. A routing protocol must be generic enough that its behavior can be maintained in both urban and highway environments. Also, it must support different traffic density conditions for both running scenarios. Other challenges that these protocols must overcome are as follows:

Table 5.1 Availability and evaluation of routing protocols

Protocol	Type	Forwarding strategy	Scenario	Location services	Map-based	Vehicular localization	Store-carry-forward	Drawbacks
OLSR	Ad Hoc	Multihop	City					Overhead in update of route table
TBRPF	Ad Hoc	Multihop	City					Overhead in update of route table
PRAODV	Ad Hoc	Multihop	City				✓	Overhead in update of route table
PGB	Ad Hoc	Multihop	City				✓	Overhead in update of route table
HARP	Ad Hoc	Multihop	City					Overhead in update of route table
GPSR	Position-based	Greedy	Highway	✓		✓		Does not address network partition
GSR	Position-based	Greedy	City	✓	✓	✓		Does not address network partition
GPCR	Position-based	Greedy	City	✓	✓	✓		Does not address network partition
A-STAR	Position-based	Greedy	City	✓	✓	✓		Does not address network partition
GPGR	Position-based	Greedy	City	✓		✓		Does not address network partition
VADD	Position-based	Greedy	City	✓		✓	✓	It is difficult to select an outgoing edge freely
CBF	Position-based	Greedy	City	✓				Does not address network partition and higher overhead

(continued)

Table 5.1 (continued)

Protocol	Type	Forwarding strategy	Scenario	Location services	Map-based	Vehicular localization	Store-carry-forward	Drawbacks
GeoDTN + Nav	Position-based	Greedy	City	✓	✓		✓	Greedy forwarding often restricted to urban scenario because direct communication typically does not exist
LORA CBF	Cluster	Greedy	City	✓	✓		✓	Overhead to generate clusters
MoZo	Cluster	Greedy	City	✓	✓		✓	Overhead to generate clusters
MCA-VANET	Cluster	Greedy	City	✓	✓		✓	Overhead to generate clusters
BROADCOMM	Broadcast	Multihop	Highway				✓	Naive performance evaluation
UMB	Broadcast	Multihop	Highway				✓	Solution performs well only in dense scenario
PREDAT	Broadcast	Multihop	City and highway			✓	✓	Duplication message
DV-CAST	Broadcast	Multihop	Highway				✓	Duplication message

SRD	Broadcast	Multihop	Highway				✓	Duplication message
HyDi	Broadcast	Multi-hop	Highway				✓	Only works in highway environments
MAODV	Multicast	Multihop	City					Overhead to create multicast group
MAV-AODV	Multicast	Multihop	City		✓	✓		Overhead to create multicast group
UGAD	Geocast	Multihop	City			✓		In some scenarios, can be affected by network partition
Mobicast	Geocast	Multihop	Highway			✓		Simple solution that depends on GPS equipment
ROVER	Geocast	Multihop	Highway			✓		In some scenarios, approach can be affected by network partition

- **Network Disconnection**. Although several methods exist for dealing with these problems, a mechanism is needed to reduce the delay of messages when the network becomes disconnected. This involves an analysis of the behavior of the driver in attempting to predict network actions, which makes it possible to extend the lifetime of the connection and road conditions based on human behavior. Another solution is to use the infrastructure to aid in routing for coping with the lack of connectivity in V2V communications; this requires a generic protocol that allows hybrid communication in vehicular networks.
- **Security**. Information security in mobile networks is a major challenge. Because information transferred in a network can affect life-or-death decisions and illegal interference may have disastrous consequences. Thus, the inclusion of security mechanisms in routing protocols becomes crucial to prevent false and malicious information from compromising not only the routing of information but the secrecy of the information being routed.
- **QoS Metrics**. Most routing protocols do not consider the minimum quality of service requirements of a particular application or stream set that is transmitted. Thus these routing protocols must consider not only the limitations of vehicular networks but also the parameters of QoSs such as available bandwidth, end-to-end delay, and jitter so that the application can be executed in the best possible way.
- **Scalability**. With the increasing number of vehicles in cities, it is essential that these protocols offer scalability. Even if a huge amount of vehicles is encountered on roads, the amount of control messages in networks or duplicate messages cannot impact performance.

5.5 Final Discussion

In this chapter, we have introduced the concept of V2V communication. We described routing and data dissemination protocols in vehicular networks, illustrating the problems of some of the traditional techniques already known in wireless networks but applied in vehicular networks. These issues include traditional protocols for wireless networks as well as new protocols developed especially for vehicular networks. We also classify these protocols routinely as ad hoc, position-based, cluster, broadcast, multicast, and geocast, showing the benefits of using this technology in the application of routing and data dissemination protocols. We also discussed the challenges facing such technology. Then we listed and explained the state-of-the-art techniques for routing and data dissemination protocols. Finally, we discussed the significant challenges in the field and research opportunities.

References

1. Akamatsu R, Suzuki M, Okamoto T, Hara K, Shigeno H (2014) Adaptive delay-based geocast protocol for data dissemination in urban vanet. In: Proceedings of the seventh international conference on mobile computing and ubiquitous networking, pp 141–146
2. Aparecido L (2015) Data dissemination in vehicular networks: challenges, solutions, and future perspectives. In: Proceedings of the 7th international conference on new technologies, mobility and security, pp 1–5
3. Bronsted J, Kristensen LM (2006) Specification and performance evaluation of two zone dissemination protocols for vehicular ad-hoc networks. In: Proceedings of the 39th annual symposium on simulation. IEEE Computer Society, Washington, pp 68–79
4. Cha SH, Lee KW, Cho HS (2012) Grid-based predictive geographical routing for inter-vehicle communication in urban areas. Int J Distrib Sens Netw 8(3):819497
5. Chaqfeh M, Lakas A, Jawhar I (2014) A survey on data dissemination in vehicular ad hoc networks. Veh Commun 1(4):214–225
6. Chen YS, Lin YW, Lee SL (2009) A mobicast routing protocol in vehicular ad-hoc networks. In: Proceedings of the IEEE global telecommunications conference, pp 1–6
7. Chen YS, Lin YW, Lee SL (2010) A mobicast routing protocol with carry-and-forward in vehicular ad-hoc networks. In: Proceedings of the 5th international ICST conference on communications and networking in China, pp 1–5
8. Chen W, Guha RK, Kwon TJ, Lee J, Hsu YY (2011) A survey and challenges in routing and data dissemination in vehicular ad hoc networks. Wirel Commun Mob Comput 11(7):787–795
9. Cheng PC, Weng JT, Tung LC, Lee KC, Gerla M, Haerri J (2008) Geodtn+ nav: a hybrid geographic and dtn routing with navigation assistance in urban vehicular networks. MobiQuitous/ISVCS 47
10. Cunha F, Villas L, Boukerche A, Maia G, Viana A, Mini RA, Loureiro AA (2016) Data communication in vanets: protocols, applications and challenges. Ad Hoc Netw 44:90–103
11. Durresi M, Durresi A, Barolli L (2005) Emergency broadcast protocol for inter-vehicle communications. In: Proceedings of the 11th international conference on parallel and distributed systems, vol 2, pp 402–406
12. Füßler H, Widmer J, Käsemann M, Mauve M, Hartenstein H (2003) Contention-based forwarding for mobile ad hoc networks. Ad Hoc Netw 1(4):351–369
13. Ghazal A, Wang CX, Ai B, Yuan D, Haas H (2015) A nonstationary wideband mimo channel model for high-mobility intelligent transportation systems. IEEE Trans Intell Transp Syst 16(2):885–897
14. Jacquet P, Muhlethaler P, Clausen T, Laouiti A, Qayyum A, Viennot L (2001) Optimized link state routing protocol for ad hoc networks. In: Proceedings of the IEEE international multi topic conference, pp 62–68
15. Johnson DB, Maltz DA, Broch J et al (2001) DSR: the dynamic source routing protocol for multi-hop wireless ad hoc networks. Ad Hoc Netw (5):139–172
16. Karp B, Kung HT (2000) GPSR: greedy perimeter stateless routing for wireless networks. In: Proceedings of the 6th annual international conference on mobile computing and networking. ACM, New York, pp 243–254
17. Kaur N, Singh A (2015) Article: a survey on data dissemination protocols used in vanets. Int J Comput Appl 120(23):43–50
18. Kihl M, Sichitiu M, Ekeroth T, Rozenberg M (2007) Reliable geographical multicast routing in vehicular ad-hoc networks. Springer, Berlin, pp 315–325
19. Korkmaz G, Ekici E, Özgüner F, Özgüner U (2004) Urban multi-hop broadcast protocol for inter-vehicle communication systems. In: Proceedings of the 1st ACM international workshop on vehicular ad hoc networks. ACM, New York, pp 76–85
20. LeBrun J, Chuah CN, Ghosal D, Zhang M (2005) Knowledge-based opportunistic forwarding in vehicular wireless ad hoc networks. In: Proceedings of the 61st vehicular technology conference, vol 4, pp 2289–2293

21. Li F, Wang Y (2007) Routing in vehicular ad hoc networks: a survey. IEEE Veh Technol Mag 2(2):12–22
22. Lin D, Kang J, Squicciarini A, Wu Y, Gurung S, Tonguz O (2017) Mozo: a moving zone based routing protocol using pure v2v communication in vanets. IEEE Trans Mobile Comput 16(5):1357–1370
23. Liu G, Lee BS, Seet BC, Foh CH, Wong KJ, Lee KK (2004) A routing strategy for metropolis vehicular communications. In: Information networking. Networking technologies for broadband and mobile networks, pp 134–143
24. Lochert C, Hartenstein H, Tian J, Fussler H, Hermann D, Mauve M (2003) A routing strategy for vehicular ad hoc networks in city environments. In: Proceedings of the intelligent vehicles symposium, pp 156–161
25. Lochert C, Mauve M, Fussler H, Hartenstein H (2005) Geographic routing in city scenarios. SIGMOBILE Mob Comput Commun Rev 9(1):69–72
26. Maia G, Aquino AL, Viana A, Boukerche A, Loureiro AA (2012) HyDi: a hybrid data dissemination protocol for highway scenarios in vehicular ad hoc networks. In: Proceedings of the second ACM international symposium on design and analysis of intelligent vehicular networks and applications. ACM, New York, pp 115–122
27. Maihofer C, Eberhardt R (2004) Geocast in vehicular environments: caching and transmission range control for improved efficiency. In: Proceedings of the IEEE intelligent vehicles symposium, pp 951–956
28. Meneguette RI (2016) A vehicular cloud-based framework for the intelligent transport management of big cities. Int J Distrib Sens Netw 12(5):8198597
29. Meneguette RI, Boukerche A, Maia G, Loureiro AA, Villas LA (2014) A self-adaptive data dissemination solution for intelligent transportation systems. In: Proceedings of the 11th ACM symposium on performance evaluation of wireless ad hoc, sensor, and ubiquitous networks. ACM, New York, pp 69–76
30. Moy J (1997) OSPF version 2. Internet Request for Comments: 2328, pp 1–244
31. Murthy S, Garcia-Luna-Aceves JJ (1996) An efficient routing protocol for wireless networks. Mob Netw Appl 1(2):183–197
32. Namboodiri V, Gao L (2007) Prediction-based routing for vehicular ad hoc networks. IEEE Trans Veh Technol 56(4):2332–2345
33. Namboodiri V, Agarwal M, Gao L (2004) A study on the feasibility of mobile gateways for vehicular ad-hoc networks. In: Proceedings of the 1st ACM international workshop on vehicular ad hoc networks. ACM, New York, pp 66–75
34. Naumov V, Baumann R, Gross T (2006) An evaluation of inter-vehicle ad hoc networks based on realistic vehicular traces. In: Proceedings of the 7th ACM international symposium on mobile ad hoc networking and computing. ACM, New York, pp 108–119
35. Nikaein N, Labiod H, Bonnet C (2000) DDR-distributed dynamic routing algorithm for mobile ad hoc networks. In: Proceedings of the first annual workshop on mobile and ad hoc networking and computing, pp 19–27
36. Ogier R, Templin F, Lewis M (2004) Topology dissemination based on reverse-path forwarding (TBRPF). Internet Request for Comments: 3684, pp 1–46
37. Perkins C, Belding-Royer E, Das S (2003) Ad hoc on-demand distance vector (AODV) routing. Tech. Rep
38. Royer EM, Perkins CE (1999) Multicast operation of the ad-hoc on-demand distance vector routing protocol. In: Proceedings of the 5th annual ACM/IEEE international conference on mobile computing and networking. ACM, New York, pp 207–218
39. Santos RA, Edwards A, Edwards RM, Seed NL (2005) Performance evaluation of routing protocols in vehicular ad-hoc networks. Int J Ad Hoc Ubiquitous Comput 1(1/2):80–91
40. Schwartz RS, Barbosa RRR, Meratnia N, Heijenk G, Scholten H (2011) A directional data dissemination protocol for vehicular environments. Comput Commun 34(17):2057–2071
41. Sharef BT, Alsaqour RA, Ismail M (2014) Vehicular communication ad hoc routing protocols: a survey. J Netw Comput Appl 40:363–396
42. Sichitiu ML, Kihl M (2008) Inter-vehicle communication systems: a survey. IEEE Commun Surv Tutorials 10(2):88–105

43. Sivaswamy S, Wang G, Ababei C, Bazargan K, Kastner R, Bozorgzadeh E (2005) Harp: hard-wired routing pattern FPGAs. In: Proceedings of the ACM/SIGDA 13th international symposium on Field-programmable gate arrays. ACM, New York, pp 21–29
44. Sladkowski A, Pamula W (2015) Intelligent transportation systems - problems and perspectives. Springer, Berlin
45. Souza AB, Celestino J, Xavier FA, Oliveira FD, Patel A, Latifi M (2013) Stable multicast trees based on ant colony optimization for vehicular ad hoc networks. In: Proceedings of the international conference on information networking, pp 101–106
46. Toh CK (1996) A novel distributed routing protocol to support ad-hoc mobile computing. In: Proceedings of the IEEE fifteenth annual international phoenix conference on computers and communications, pp 480–486
47. Tonguz OK, Wisitpongphan N, Bai F (2010) DV-cast: a distributed vehicular broadcast protocol for vehicular ad hoc networks. IEEE Wirel Commun 17(2):47–57
48. Vahdat A, Becker D et al (2000) Epidemic routing for partially connected ad hoc networks. Technical Report CS-200006, Duke University, pp 1–14
49. Villas LA, Boukerche A, Maia G, Pazzi RW, Loureiro AA (2014) Drive: an efficient and robust data dissemination protocol for highway and urban vehicular ad hoc networks. Comput Netw 75:381–394
50. Vodopivec S, Bešter J, Kos A (2014) A multihoming clustering algorithm for vehicular ad hoc networks. Int J Distrib Sens Netw 10(3):107085
51. Zeadally S, Hunt R, Chen YS, Irwin A, Hassan A (2012) Vehicular ad hoc networks (vanets): status, results, and challenges. Telecommun Syst 50(4):217–241
52. Zhao J, Cao G (2008) VADD: vehicle-assisted data delivery in vehicular ad hoc networks. IEEE Trans Veh Technol 57(3):1910–1922

Chapter 6
Vehicular Cloud

Abstract A vehicular cloud (VC) consists of a set of vehicles that share their computation resources through the cloud paradigm. Cooperation among vehicles and with roadside units allows on-demand scheduling of their resources. These clouds can adapt dynamically according to the quality of service requirements of applications. Consequently, resource management represents a truly crucial for this particular kind of cloud. In this chapter, we discuss the relevant aspects of the major concepts of VCs, as well as the challenges in enabling resource management for building and maintaining such clouds. A comprehensive description is also presented covering the existing techniques that require consideration in the context of resource management for VCs. Finally, we discuss the current issues and challenges that may ignite potential future work.

6.1 Introduction

In the past few decades, vehicular clouds (VCs) have been receiving significant attention from not only the service and automotive industries but also the scientific community. This heightened interest in this type of cloud stems from the opportunities, services, and applications that such clouds can offer. A VC provides dynamic allocation of resources, reliable services, and guaranteed delivery. Vehicles can take advantage of cloud services through the provision of provided resources; thus, a VC must consider resource management so that it can enable the sharing of its resources. Proper management allows vehicles to request available, idle resources in the VC for authorized access.

Transiting vehicles that casually cooperate to share their resources among themselves in the form of a cloud create a VC [25]. The set of these resources creates a pool of services that are made available to users and other vehicles. Therefore, these clouds need to provide dynamic resource allocation, resource discovery, and reliable service delivery. To achieve this, a VC can access a wired infrastructure through roadside units (RSUs), a cellular network, or any other external support. Furthermore, these clouds can benefit from the collaboration and cooperation among vehicles supported through the communication among them [14].

© Springer International Publishing AG, part of Springer Nature 2018   113
R. I. Meneguette et al., *Intelligent Transport System in Smart Cities*, Urban Computing, https://doi.org/10.1007/978-3-319-93332-0_6

However, owing to vehicular networks' features, such as high vehicle mobility and constant changes in topology, resource management and discovery become very challenging. The issues with these aspects worsen when the VC does not present a central control to address detection and management because vehicles need to create an infrastructure to manage the resource and request of the cloud. Moreover, cooperation is essential among VCs to meet service demands without violating their quality of service (QoS) requirements.

In this chapter, we discuss the concepts of the VC, as well as the problem of resource management and discovery, considering both primary types of architectures of VCs. Since these two elements are essential parts of creating and maintaining such clouds, this chapter classifies the existing works into these two categories.

The remainder of this chapter is organized as follows. Section 6.2 describes the concept of VC. Section 6.3 presents the basic methods that address resource management for VCs and a discussion on the predominant challenges and issues for future works. Section 6.4 presents the primary methods that address resource discovery for VCs and a discussion on the predominant challenges and issues for future works. Finally, Sect. 6.5 briefly summarizes the chapter.

6.2 Vehicular Cloud Concepts

The VC has introduced a novel paradigm in resource discovery and provisioning. The novelty in the field has motivated several pioneering works, as well as definitions that delimit this particular cloud and its properties. The works described in [29] initially defined a VC as a group of vehicles that autonomously and cooperatively coordinate authorized access to resources. Consequently, their corporate computing, communication, sensing, and physical resources allow for dynamic allocation.

Similarly, we define a VC within the scope of this chapter as a group of vehicles that have embedded resources, such as storage, computation, and physical resources. These vehicles share and dynamically schedule their resources based on the communication between them and with an external infrastructure. This type of cloud can dynamically adapt according to the availability of resources and the application requirements for QoS [39].

Analyzing the most significant previous works [1, 7, 39], we observed that they commonly proposed architectures to create and manage VCs. Most of these works split the architectural structure into three main layers: onboard, communication, and the cloud. Figure 6.1 shows an abstraction of a general VC architecture that generalizes these primary segments based on these previous works.

The first layer—the *onboard layer*—is responsible for abstracting information of embedded sensors, GPS, camera, radar, and other devices that vehicles can contain. The collected information can be sent to the cloud to be stored or to serve as input for several services in the application layer. Therefore, this layer can promote sensing of not only the environment but also the behavior of passengers and drivers in vehicles.

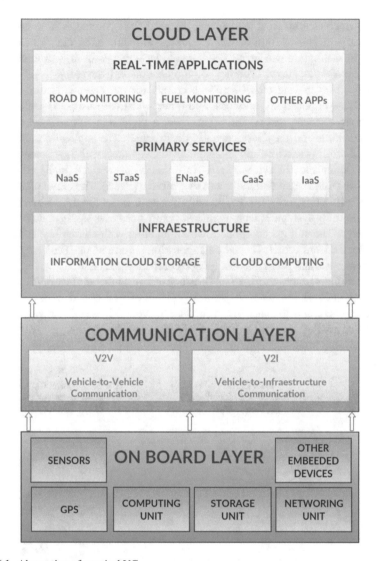

Fig. 6.1   Abstraction of a typical VC

The second layer—the *communication layer*—ensures a connection between the onboard layer located in the layer below and the cloud layer located in the layer above. To achieve this, vehicles are equipped with devices that make use of wireless communication protocols, such as 802.11p, 3G, and 4G. These devices enable the classification of this layer into two parts: communication of vehicles with vehicles, or vehicle-to-vehicle (V2V) communication, and communication of vehicles with an external infrastructure, or vehicle-to-infrastructure (V2I) communication. V2V communication relates to vehicles that are in the same range of communication, so information can be propagated through vehicles until it arrives at the cloud if any vehicle perceives a noticeable event on the road. V2I communication consists of the exchange of information between vehicles, infrastructures, and the cloud. The external infrastructure can be an RSU, a cellular antenna, or any structure on the side of the road that allows bridging communication with the cloud.

The third layer—the *cloud layer*—accounts for the aggregation of resources and furnishes applications, services, and other systems to users, as well as other applications, services, and systems. This layer is divided into three sublayers: real-time applications, primary service, and infrastructure. The applications sublayer is capable of offering services and applications that can meet real-time constraints and support essential cloud services, such as information as a service (IaaS), cooperation as a service (CaaS), and entertainment as a service (EaaS). The cloud platform and cloud infrastructure, on the other hand, serve as a basis for a traditional mobile cloud computing system. The cloud infrastructure possesses storage and computing components. The storage component works together with an application; it stores data collected from vehicles based on application requirements. The computational component hosts and processes designated computational tasks.

Some authors, such as [4, 17, 24], proposed an architecture of VC based on underlying network elements. A generic VC can consist of a data center (central cloud), cloudlets, and an underlying vehicular network. Figure 6.2 shows the generic elements of a VC.

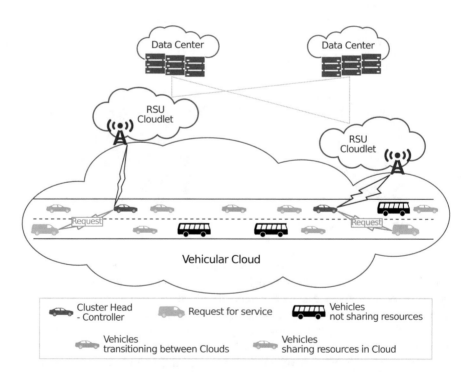

Fig. 6.2 Vehicular cloud defined based on its network elements

In this architecture, the data center provides a group of services offered by the traditional cloud, such as Microsoft Azure and Amazon EC2. These data centers rely on traditional wired networks to connect them and to provide services and resources to users (vehicles). In this case, vehicles connect with data centers through RSUs or any other external infrastructure. These RSUs can have computational features that assist the data center in the management and discovery of resources. Therefore, RSUs work as brokers between VCs to share and manage resources and services among different clouds [1]. These groups of computing resources in an RSU are known as cloudlets, which consist of a set of vehicles equipped with available resources that can share those resources with each other via hybrid communication [17].

The VC corresponds to the other end of the architecture, which is assembled through collaboration and coordination among vehicles through communication that takes place between them. Consequently, the VC creates an infrastructure to provide resources to data centers, cloudlets, and other vehicles. Thus, if an RSU or any other external connection is available, the VC by itself must enable the discovery and management of resources, providing the resources like a datacenter. Otherwise, vehicles create an infrastructure that addresses resource discovery and management for users in the vehicular environment.

6.2.1 Cloud Formation and Services

A VC can be formed through the consolidation of computing resources of a group of vehicles geographically colocated in parked position [30]. Therefore, grouping vehicles parked in a mall or airport or a private parking lot may form a cloud through the aggregation of their resources. This type of cloud formation is similar to the conventional cloud, which consists of virtualized resources in geographically colocated physical hosts at a data center [32]. VCs can also be a traditional cloud bound to a shoreline infrastructure that provides access to the Internet where it provides service access and abstraction of relevant information from vehicular networks. However, a pure VC is established through intercommunication among vehicles. Such a cloud needs to deal not only with the unique characteristics of vehicular networks but also with the limitations on training and resource management of a mobile cloud, such as resource migration between hosts.

Like a traditional cloud, VCs also offer the services generally offered by conventional clouds, such as computing services through the aggregation of devices embedded in vehicles and the use of a regular cloud with the purpose of increasing its computing power. Networks act as a service by which a VC can provide network resources such as bandwidth and Internet access to its users. Storage as a service that provides information storage mechanisms. However, when it comes to storage, it is necessary to consider which vehicles' information will be stored, such as how long a vehicle has been in a parking lot. To overcome these limitations, the use of peer-to-peer (P2P) applications makes it possible to store multiple replicas of the same file block on many cars. Moreover, owing to the short transmission time between vehicles, the size of these blocks can be small, facilitating their sharing.

In addition to the traditional services, new cloud services have been developed such as sense-as-a-service (SenaaS) that makes available its components, including vehicle sensors and devices, for vehicle monitoring applications such as cloud computing capabilities called sensor cloud service. Zingirian and Valenti [46] proposed this service, which uses the sensors embedded in vehicles as well as communication between vehicles to sense urban roads.

SenaaS can be utilized to assist smart cities in sensing and monitoring roads. In addition to this service, smart cities can use other services to assist in the management of urban mobility through the dissemination of traffic condition information or events that might be occurring in the city or on its streets, among other information. This helpdesk corresponds to:

- Cooperation as a service (CaaS): vehicular networks provide a variety of new services, such as driver safety, traffic information, traffic and traffic alerts, weather or traffic conditions, parking availability, and advertisements. To disseminate such information, data are collected for use by these services as a data dissemination mechanism. To this end, connectivity must be established not only between vehicles but also between vehicles and a shoreline infrastructure, a hybrid communication for the discovery and dissemination of services offered by the cloud. This medium deals with denser networks, covering regions with a large number of cars as a result of some event. Because of this, the network experiences huge data traffic, causing transmission congestion. A mechanism for the proper selection of relay node may present a solution to this problem. Only selected vehicles or infrastructures retransmit messages; under this approach, the area of coverage of the vehicle transmitting a message serves as a basis for selecting a retransmitter. The retransmitter may be in regions within coverage area of communication or by the greater distance between the transmitter and the nodes connected to it. To aid communication, the node location of both the transmitter and the possible retransmitter is used. This location is also used to monitor the routes of the regions close to an event to check traffic congestion and to come up with alternative routes to the nodes by monitoring and interpreting the data from the event region and neighboring regions.
- INaaS: The cloud should offer services to capture vehicle information in connection not only with traffic conditions but also events happening on the road, such as an accident. This capture service is provided by the dissemination of data on some event and by the messages establishing connections among vehicles. This service receives information from mobile devices to obtain more data about a particular region, allowing for better inferences about what is happening. The cloud possesses geographic data about events from nearby regions, which allow for analysis and interpretation of data. This analysis and interpretation of the data occurs using mathematical methods that calculate congestion, make predictions about the mobility of individuals, estimate alternative routes to bypass any congestion, and estimate the computational demand that the next event will

require. After an interpretation is made about resource allocation that involves reprogramming of traffic lights, computational resources are allocated so that the next event and regions close to this event can support the information demand.

The applications developed as a result of the services described can be found in more detail in Chap. 7, which describes the main applications used by intelligent transport systems (ITSs) and the challenges involved in these applications. However, it should be noted that one of the significant research challenges in VCs is to identify conditions under which VCs can support big data applications. It is apparent that big data applications, with stringent data processing requirements, cannot be supported by ephemeral VCs, where the residency time of vehicles in the cloud is too short to support virtual machine (VM) setup and migration. Quite recently Florin et al. [12] identified sufficient conditions under which big data applications could be effectively supported by data centers built on top of vehicles in a parking lot. This work represented the first time researchers considered evaluating the feasibility of the VC concept and its suitability for supporting big data applications. The main findings of [12] are that if the residency times of vehicles are sufficiently long, and if the interconnection fabric has a sufficient amount of bandwidth, then big data applications can be supported effectively by VCs. In spite of this result, a lot more work is needed to understand what it takes for VCs to be able to support, in a graceful way, data- and processing-intensive applications.

6.2.2 *Virtual Machine Migration*

To provide greater flexibility and scalability to physical resources, clouds use VMs that allow users to use an environment capable of executing their processes without reoccupying the physical resources involved [33]. Therefore, servers are divided into multiple VMs, in which users are assigned VMs allowing the use of the fully isolated physical environment of other machines [32]. The management of VMs is performed through hypervisors that introduce, virtually, isolation from VMs. Although the VMs are on the same machine, the hypervisors allocate resources separately for each VM according to usage.

During the execution of a service in a cloud, the VMs allocated to a given user can be shifted between physical hosts for several purposes such as energy efficiency, enhanced utilization, and hotspot mitigation, among others [40]. Thus, virtualized resources allow the migration of logical resources (VMs) from one machine to another. The movement of a VM from one physical location to another is simple relativity and potentially seamless [33]. Several works bring the challenges and solutions to deal with the issues encountered in the migration of VMs into a workable cloud. Reliability and efficiency are important aspects when dealing with VM migration [2]. In the literature, one can find several works that propose solutions to the limitations and challenges of a traditional cloud [8]. However, VCs present new challenges and limitations that result in traditional cloud techniques not performing the same as in a VC. One difference between the two is in the initialization of VM migration, where the traditional cloud can be triggered by the prevention of hotspots, load balancing, and maintenance. The mobility and ubiquity of resources consist of inherent and major aspects of VCs due to the characteristics of vehicular networks. Thus, a VC data center is a more dynamic environment, due to the mobility of the physical servers, usually connected vehicles. Also, the topology of a VC data center network changes more rapidly due to the high mobility of vehicles.

Refaat et al. [33] proposed three vehicular VM migration mechanisms called vehicular virtual machine migration (VVMM). These mechanisms aim to bring greater efficiency to migration due to mobility data center topology and host heterogeneity, all with minimum RSU intervention. The first proposed model, VVMM-U, performs uniformly, selecting destinations for VM migrations, which take place shortly before a vehicle's departure from RSU coverage. The second model proposed, VVMM-LW, aims to migrate VMs to vehicles with the lightest workload. Finally, the VVMM-MA model incorporates mobility awareness by migrating VMs to vehicles with the lightest workload and projected to be within the geographic boundaries of the VC. Results showed that the last model, VVMM-MA, obtained a significant reduction in unsuccessful migration and resulted in increased fairness in vehicle capacity utilization across the VC system.

Yu et al. [42] proposed efficient VM live migration mechanisms to deal with the problem. In particular, the selective dirty page transfer strategy is designed to enhance the efficiency of data transfer in VM live migration. Also, the authors proposed an optimal resource reservation scheme to ensure sufficient physical resources at a target cloud site such that migration dropping is significantly reduced. In the paradigm used by the authors, vehicles are allowed to access three types of cloud sites for services: VC, roadside cloud, and central cloud. Due to vehicle mobility, cloud services must shift from one cloud to another to maintain ongoing services. The resulting mechanism reduced migration dropping, decreasing the dropping rate.

One of the major challenges of VM migration in a VC is related to network overhead and the search and management of resources [5]. As a result, VM migration methods must consider not only the issue of vehicle mobility but also the number of resources that these vehicles have available for the creation of VMS. Also, migration must have a significant impact on the network so that migration overhead does not impact the use of services and resources made available by the cloud.

6.2.3 Job Assignment in VCs

The dynamically changing availability of computing resources due to vehicles joining and leaving VCs unexpectedly leads to a volatile computing environment where the task of assigning incoming user jobs to vehicles is quite challenging. To understand the challenge, assume that a job was just assigned to a vehicle currently in a VC. If the vehicle remains in the VC until the job is completed, then all is well. Difficulties arise when the vehicle leaves the VC before job completion. In this case, unless special precautionary measures are taken, the work is lost, and the job must be restarted, taking chances on another vehicle until eventually the job is completed. Losing the entire work of a vehicle, in case of premature departure, must be mitigated. One possible method is to use checkpointing, a strategy originally proposed in databases. This strategy requires making regular backups of a job's state and storing them in a separate location. In the event a vehicle leaves the VC before job completion, the job can be restarted, on a new vehicle, using the last backup. Alternatively, reliability and availability can be enhanced, as is often done in conventional clouds and other distributed systems, by employing various forms of redundant job assignment strategies. Indeed, the volatility of resources in VCs suggests the use of job assignment strategies wherein each job is assigned to, and executed by, two or more vehicles in a VC.

Some works in the literature use this mechanism. For example, Ghazizadeh et al. [15] have studied redundancy-based job assignment strategies in VCs and have derived analytical expressions for the corresponding mean-time-to-failure MTTF. Similarly, Florin et al. [11] have studied reliability issues in military vehicular clouds (MVCs), the version of VCs that suits the needs of tactical applications. These works describe how to enhance system reliability and availability in these types of VCs through a family of redundancy-based job assignment strategies that attempt to mitigate the effect of computing resource volatility. These scheduling strategies demonstrate the efficiency of the MTTF for job assignments in VCs.

Another important issue for a VC is the job completion time, one of the fundamental QoS attributes of VCs. Among all existing related works, some approaches attempt to estimate job completion time [13, 16, 21, 44]. Of these works, it is worth mentioning that of Florin et al. [13], who developed an analytical model for estimating job completion time in VCs assuming a redundant job assignment strategy.

Due to the characteristics not only of vehicular networks but also of human behavior, the estimation of time allocation of resources in a vehicle as well as the time of execution of a work has become an increasingly important factor in the performance of VCs seeking to maintain greater usability of resources, thereby meeting the needs of cloud users.

6.3   Resource Management in Vehicular Clouds

Resource management in a cloud carrier must consider a series of factors. These factors are essential and include efficiency, QoS, and correctness. (1) Efficiency relates to the fact that a resource allocation strategy should optimize resource utilization so resources are used in their entirety. (2) QoS has to do with the fact that the resources allocated need to be sufficient to meet QoS requirements. (3)

Correctness indicates that a resource must have the same possibility and time to be executed.

This chapter presents a comprehensive study that was conducted on resource management in VCs, in which the relevant works are divided into two groups that define the resource management by (1) infrastructure or (2) vehicles. The first group refers to works in which resource management is connected directly to the static structure of the cloud, which means that the processing and management of resources are carried out by both the cloud (data center) and cloudlets (computational resources made available by RSUs). The second group relates to the focus of this work, in which the management and processing of resources are performed only by vehicles, where the intervention of external elements, such as an RSU, is minimal. In other words, resource management entails using only some of the features offered by an RSU structure, such as signal strength.

6.3.1   Resource Management by Infrastructure

Resource management in a VC-based infrastructure needs to deal with resource allocation, which is typically achieved by creating VMs. Furthermore, a resource management engine must allow for data transfer between RSUs (cloudlets) and avoid resource failure resulting from the lack of meeting QoS requirements or high vehicle mobility. Another aspect to consider is the analysis of resources, which indicates the order in which requests are met. Figure 6.3 describes an abstraction of resource management executed by the infrastructure of a VC.

From the scenario depicted in the figure, vehicle 1 first requests a cloud service from the data center (central cloud) and the cloudlet. Thus, VMs are reserved in the data center and cloudlet. Once resources are provided by this central cloud, the VM running in the cloudlet pushes messages to vehicle 1, allowing its driver to make use of the requested resource. When vehicle 1 moves along the road and comes into the coverage area of cloudlet 2, the VMs present in cloudlet 1 must migrate to cloudlet 2. As a result, the requested resources are active until it is no longer necessary.

The following section describes some of the techniques and works that address the optimization of the resource management process in an infrastructure-based VC.

6.3.1.1   Integer Linear Programming

One of the techniques used to manage resources in VCs is integer linear programming (ILP), which consists of a mathematical optimization in which some or all variables must be integers. ILP seeks the efficient distribution of limited resources to meet a particular goal, generally maximizing profits or minimizing costs [10]. Therefore, this objective is expressed through a linear function, called an *objective function*. Furthermore, it is necessary to define which activities consume resources and in what proportions the resources are consumed. This information is presented in the form of linear equations, one for each resource. For the set of these equations and inequalities it is called *model restrictions*.

There are generally many ways of distributing scarce resources among various activities, provided that these distributions are consistent with the constraints of a given model. However, what is investigated is the objective function, focusing on the maximization of profit or the minimization of costs. This solution is called the optimal solution. Thus, linear programming is used to find the optimal solution to a problem once the linear model is defined, delimiting the objective function and the linear constraints.

In a VC, ILP is used to minimize the cost of resource management operations, so as to reduce the need to migrate a VM from one cloud to another or from one network element to another. For this, the strategy uses network parameters, such as overhead, bandwidth, and VM size, among other elements of vehicular networks, and the elements in question as constraint models. We describe a work that uses this strategy to conduct resource management in VCs.

For instance, consider a VC that has the capacity to attempt service requests of T. The VC provides the services of a traffic management, event alert, or a combination of these two. This VC has a limited capacity for available processing resources R_p and the storage R_s that can be used to attempt these services. These resources can be allocated in different amounts depending on whether the request is one for traffic management (R_{p1}, R_{s1}), or for event alert (R_{p2}, R_{s2}). Suppose that the allocation of the processing resource has a cost of C_p for the system and a cost of C_s for allocating the storage resources. Thus, if we assume that the vehicles make requests for traffic management (*tm*) or event alert (*ea*) services, then the ideal number of

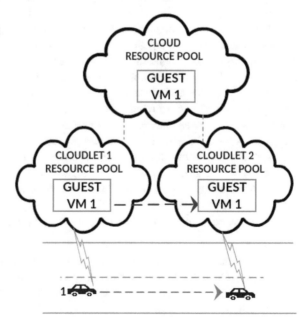

Fig. 6.3 Abstraction of resource management carried out by VC infrastructure

services provided by the system can be described as a linear programming problem:

Minimize: $C_p * tm + C_s * ea$ (This is the objective function)
Subject to: $tm + ea \leq T$ (Total limit of requests met)
                  $R_{p1} * tm + R_{p2} * ea <= R_p$ (Processing resource limit)   (6.1)
                  $R_{s1} * tm + R_{s2} * ea <= R_s$ (Storage resource limit)
                  $tm \geq 0 \; and \; ea \geq 0$ (Vehicles request services)

In what follows we describe some works that use this strategy to perform resource management in VCs.

The work described in [34] proposed a cloud resource management (CRM) method based on ILP that minimizes the reconfiguration overhead. CRM aims to reduce infrastructure delays and service replications. The ILP model consists in jointly minimizing the reconfiguration overhead, VM migrations, control plane modifications, number of service hosts, and cloud infrastructure delays. To achieve this, the authors used weights to control the priority of reconfiguration overhead so that minimizing VM migrations takes priority over control plane modifications. Furthermore, ILP considers the delay among messages in the system, as well as network bandwidth, to achieve a balanced network load and minimize the number of service hosts and infrastructure.

6.3.1.2 Semi-Markov Decision Process

Markov decision processes (MDPs) [6] aim to model decision making in situations where outcomes are partly random and partly under the control of a decision maker. MDPs provide a mathematical framework to model processes where transitions between states are probabilistic; it is possible to observe what state a process is in, and it is possible to interfere in the process periodically in *decision times* by performing actions [31]. Each action has a reward or cost, depending on the state of the process. Alternatively, rewards can be defined by the state only, without relying on the action performed. They are called *Markov* or *Markovians* because the modeled processes obey Markov's property: the effect of an action on a state depends only on the action and the current state of the system and not on how the process came to the state. A *decision process* comes from the possibility that is modeled by an agent or *decision maker*, which periodically interferes with the system performing actions, unlike Markov chains, where it is not about how to interfere in the process.

Therefore, an MDP is defined as a tuple (S, A, T, R), where

- S is a set of states where the process can be present;
- A is a set of actions that can be performed in different decision periods;
- $T : SXAXS \mapsto [0, 1]$ is a function that gives the probability that the system will pass to a state $s' \epsilon S$. This function assumes that the process was in a state $s \epsilon S$ and the agent decided to take action $a \epsilon A$ (denoted $T(s'|s, a)$);

- $R : SXA \mapsto \mathbb{R}$ is a function that gives the cost (or reward) for making a decision $a \epsilon A$ when the process is in a state $s \epsilon S$.

To illustrate the use of MDPs, we assume that a VC can offer a resource pool that contains R units of resources that support a K service class. Additionally, the service class $i, i \epsilon \{1, 2, \ldots, K\}$ requires b_i resources to meet its service requirement. Furthermore, the arrival time of a new request is modeled as a Poisson process at a rate of λ_n.

Therefore, the system state can be described by the resource occupation in the VC. Thus, the state space can be denoted as follows:

$$S = \{s|s = (n, e)\}, \ e \epsilon E = \{Req, Ter\} \tag{6.2}$$

where n is defined as

$$n = \{n_1, n_2, \ldots, n_i\}, \tag{6.3}$$

and n_i represents the number of vehicles in a VC that requests the service class i. In the same way, the sum of allocated resources in the local cloud is $\sum_{k=1}^{K} b_k * n_k \leq R$. e represents an event that occurs in the system, and the event set E is described as follows:

- Req represents the arrival of a new request,
- Ter represents the terminal of a requested service of class k that the request come from the cloud.

In an MDP environment, the cloud has to make a decision based on its action space after a known period of time. Thus, in each decision epoch, the cloud chooses an action a from the action space A_s, which is defined as follows:

$$A_s = \begin{cases} \{-1\}, & e \neq Req \\ \{0, 1, 2, \ldots, K\}, & e = Req \end{cases} \tag{6.4}$$

$a = -1$ indicates that the controller needs, not to make decisions, but update the resource consumption in the system. $a = 0$ indicates that the request of service of class k was rejected by the controller. $a = k$ indicates that the request is accepted and the service of class k was allocated in the system.

The transition probability from state s to states s' under action a is defined by $p(s'|s, a)$

$$p(s'|s, a) = \begin{cases} \frac{\lambda_n}{\varphi(s', a)} & e' = Req \\ \frac{\mu_k n_k}{\varphi(s', a)} & e' = Ter_k \end{cases} \tag{6.5}$$

where $\varphi(s, a) = \gamma(s, a)^{-1}$. $\gamma(s, a)$ represents the expected time until the next decision epoch, which can be given by

$$\gamma(s, a) = \frac{1}{\lambda_n + \sum_k^K \mu_k * n_k} \tag{6.6}$$

Given a state s and an action a, the system reward is defined as

$$r(s, a) = k(s, a) - g(s, a) \tag{6.7}$$

where $k(s, a)$ is the lump sum income of the system by taking action a, and $g(s, a)$ is the expected system cost. $k(s, a)$ can be defined as

$$k(s, a) = \begin{cases} P & e \in Req, a = 0 \\ G_{Req} & e \in Req, a = 1 \dots K \\ G_{Ter} & e \in Ter, a = -1 \\ 0 & \text{otherwise} \end{cases} \tag{6.8}$$

P denotes a system penalty resulting from the rejection of the service or by the departure of a vehicle from the cloud. In P_r, a request has been made to reject the resource of a vehicle still in the cloud pool, but the system has been penalized by the exchange of messages between clouds. Thus, P is defined as $P - \sum_{k=1}^{K} b_k$, where P is the system penalty. G_{Req} represents the system income for accepting a new request or migration request. G_{Req} is defined as $G - b_k$, where G is the income from the cloud's use of the resource shared by the vehicle. Although the resource of this vehicle increases the pool of resources of the local cloud, the vehicle uses the b_k resource of the available resources in the cloud. G_{Ter} stands for the system income for termination of a service (a request) or by a migration request. G_{Req} is defined as $G + b_k$. The expected system cost $g(s, a)$ is defined as

$$g(s, a) = c(s, a)\gamma(s, a) \tag{6.9}$$

where $c(s, a)$ is the cost rate of the system, which can be characterized by the number of resource allocations in the dynamic VC; consequently, it is represented as

$$c(s, a) = \sum_{k=1}^{K} b_k * n_k \tag{6.10}$$

Thus, this modeling aims to control the acceptance or rejection of requests for service in the system, seeking to maximize the use of these resources in the cloud. In the literature, some models have been proposed to consider not only services but also characteristics of the entrance and departure of vehicles in the cloud. In what follows, we describe some works that use this strategy to perform resource management in VCs.

In [45], an allocation resource scheme for maximizing the reward of a VC was proposed. This approach is based on an infinite-horizon semi-Markov process that uses four stages to formulate the resource allocation problem. (1) The state space represents the current resources and request states in a VC. (2) The action space is a set of actions that can be used by a VC based on its current state. (3) A reward consists of the income and costs that allow for applying a discounted model that computes and analyzes the sum of the rewards. (4) A transition probability calculates the probability that one system state will change to another state under a specific action. This approach uses an iteration algorithm to solve the optimization problem. The algorithm aims to maximize the long-term expected total reward of the VC.

An optimal method was proposed in [27] for maximizing the reward of a proposed solution and improving the quality of experience with vehicles. The authors formulated a semi-Markov decision process (SMDP) to optimize the decision-making process to obtain an optimal scheme. In this optimal method, rewards are computed using the average rate of events. The SMDP uses a uniformization that modifies the formula for a discrete-time model. This approach also employs an iteration algorithm. To maximize the average reward, it is based on the model defined in [45]. However, the authors attempted to improve the processing power to save more energy, as seen in [45].

6.3.1.3 Game Theory

Game theory is a mathematical strategy designed to model phenomena that can be observed when two or more *decision makers* interact with each other. This scheme is used in situations where the decisions of one agent or player depend on or influence the choices of others.

Therefore, a game consists of a set of players represented by $G = g1, g2, \ldots, g_n$. Each player g_i has a finite set S_i of options called the player strategy it can use. We denote by S a set of all strategy profiles, defined as follows:

$$S = \prod_{i=1}^{n} S_i = S_1 X S_2 X \ldots X S_n \tag{6.11}$$

Each element $s \in S$ represents a result of the game, also called a strategy vector or strategy profile of the game. Also, each player must have a preference order, which must be a complete, transitive, reflexive, and binary relationship for the possible outcomes of the game. This relationship indicates that the player prefers to change its strategy, and with that the result of the game changes from one vector of strategies to another. A simple way to represent this is a utility function or benefit $u_i : S \to R$ for each player i, which returns a numeric value for each strategy vector. Thus, if i changes its strategy, migrating from a strategy vector s for a vector s', this action only happens because $u_i(s') > u_i(s)$.

When players reach a result where each player has no interest in changing its strategy, a stable result is achieved. We say that a vector of strategies representing such a result is a Nash equilibrium in strategies.

To illustrate how this strategy works, consider a VC in which two services (players) have been requested by the user. These services can be *attempted* or *blocked*. If both are attempted, they have a cost of 4 for each service. If only one service (A) is attempted and the other (B) is blocked, then service A costs 1 and the other costs 5. Likewise, if B is attempted and A is blocked, B has a cost of 1, and A has a cost of 5. If both are blocked, the cost is 2.

A set with two players $G = A, B$ has the following sets of strategies for each player:

$$S_A = \text{Attempted, Blocked}$$

$$S_B = \text{Attempted, Blocked}$$

$$u_A(\text{Attempted, Attempted}) = 4, u_A(\text{Attempted, Blocked}) = 1,$$

$$u_A(\text{Blocked, Attempted}) = 5, u_A(\text{Blocked, Blocked}) = 2,$$

$$u_B(\text{Attempted, Attempted}) = 4, u_B(\text{Attempted, Blocked}) = 1,$$

$$u_B(\text{Blocked, Attempted}) = 5, u_B(\text{Blocked, Blocked}) = 2$$

Thus, for this example, the result where both statuses are attempted is a Nash equilibrium because, achieving this result, none of them minimizes the system cost by changing their choices individually.

The work presented in [43] proposed a mechanism for resource management and cooperative sharing of idle resources based on two-sided matching theory. This approach is divided into two steps. First, the cloud service provider analyzes the revenue and verifies whether it works alone or integrates with a cloud market. Then the service provider leases or rents its resources from other service providers. This approach must consider certain options: (1) A service provider can participate in a coalition whether its utility is better. (2) A service provider can change coalitions to improve its utility; in other words, the provider can leave coalition A and join coalition B. (3) A service provider prefers to work alone regardless of whether it improves utility. In this approach, the authors used a *Pareto optimality* to assist service providers in their actions, which ensured that their utility would increase or at least not decrease. The Pareto optimal collection consolidates gradually in each round.

In another work [41], a cloud architecture for vehicular networks is presented; it is divided into three layers: (1) vehicular cloud, (2) roadside cloud, and (3) central cloud. This approach aims to integrate redundant physical resources in ITS infrastructures. For this, the authors used a game-theoretical approach to maximize the allocated cloud resources. To illustrate the use of this theory, consider a set of VMs available in a cloudlet that aims to obtain as many resources as possible. The VMs are allocated based on the number of requested resources. In this case, the cloud sets up two virtual resource counters (VRCs) for each VM. Since the VRCs achieve their maximal threshold, the VMs cannot allocate different types of resources. Therefore, the total amount of allocated resources is the same for all VMs.

A noncooperative cloud resource allocation scheme is presented in [37] for urban scenarios using the Gauss–Seidel (G–S) iteration method, which reduces the calculation time of the Nash equilibrium point (NEP). The work then considers the joining and leaving processes of nodes. Therefore, an analysis was conducted to investigate the noncooperative cloud resource allocation game based on the G–S iteration method. A precision control was modeled to improve the iteration of the flow. To this end, the approach exploited the game theory to model the transmission behaviors of the vehicle nodes, also known as the cloud resource allocation game. Also, cloud RSUs were used to increase the communication time between vehicle nodes and the data server, which is sufficient for selfish vehicles to finish the equilibrium calculation of the cloud resource allocation game and access data at the calculated transmission rate. In a cloud resource allocation game, each vehicle node attempts to minimize its cost or maximize its utility. This approach can allocate cloud resources among the vehicles using the G–S iteration method. The G–S iteration method is usually used to resolve first-order partial differential equations. This method computes the optimal utility and flow rate of nodes. To deal with the convergence problem of resource allocation in vehicular networks, a convergence of the G–S iteration method was used.

6.3.1.4 Communication Layers

Some strategies only manipulate information coming from protocols already established in computer networks. Other approaches are focused on capturing information from delay, jitter, and packet loss. Some strategies are aimed at analyzing information coming from the TCP and information derived from the routing table at the network layer. Using this information, some works define their mathematical models to manage the flow of information and services requested. Through such models, they are capable of manipulating and managing resources available in the cloud to offer services to their users.

Another way to accomplish this manipulation of resources is through strategies already known in networking, such as in cognitive networks. According to the definition presented in [38], a cognitive network is a network endowed with cognitive ability, which can perceive the current conditions of the network and then plan, decide, and act on those conditions. The network can learn from these adaptations and use this information to make future decisions while taking end-to-end transmission goals into account. Like cognitive networks, cognitive radios provide the ability to use or share the spectrum in an opportunistic way.

Some works employ information not only of radio but also of other protocols for performing resource management. In what follows, we describe some works that use this strategy.

A resource scheduler for networked fog centers (NetFCs) was proposed in [35]. NetFCs determine that QoS requirements are met, seeking minimum/maximum rate jitters, process delay, and jitter rate. This approach uses an infrastructure-to-vehicle strategy to communicate in vehicular networks: vehicles communicate with the infrastructure through TCP/IP-based single-hop mobile links. The objective of this approach is to minimize the average communication-plus-computing energy wasted by the overall TCP/IP-based fog platform under hard QoS requirements are met, such as hard bounds. The energy-efficient schedule jointly performs the following functions: (1) management of input traffic; (2) minimum-energy dispatching of admitted traffic; (3) setting and maintaining configuration of VMs hosted; and (4) adaptive control of traffic injected into TCP/IP mobile connections. Also, NetFCs use the adaptive control of input and output traffic flows by managing the random, and possibly unpredictable, fluctuations of the input traffic to be processed and the states of the utilized TCP/IP connections. This approach also considers an adaptive reconfiguration of per-VM task sizes and processing rates and an adaptive reconfiguration of intrafog per link communication rates.

An adaptive resource management controller based on cognitive radio (CR) and soft-input/soft-output data fusion for vehicular networks is presented in [9]. Under this approach, an optimal controller dynamically manages the access time windows at the serving RSU, as well as the access rates and traffic flows at the served VC in a distributed and scalable way. Furthermore, this approach provides hard reliability guarantees to the primary traffic transported by the wireless communication backbone. To support CR-based access of the VC to the serving RSU in a fully distributed and scalable way, the approach adopts the frame format reported in sync with an intracluster access protocol. Therefore, an intracluster access protocol was designed and employed. This approach consists of seven phases: (1) channel estimation, (2) propagation, (3) sensing, (4) data fusion, (5) client scheduling, (6) client upload, and (7) acknowledgment. Furthermore, time slots are partitioned into nonoverlapping mini slots.

6.3.1.5 Discussions and Challenges Encountered

To summarize the characteristics of existing works, a table was compiled to describe the aspects of those works that are addressed. The table considers the most relevant aspects for delimiting the works: resource allocation, resource migration between RSUs, and scheduling resources. Table 6.1 also describes the probabilistic mechanisms used in the works.

One of the problems of this type of resource management is the complexity and time that the mechanisms of resource allocation and migration need to converge. These two aspects impose hard constraints on speed and efficiency so that the mechanisms are not affected by the speed of vehicle mobility and computing resources are not wasted. This complexity increases when you add the resource scheduler, which increases the time for resource availability. Another important problem consists of the high computational load required to calculate the required

Table 6.1 Works that deal with resource manager based on infrastructure

Work	Allocation Resource	Resource Scheduling	Resource Migration	Probabilistic method
Salahuddin et al. [34]	✓		✓	ILP
Zheng et al. [45]	✓		✓	SMDP Bellman Equation
Meng et al. [27]	✓		✓	SMDP Bellman Equation
Yu et al. [43]	✓		✓	Game Theory
Yu et al. [41]	✓	✓	✓	Game Theory
Tao et al. [37]	✓		✓	Game Theory
Shojafar et al. [35]	✓	✓	✓	Own Method
Cordeschi et al. [9]	✓		✓	Access Rate Allocation, Combined Time-Flow Allocation, and Network-Wide Optimization

optimization. This high computational load may impact the power consumption of the unit, creating a need for a more efficient cooling mechanism.

Although some work addresses the resource management problem in VCs affected by infrastructure, the challenge of integrating the three fundamental aspects of management remains because of the complexity of allocation mechanisms, scheduling, and resource migration. Therefore, there is a need for an effective structure that includes the three mechanisms: a solution that allocates resources quickly, respecting the resource requirements of quality requested. This minimizes or facilitates the migration of resources between RSUs, allowing migration to occur quickly without losses in resource utilization and providing fair allocation without loss of requests.

Another point for consideration is the precise assessment of time and computation consumption. Related to the efficiency with which assigned tasks are processed, optimization techniques are highly necessary for working out the issues involved in resource management.

6.3.2 Resource Management by Vehicles

Because existing resource managers that are based on infrastructure rely on the aspects of resource allocation, the transfer and scheduling of resources between RSUs must also be considered in the resource management conducted by the communication between vehicles. As a result, the method in which communication is established among transiting vehicles is an essential element in this type of management. Figure 6.4 depicts the operation of resource management by vehicles.

For example, consider that vehicle 1 requires some available resource from another cloud vehicle, so it initially sends a request for that resource and needs to continue sending requests to a particular resource cloud until a reply is received.

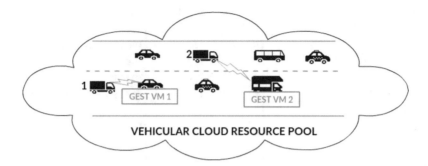

Fig. 6.4 Resource management by vehicles

This messaging can be a data dissemination mechanism or clustering mechanism. Once another vehicle receives the request, and the requested resource becomes idle, it creates and reserves a VM; then it assigns these virtual resources to the requester and begins to send messages to vehicle 1. Data dissemination or clustering mechanisms are used for the creation and maintenance of this form of management, as we can see in the work described in what follows.

6.3.2.1   Bayesian Coalition Game

Coalition game is a category of game theory in which a group of players is instructed to demonstrate cooperative behavior, transforming the game into a competition between groups rather than a competition between individuals, as described in Sect. 6.3.1.3.

The coalition game consists of a finite set of players G called the grand coalition and a characteristic function $v : 2^N \rightarrow \mathbb{R}$, which maps a set of coalitions to a set of rewards. This function describes how much a set of players can accumulate if they form a coalition. This game is known as a game of value or a game of profit. Thus, players must choose which coalitions to form according to their expectations about how the reward will be divided among coalition members. Therefore, the coalition game can be considered a study of payoff division within groups of agents [18].

Similarly, a cooperative game can be defined as a characteristic cost function $v : 2^N \rightarrow \mathbb{R}$ that satisfies $v(0) = 0$. In this case, players must fulfill some task, and the function represents the value that the set of players requires performing the task together. A game of this type is known as a cost game.

This technique can be used to calculate the cost of the cloud when migrating a VM in which it has several parameters that must be analyzed, such as overhead, the size of the VM, and the necessary bandwidth.

A work that employs such strategy is that in [19]. In this work, an algorithm called Learning Automata-based Contention Aware Data Forwarding (LACADF) is proposed. The algorithm deals with reliable data forwarding as a Bayesian coalition game (BCG) based on learning automata concepts. LACADF assumes that vehicles are players, and each vehicle analyzes the play of the other vehicles; thus, the vehicles can determine the movement to be performed. At the beginning of the game, each vehicle has a payoff pay value, and this value can increase or decrease based on the vehicle's actions. The actions can make the vehicle earn a reward or incur a penalty according to the updates of its action probability vector. After some iterations, the proposed approach selects an action based on the different disjointed sets that are analyzed by Bayes' theorem. All these actions are performed by an automaton process that can yield optimal inferred results if a solution is convergent.

6.3.2.2 Semi-Markov Decision Process

An MDP can also be used when there is not a central element to control cloud services. The MDP can be modeled in such a way that it takes into account not only the unique parameters of the resources being managed but also all the characteristics of the vehicular network, such as high mobility, a highly dynamic topology, and a low connectivity time between vehicles. Few works perform this modulation with MDPs. In what follows, we describe a work that considers not only the QoS requirements requested but also the mobility of a vehicle when entering and exiting a VC.

An optimal resource allocation scheme was proposed in [26] to maximize the utilization of available resources. The optimal solution for the problem of maximizing the system expected average reward is formulated as a SMDP. The SMDP problem is solved by an iteration algorithm. The authors consider a dynamic VC consisting of vehicles with resources that can be shared with a vehicular network. This cloud is formed through a set of vehicles that are grouped into a cluster. The cluster is constructed and maintained according to the strategy defined in [25], which considers that allocation requests are managed by a controller.

6.3.2.3 Discussions and Challenges

One of the problems of this form of management relates to the allocation of resources without overloading a vehicle with heavy computing, which consists of basically determining the best way of allocating the use of a vehicle. The management of allocated resources may not be straightforward due to the characteristics of the carrier network. For example, if a resource is allocated through a VM, computational power and significant network capacity are necessary to support the migration of the VM. Another problem characteristic of vehicular networks is related to the transmission time, such as in the presence of network fragmentation. Some auxiliary solutions may be used for data dissemination, although such solutions may introduce a high degree of overhead and package collisions. Clustering may be used to preventing this condition. In addition to reducing the number of network messages, this mechanism distributes resources better. However, such a solution

Table 6.2 Works that deal with resource management by vehicles

Work	Resource Mechanism	Resource Scheduling	Resource Migration	Probabilistic Method
Arkian et al. [3]	√	√	√	Fuzzy and Learning Methods
Kumar et al. [19]		√		Bayesian Coalition Game
Sibai et al. [36]	√	√		Spatiotemporal Similarity

might be constrained by the allocation time as the provision of resources is directly dependent on the time necessary to build a cluster, which is high.

A summary of features and mechanisms used in the described works is listed in Table 6.2.

Due to the characteristics of vehicular network resource management, vehicle speed, mobility, and transmission times must be addressed. Therefore, an efficient resource allocation mechanism must be developed so that the allocation can take place in a rapid manner due to short communication times between vehicles. Thus, the allocated resources must be performed efficiently and without computational overhead for the vehicle due to the limitations of vehicle resources.

The structure used for allocation has a direct impact on the form of migration of resources between vehicles. Consequently, this structure should be simple to the point that the migration of this feature is fast and efficient, does not impact the use of the resource, and does not overload the network with control messages. Thus, the challenges relate to communication and aggregation of information to provide a rapid cooperation mechanism between vehicles to meet the service quality requirements of the requested resource.

Another challenge involves the optimization of features of a scheduling mechanism, which must take into account not only the requirements for the request execution but also the mobility characteristics of the vehicle. Thus, this mechanism should not only optimize the choice of vehicles that suit a particular resource but also serve as a support tool at the time of resource migration.

6.4   Service Discovery in a Vehicular Cloud

Resource discovery is defined in this work as the process of requesting a resource and receiving a response back from the cloud controller. We formulate it as being dependent on resource requests. Consider a vehicle or a group of vehicles that need a specific resource r that is available from a VC. The VC has a set of available resources R that are available for users to request. Thus, these users send a request to the component of the VC that is responsible for managing resource requests. After the component receives the request, it verifies the availability of the resource; then it sends a response back to the user. The component can be a controlled cloud when considering only one VC or a broker when considering a group or a federation of VCs.

We consider a series of VCs interconnected through RSUs or vehicles that work to build alternative paths to reach data centers or cloudlets when there is no external infrastructure available. For this, we divide the study about resource discovery into two parts: (1) RSU as resource discovery manager and (2) vehicles as resource discovery manager. By the fact that the VC is a novel area, there are few works that deal with VC resource discovery. Consequently, we have also included techniques having to do with the discovery of resources in a VC.

6.4.1 RSU as Resource Discovery Manager

When more than one cloud is connected to a single RSU, this RSU can be used as a broker among these clouds to manage and discover resources in a vehicular network. Therefore, when a vehicle requests a service from the RSU, it can check the best cloud to process the service request, allocating and managing the resources in case the request is accepted. In what follows, we describe works that address resource discovery in this context.

6.4.1.1 Data Dissemination

The dissemination protocols aim to transfer relevant information to both vehicles and a control center quickly and efficiently. However, such dissemination protocols must deal with broadcast storms in order not to overload the network with control messages or previously disseminated information.

Such dissemination protocols can be used to disseminate search information of a particular resource. Because an RSU has a broader view of a network than vehicles, it can select a set of vehicles to carry out the dissemination of the resource search. Thus, this control through the RSU reduces the number of request messages in the network because only a few vehicles disseminate the message, thereby reducing the broadcast storm.

In what follows, we describe some solutions that use the dissemination of data as a resource search mechanism.

A cloud service discovery protocol was proposed in [28] to use RSUs as a cloud directory to store information about VC servers. As a result, this protocol forms a distributed dynamic index of such servers. The protocol defines a cloud server as a tranSporTAtion seRver (STAR) that provides services or resources via RSUs. Furthermore, the proposed approach includes an identification of services and their attributes that can be offered by the STAR. The RSUs store information about the services that it offers, such as the attributes of each service, the cost per resource unit, and the quality of each service. Also, the RSUs select the best candidate STAR to match user requirements. The STAR in this case is a vehicle that helps the RSU to manage and discover new resources and services in a VC. A STAR can offer higher QoS in a dense network because it can be closer to the requester than an RSU, speeding up the communication with the RSU and the cloud.

A service-oriented architecture-based middleware called VsdOSGi was proposed in [23] to address resource discovery directly. This, middleware is based on an OSGi framework, and it contains four layers: device bundle, service discovery bundle, DssOSGi bundle, and app bundles. VsdOSGi focuses on discovering the most suitable and intelligent transport application services. The resource discovery algorithm based on QoS (SDQ) employs different calculation methods of service quality according to service requirements. Thus, this algorithm provides an optimal service to satisfy the requirements and constraints of many requesters. For this, the service discovery algorithm is divided into four phases. (1) Vehicles that make their resources available send a message to the service directory of an RSU to notify it that the RSU provide a service. (2) Vehicles send requests to the service directory of an RSU to subscribe to its services. (3) The RSU matches the subscribed service with a published service and replies back to the service request. (4) The vehicle receives the response to its request and selects the final service provider to bind the required service.

6.4.1.2   Clustering

Clustering is a technique for grouping vehicles to facilitate communication. There are several criteria involved in the grouping of vehicles, such as speed, direction, number of vehicles, and follow-up vehicles. The simplest way to group vehicles in a city is through the localization in which the vehicles are, so all vehicles that are on the same street, following each other, or on a block are placed in the same cluster. Thus, each street has its cluster. Another common way of grouping is through steering, so all nearby vehicles that are going in the same direction in a given region are placed in the same cluster.

A cluster consists of the following elements:

- *Cluster head*, which manages the cluster and its resources;
- *Gateway*, which is responsible for facilitating communication between several clusters;
- *Member vehicles*, which are those vehicles that participate in a particular cluster;
- *Unknown vehicles*, which are vehicles that do not participate in any cluster.

The cluster head and gateways are chosen through a selection process among the vehicles belonging to the cluster. After the selection, this information is disseminated to all the elements of the cluster so that they can know who the gateways are and who the controller of that cluster is.

The clustering technique is widely used to create a communication structure among vehicles to reduce the number of messages sent over the network. Any request or communication in the cluster first passes through the cluster head for later forwarding to the destination vehicle. Some studies that follow this strategy are described in what follows.

A VC called COHORT was proposed in [3]; it employs RSUs to provide services to vehicles. COHORT also assists RSUs in managing and discovering new resources in vehicular networks. However, an RSU is accessible to the vehicles located within its transmission range. Thus, COHORT makes use of CaaS as a cloud service for increasing the coverage of the available service. CaaS is created using cluster theory through communication among vehicles. These clusters are dynamically formed, in which one member of a cluster is selected as a cluster head. These cluster heads communicate with the RSU and with other vehicles, functioning as a communication bridge between vehicles with RSUs. A cluster head is responsible for the creation, maintenance, and deletion of services, so cluster heads help an RSU in the management and discovery of services and resources of vehicles in a cloud.

6.4.1.3 Discussions and Challenges Encountered

When we consider RSUs as the elements responsible for the management and discovery of new resources, we can consider the use of well-known resource discovery solutions in traditional clouds. This is because the communication between the cloud and RSUs can be wired and the elements are not moble. However, a VC can use the vehicle network as a provider of resources and services. Thus, these solutions certainly require novel aspects and components that deal with the high mobility of vehicles, the time of connection between RSUs and vehicles, and other aspects of vehicular networks.

Table 6.3 summarizes the characteristics of the existing main works, listing the major aspects of each work mentioned. A description of such aspects is presented in what follows.

Although the solution presented in [28] uses STARs to aid in the discovery of resources, it is still limited to the time of communication between STARs and an RSU, hindering the mechanism of resource management and discovery. The same thing occurs in [3], which presents a solution involving intense communication between vehicles and RSUs that can cause a considerable amount of collisions among control management messages. VsdOSGi [23] shows a dynamic aiding mechanism that takes into account the high mobility of vehicles, the time of connection between vehicles, and RSUs. However, the proposed mechanism has a high computational complexity for the choice of cluster heads as well as the mechanisms that select the vehicles that help in the communication between vehicles and between the head cluster and the RSU.

Therefore, the mechanism can make use of information storage elements in a traditional cloud and can assist brokers (RSUs) on the discovery and management of resources. This auxiliary mechanism must consider the high mobility of vehicles and the time of communication between the RSU and the vehicle. Also, the mechanism must not introduce high computational overhead so that it does not impact the computational resources in the VC.

As RSUs are interconnected via the Internet and supposedly present a connection with a data center, they are capable of employing the same protocols as are used

Table 6.3 Works dealing with service discovery by RSUs

Work	Major feature	Assistance	Weaknesses
Service Discovery Protocol [28]	Vehicle Cloud Server Search and Service Discovery	STAR	Mobility of Vehicles
COHORT [3]	Service Provider Selection	Cluster Head	Complexity of Cluster Head Selection
VsdOSGi [23]	Service Discovery Middleware	–	Lack of Service Discovery Support

in clouds. However, to achieve this, any proposed solution must deal with all the limitations found in vehicular networks. As a result, protocols need to aggregate resources made available by vehicles and meet the demands of services requested by vehicles.

Therefore, one of the great challenges in this scenario is the creation of an information storage structure that does not impose high complexity on computational resources since the RSUs may have a low computational capacity to support such structures. Also, simple and dynamic mechanisms must be designed to enable aggregation, search, and management of resources that match with the needs of a data center and the unique constraints of vehicular networks. Also, it is assumed that such new resource discovery approaches will not overload a network with control messages.

6.4.2 Vehicles as Resource Discovery Managers

Consider a scenario in which vehicles cannot connect with an RSU or even a data center. Vehicles need to cooperate and collaborate among themselves to generate an infrastructure able to aggregate resources and make services available to other vehicles. In such a scenario, we consider two possible situations:

- *A vehicle is its own cloud.* A vehicle represents a set of resources that can be available to other vehicles in a vehicular network. In this case, each vehicle needs to perform resource discovery through interconnections with other VCs with the propagation of control messages. Therefore, a vehicle (control cloud) can verify if it has the resources that match a service request or indicates other clouds (vehicles).
- *A set of vehicles form a cloud.* A set of vehicles create a cloud through by communicating among themselves. In this set, a vehicle is selected to control requests and resources in the cloud. Furthermore, the vehicles can select an element (vehicle) that serves as a gateway between different groups of vehicles (VCs), so these gateways are considered brokers among the clouds.

6.4.2.1 Data Dissemination

One of the simplest ways to search for resources in a VC is to disseminate a requisition among vehicles. Consequently, the flooding of control messages on the network consists of the simplest technique for resource discovery when we consider each vehicle as a cloud. Using this technique, messages are propagated until they arrive at a cloud that contains the desired resource. However, this mechanism causes an overload in the network because it necessarily generates a broadcast storm. Another strategy entails the use of existing data dissemination protocols for vehicular networks. However, most of these protocols are aimed at disseminating accident and traffic information on the roads of a given city.

Some works, for example [36], adopt a traditional data dissemination protocol to address resource discovery. A service provision is developed and based on the mobility of vehicles, the availability of the requested service, and other network parameters. The service provision selects the vehicle that can provide the requested resource. For this, the scheme assumes two categories of vehicle: (1) a requester vehicle and (2) a service provider vehicle. The requester vehicle solicits one or multiple available services in the cloud. The requestor vehicle is the initiator of the VC; thus, it is named the leader vehicle. The leader vehicle is responsible for (1) searching candidate vehicles willing to provide services, (2) initiating the cloud, (3) maintaining the cloud, and (4) destroying the cloud.

The service provider vehicle, on the other hand, provides services to a requester vehicle. A service provider may be a stationary or mobile vehicle in a vehicular network. This approach uses a spatiotemporal similarity algorithm to calculate the common interval of communication between two vehicles, where there is a requester/service provider relation. The output of the spatiotemporal algorithm returns the communication duration, given by the communication duration and the delimited communication interval. These values are used to search for and allocate resources in a VC, achieved when the requester sends a request message via a retransmission mechanism that attempts to resolve the broadcast storm and decrease overhead in the network.

6.4.2.2 Publish-Subscribe

One way to reduce the amount of network messages due to packet dissemination is through the publish-subscribe mechanism. In this strategy, a group of vehicles publishes their offer of a set of features or services in the cloud. This method of publication is done through a broadcast on the network. The vehicles that want to use these resources subscribe to use or receive information about the service. Subsequently, the communication is restricted only to the vehicle that publishes the service or resource and the vehicles that subscribe to it, reducing the amount of messages propagated on the network.

A novel Distributed Location-Based Service Discovery Protocol (DLSDP) was proposed in [22]. This protocol classifies vehicles into three classes: (1) distributed directory service vehicles, (2) gateway vehicles, and (3) member vehicles. The approach employs regions of interest to organize the infrastructure of resource discovery. The infrastructure is based on multiple spanning trees. The root of the trees is the leader that uses the service discovery function based on its region of interest. The location-based requests are replied to independently of service demand providers being found by the corresponding leader vehicle.

6.4.2.3 P2P

P2P is an architecture of computer networks where each of the points or nodes of the network works both as client and server, allowing the sharing of services and data without the need for a central server. This kind of network typically creates an abstraction layer between vehicles on the network to facilitate communication and resource management. This architecture can be decentralized or hybrid. The decentralized architecture does not contain a central element to perform control of the resource, and all nodes have the same capacity. In this architecture, when a peer needs a service, it broadcasts a message to its neighbors. If the neighbor contains the requested resource, it sends a response to the requester. Otherwise, the neighbors broadcast the request to their neighbors.

In the hybrid, the nodes can be divided into superpeers and peers. Superpeers are nodes that possess greater processing capacity, memory, and other resources. Peers consist of nodes possessing a capacity common to all other nodes. Superpeers have some resources available, so they manage only part of the resources available in the cloud. Therefore, once a peer needs a certain resource, it sends a request to the superpeer to which it is attached. The superpeer, upon receiving this information, verifies whether it can answer the request. If so, the superpeer sends a response to the peer. Otherwise, it checks to see whether other superpeers have the requested resource.

This technique is used not only to facilitate communication between vehicles but also to create a connection layer. The technique also allows distribution of resources among vehicles so that it enables a search for resources without overloading networks with control messages.

In what follows, we describe some of the works that use a P2P architecture to facilitate resource discovery in the cloud.

A VC architecture based on the publish-subscribe paradigm has been proposed to deal with resource management and discovery [20]. In this work, resources are purely interconnected via P2P communications. Thus, negotiations about resource sharing occur directly between vehicles. However, one vehicle in the cloud can be selected and serve as a broker to manage and discover resources among other vehicles (clouds). In the architecture, a cloud leader is defined as a vehicle that runs an application. The leader recruits members that can provide resources to generate a vehicular cloud based on this application's requirements. After the leader assesses the necessary resources for the application, it broadcasts a resource request message to vehicles within the search range. The search range is delimited by a road section, an intersection, or a predefined distance. The vehicles that are willing to share their resources respond to the leader's request with their resource capabilities.

A P2P protocol for the search and management of resources in a VC is defined in [25]. This protocol is based on Gnutella concepts and introduces an overlay to assist the discovery and management of resources in the cloud. The protocol is divided into two main components: (1) resource management, which creates and controls an overlay and helps in the discovery and management of resources; (2) routing, which deals with the propagation of request and response messages. The proposed protocol treats gateways as brokers that help a requester or a controller to interconnect in the VC. Therefore, vehicles and the cloud controller employ gateways to find resources in other clouds that meet the service demands. Resource discovery considers the location of vehicles, average speed, time delay of messages, and other parameters to estimate the position of vehicles and facilitate the search for resources.

6.4.2.4 Discussions and Challenges Encountered

A summary of features and mechanisms used in the works presented in this chapter is described in Table 6.4. A more detailed description of such aspects is presented in what follows.

One of the major challenges in resource discovery in VCs is the lack of an external infrastructure that can support and facilitate the search and management of available resources in the VCs. A *centralized* approach aids in the sense that vehicles need to communicate quickly and without overloading the network with control messages. The works described in [20, 36] presented a mechanism for resource discovery that meets the proposed need; however, these solutions demand a large number of messages to deal with network disconnections and maintain the support structure constant. The works discussed in [22, 25] make use of a more efficient mechanism of communication; nevertheless, the approaches present greater complexity in the creation and maintenance of the cloud, consequently requiring a greater number of computing iterations.

Table 6.4 Summary of works dealing with service discovery by vehicles

Works	Support Technology	Propagation Method	Weaknesses
MAP	Data Dissemination	Broadcast Limited	Overhead
Pub/sub VC Architecture [20]	Publish-Subscribe	Broadcast	Overhead
DLSDP [22]	Spanning Trees	Hierarchical	Protocol Complexity
Peer-to-Peer Protocol [25]	Gnutella	Cluster	Protocol Complexity
Data Dissemination Protocol [36]	Data Dissemination	Broadcast Limited	Overhead

Thus, an ideal protocol to address resource discovery in a VC must be simple, minimizing the number of control messages. This envisioned protocol needs to create an infrastructure that meets the needs of VCs and overcomes mobile network limitations.

Due to the characteristics of vehicular networks, addressing resource discovery without any external infrastructure becomes the most complex challenge in VCs. Vehicles must self-manage and coordinate their embedded resources and dynamically create a structure that aggregates resources from other vehicles to provide demanded services. From this standpoint, a VC can be composed of an individual vehicle or a set of vehicles. Each vehicle can build a VC, managing its resources and making them available to neighboring vehicles. On the other hand, vehicles can collaborate and cooperate to create a structure that aggregates and manages many available resources in a coordinated manner.

If we consider a vehicle as a cloud, the resource discovery solution needs to be simple to avoid sending unnecessary messages that may cause overhead on the vehicular network. Furthermore, these solutions need to be light on vehicular devices so that they can run without concurrently overloading local resources. As a result, the challenges are related to communication aggregation of information to provide a rapid cooperation mechanism among vehicles to create broker services to facilitate resource discovery among other clouds (vehicles).

Another challenge involves the creation of a structure that aggregates available resources of different vehicles to provide cloud services. This structure needs to be dynamic enough to support the arrival and departure of vehicles in the cloud. Furthermore, simple selection algorithms must be developed to choose which vehicle will be the set leader and which ones can serve as gateways to communicate with other VCs, assisting communication as a broker for resource discovery. In the end, maintenance of this kind of structure should be such that it does not affect the performance of the vehicular network.

6.5   Final Discussion

In this chapter, we have introduced the concept of a VC, presenting not only an architectural vision of cloud elements but also a vision of the network elements that make up the VC. We described the resource management problem in VCs, which turns out to be a problem with many challenges to overcome; these challenges concern resource allocation, migration resources within the cloud, and the scheduling of resources that consider the singular characteristics of the carrier network. We also presented the resource discovery problem in VCs, which is a novel subject in this research field, showing potential opportunities and several issues that could be explored. These challenges involve the structure of information storage, communication mechanisms, coordination, and cooperation mechanisms among vehicles. We then listed and explained the state-of-the-art techniques for resource management and discovery. We also discussed the major challenges, as well as research opportunities, in identifying resources dynamically and coordinating them for VCs.

References

1. Abdelhamid S, Benkoczi R, Hassanein HS (2017) Vehicular clouds: ubiquitous computing on wheels. Springer, Berlin, pp 435–452
2. Arif S, Olariu S, Wang J, Yan G, Yang W, Khalil I (2012) Datacenter at the airport: reasoning about time-dependent parking lot occupancy. IEEE Trans Parallel Distrib Syst 23(11): 2067–2080
3. Arkian HR, Atani RE, Diyanat A, Pourkhalili A (2015) A cluster-based vehicular cloud architecture with learning-based resource management. J Supercomput 71(4):1401–1426
4. Baby D, Sabareesh RD, Saravanaguru RAK, Thangavelu A (2013) VCR: vehicular cloud for road side scenarios. Springer, Berlin, pp 541–552
5. Baron B, Campista M, Spathis P, Costa LHM, de Amorim MD, Duarte OCM, Pujolle G, Viniotis Y (2016) Virtualizing vehicular node resources: feasibility study of virtual machine migration. Veh Commun 4:39–46
6. Baykal-Gürsoy M (2010) Semi-Markov decision processes. Wiley encyclopedia of operations research and management science.Wiley, New York
7. Bitam S, Mellouk A, Zeadally S (2015) VANET-cloud: a generic cloud computing model for vehicular ad hoc networks. IEEE Wirel Commun 22(1):96–102
8. Boutaba R, Zhang Q, Zhani MF (2013) Virtual machine migration in cloud computing environments: benefits, challenges, and approaches. In: Communication infrastructures for cloud computing. IGI Global, Hershey, pp 383–408
9. Cordeschi N, Amendola D, Shojafar M, Baccarelli E (2015) Distributed and adaptive resource management in cloud-assisted cognitive radio vehicular networks with hard reliability guarantees. Veh Commun 2(1):1–12
10. Dantzig G (2016) Linear programming and extensions. Princeton University Press, Princeton
11. Florin R, Ghazizadeh P, Zadeh AG, Olariu S (2015) Enhancing dependability through redundancy in military vehicular clouds. In: Proceedings of the IEEE military communications conference. IEEE, Piscataway, pp 1064–1069
12. Florin R, Abolghasemi S, Zadeh AG, Olariu S (2017) Big data in the parking lot. Taylor and Francis, Boca Raton, pp 425–450
13. Florin R, Ghazizadeh P, Zadeh AG, El-Tawab S, Olariu S (2017) Reasoning about job completion time in vehicular clouds. IEEE Trans Intell Transp Syst 18(7):1762–1771
14. Gerla M (2012) Vehicular cloud computing. In: Proceedings of the 11th annual mediterranean ad hoc networking workshop, pp 152–155
15. Ghazizadeh P, Florin R, Zadeh AG, Olariu S (2016) Reasoning about mean time to failure in vehicular clouds. IEEE Trans Intell Transp Syst 17(3):751–761
16. Gkatzikis L, Koutsopoulos I (2014) Mobiles on cloud nine: efficient task migration policies for cloud computing systems. In: Proceedings of the IEEE 3rd international conference on cloud networking. IEEE, Piscataway, pp 204–210
17. Gu L, Zeng D, Guo S (2013) Vehicular cloud computing: a survey. In: Proceedings of the IEEE globecom workshops, pp 403–407
18. Ieong S, Shoham Y (2008) Bayesian coalitional games. In: Proceedings of the AAAI, pp 95–100
19. Kumar N, Iqbal R, Misra S, Rodrigues JJ (2015) Bayesian coalition game for contention-aware reliable data forwarding in vehicular mobile cloud. Futur Gener Comput Syst 48:60–72
20. Lee E, Lee EK, Gerla M, Oh SY (2014) Vehicular cloud networking: architecture and design principles. IEEE Commun Mag 52(2):148–155
21. Li K, Zheng H, Wu J (2013) Migration-based virtual machine placement in cloud systems. In: Proceedings of the IEEE 2nd international conference on cloud networking. IEEE, Piscataway, pp 83–90
22. Liu C, Luo J, Pan Q (2015) A distributed location-based service discovery protocol for vehicular ad-hoc networks. In: International conference on algorithms and architectures for parallel processing, pp 50–63

23. Luo J, Zhong T, Jin X (2016) Service discovery middleware based on QoS in VANET. In: Proceedings of the 12th international conference on natural computation, fuzzy systems and knowledge discovery, pp 2075–2080
24. Meneguette RI (2016) A vehicular cloud-based framework for the intelligent transport management of big cities. Int J Distrib Sens Netw 12(5):8198597
25. Meneguette R, Boukerche A, De Grande R (2016) SMART: an efficient resource search and management scheme for vehicular cloud-connected system. In: 2nd Proceedings of the IEEE global communications conference: mobile and wireless networks, Washington
26. Meneguette R, Boukerche A, Pimenta A, Meneguette M (2017) A resource allocation scheme based on Semi-Markov decision process for dynamic vehicular clouds. In: Proceedings of the IEEE ICC 2017 mobile and wireless networking, Paris
27. Meng H, Zheng K, Chatzimisios P, Zhao H, Ma L (2015) A utility-based resource allocation scheme in cloud-assisted vehicular network architecture. In: Proceedings of the IEEE international conference on communication workshop, pp 1833–1838
28. Mershad K, Artail H (2013) Finding a star in a vehicular cloud. IEEE Intell Transp Syst Mag 5(2):55–68
29. Olariu S, Khalil I, Abuelela M (2011) Taking VANET to the clouds. Int J Pervasive Comput Commun 7(1):7–21
30. Olariu S, Hristov T, Yan G (2013) The next paradigm shift: from vehicular networks to vehicular clouds. In: Mobile ad hoc networking: cutting edge directions, 2nd edn. Wiley, London, pp 645–700
31. Puterman ML (2014) Markov decision processes: discrete stochastic dynamic programming. Wiley, London
32. Refaat TK, Kantarci B, Mouftah HT (2014) Dynamic virtual machine migration in a vehicular cloud. In: Proceedings of the IEEE symposium on computers and communications, Workshops, pp 1–6
33. Refaat TK, Kantarci B, Mouftah HT (2016) Virtual machine migration and management for vehicular clouds. Veh Commun 4:47–56
34. Salahuddin MA, Al-Fuqaha A, Guizani M, Cherkaoui S (2014) RSU cloud and its resource management in support of enhanced vehicular applications. In: Proceedings of the IEEE Globecom Workshops, pp 127–132
35. Shojafar M, Cordeschi N, Baccarelli E (2016) Energy-efficient adaptive resource management for real-time vehicular cloud services. IEEE Trans Cloud Comput PP(99):1–1
36. Sibaï RE, Atéchian T, Abdo JB, Tawil R, Demerjian J (2015) Connectivity-aware service provision in vehicular cloud. In: Proceedings of the international conference on cloud technologies and applications, pp 1–5
37. Tao J, Zhang Z, Feng F, He J, Xu Y (2015) Non-cooperative resource allocation scheme for data access in vanet cloud environment. In: Proceedings of the third international conference on advanced cloud and big data, pp 190–196
38. Thomas RW, Friend DH, Dasilva LA, Mackenzie AB (2006) Cognitive networks: adaptation and learning to achieve end-to-end performance objectives. IEEE Commun Mag 44(12):51–57
39. Whaiduzzaman M, Sookhak M, Gani A, Buyya R (2014) A survey on vehicular cloud computing. J Netw Comput Appl 40:325–344
40. Yao H, Bai C, Zeng D, Liang Q, Fan Y (2015) Migrate or not? exploring virtual machine migration in roadside cloudlet-based vehicular cloud. Concurr Comput Pract Exp 27(18): 5780–5792
41. Yu R, Zhang Y, Gjessing S, Xia W, Yang K (2013) Toward cloud-based vehicular networks with efficient resource management. IEEE Netw 27(5):48–55
42. Yu R, Zhang Y, Wu H, Chatzimisios P, Xie S (2013) Virtual machine live migration for pervasive services in cloud-assisted vehicular networks. In: Proceedings of the 8th international conference on communications and networking in China, pp 540–545
43. Yu R, Huang X, Kang J, Ding J, Maharjan S, Gjessing S, Zhang Y (2015) Cooperative resource management in cloud-enabled vehicular networks. IEEE Trans Ind Electron 62(12):7938–7951

44. Zhang J, Ren F, Lin C (2014) Delay guaranteed live migration of virtual machines. In: Proceedings of the IEEE INFOCOM. IEEE, Piscataway, pp 574–582
45. Zheng K, Meng H, Chatzimisios P, Lei L, Shen X (2015) An SMDP-based resource allocation in vehicular cloud computing systems. IEEE Trans Ind Electron 62(12):7920–7928
46. Zingirian N, Valenti C (2012) Sensor clouds for intelligent truck monitoring. In: Proceedings of the IEEE intelligent vehicles symposium, pp 999–1004

Chapter 7
Applications and Services

Abstract Currently, there is an observable accelerated rate of growth in the number of vehicles traveling in cities, causing not only traffic problems, such as congestion, mobility, and automobile accidents, but also environmental and financial problems as a result of gases being emitted into the atmosphere, time spent in congestion, and number of accidents. To address such urban challenges, vehicular networks are used together with intelligent transportation systems (ITSs) to develop new technologies and services and assist in urban traffic engineering. These systems and services use a combination of various technologies to identify and monitor problems and assist in resolving them. In this chapter, we describe the main applications of ITSs using techniques developed for vehicular networks such as data dissemination, vehicle clouds, and others to provide not only an infrastructure for services that are useful to drivers and passengers but also tools to be used in urban mobility management.

7.1 Introduction

The potential social impact of vehicular networks is confirmed by the increase in consortia and initiatives involving automotive manufacturers, government agencies, universities, and other institutions [33]. The benefits brought about by vehicular networks can be described by the form of communication between the vehicles in which it is a tool for the dissemination of information as an important mechanism to reduce the number of congestion and accidents on roads [29]. Another important aspect of vehicular networks is related to the set of applications that can, in addition to assisting in the safety and driving of vehicles, also aid in the comfort and entertainment of passengers.

The set of services and applications focused on transport systems and mobility management has seen a significant increase in the emergence of intelligent transport systems (ITSs). ITSs aim to optimize the mobility of a city's vehicles by providing greater safety to drivers and passengers, as well as offering services that make the journey more enjoyable and predictable for passengers and the driver [11]. ITS can

© Springer International Publishing AG, part of Springer Nature 2018   147
R. I. Meneguette et al., *Intelligent Transport System in Smart Cities*, Urban
Computing, https://doi.org/10.1007/978-3-319-93332-0_7

be defined as a set of technologies and services aimed at optimizing the transport systems of a city [48].

To verify the potential of ITSs, we take as an example some cost estimating study of vehicle congestion, such as the report by Texas Transport Institute [44], which estimates that the costs of traffic congestion in the United States exceeds US$160 billion per year. Another study showed that the cost of congestion in the European Union is approximately 2% of its gross domestic product [3]. When we consider developing countries such as Brazil, this cost reaches US$80 billion, as shown by Cintra et al. [9]. Congestion not only brings a high financial burden to people and cities but also causes environmental damage. In the United States, about 25% of the total CO2 is due to road transportation [17]. These costs of vehicle traffic tend to increase due to the growth in the rate of vehicle use in urban areas. An estimate by IBM [45] showed that the number of vehicles in the world today exceeds one billion, and this number will double by 2020. Furthermore, the US Department of Transportation [46] showed that the number of registered vehicles increased from 234 million to 253 million from 2002 to 2011.

The cost of vehicle traffic can be reduced by using the services and applications offered by ITSs, which provide up-to-date and dynamic information on traffic conditions [30]. Also, such systems can reduce the number of traffic accidents while providing drivers and passengers with applications that increase their travel comfort such as location, streaming and multimedia services, local news, tourist information, and warning messages on city streets.

Using sensors, cameras, computers, and communication resources, vehicles can collect, transmit, and interpret information to assist in data acquisition to help drivers and devices take action. With the ability to sense and act in a given environment, vehicles become an important tool for smart cities, not only in terms of vehicle management but also as a source for capturing relevant real-time information that is helpful in resource management.

This chapter describes applications and services used in traffic management and mobility in urban centers that can use data dissemination mechanisms in a cloud-based infrastructure. The rest of this chapter is organized as follows. Section 7.2 describes the classification of vehicular network applications, and Sect. 7.5 briefly summarizes the chapter.

7.2 Applications and Services

In the case of communication by vehicles with other vehicles and with the road infrastructure, vehicular networks provide its users with diverse applications and services. Although the initial impetus for vehicular ad hoc networks (VANETs) was to ensure traffic safety, other concerns arose [33]. The different types of applications can be categorized as follows [19, 39, 49]:

- **Safety** comprises the class of applications that aim to increase the safety of drivers [24] by sending and receiving pertinent information about public roads. Therefore, these application classes can disseminate information about an event that has occurred on roads or streets. This information may be informative for the drivers or may activate signage on roads. Examples include emergency warning systems, emergency video streaming, cooperative collision warnings, and others.
- **Comfort** is the class of applications that aim at passenger comfort, traffic efficiency, and route optimization such as traffic information systems [32], interactions among vehicle passengers [40] through music downloads, chats, and voice messages, and others.

In what follows, we describe some applications of each category of vehicular network.

7.2.1 Safety Application

The main aim of safety applications is to reduce the number of road accidents. These applications are sensitive to delay [15], meaning messages must arrive in time for vehicles or drivers to take some action to avoid an accident. To reduce message delays, techniques of data and vehicle-to-vehicle communication are employed.

The applications most investigated and developed by the automobile industry and in academia are as follows [21, 47]:

- **Post-Crash Notification**. This type of application is used in the context of a vehicle involved in an accident. The affected vehicle begins to propagate alert messages to other vehicles using data dissemination mechanisms, informing those vehicles about its location. This message propagation is carried out so as to inform other vehicles about the accident in a timely manner so that they can make decisions and call for a rescue crew. Applications in this class can use both vehicle-to-vehicle (V2V) and vehicle-to-infrastructure (V2I) communication. Thus, vehicles can disseminate information about an event for the benefit of both nearby vehicles and first responders, so appropriate actions can be taken. An important advantage of such communication is the reduction of false positives and false negatives to prevent incorrect information from being disseminated regarding an accident .
- **Cooperative Collision Warning**. This type of message informs drivers about a possible collision course with another vehicle. Thus, other vehicles can take action to avoid an accident. For this type of application, a set of sensors is needed to detect the approach of another vehicle and perform an analysis of the behavior of that vehicle's driver so that both drivers do not take the same course of action in attempting to avoid a collision.
- **Lane Change Assistance**. This type of application monitors the behavior of a driver when passing other vehicles or changing lanes. A message is generated on the network informing nearby vehicles of a lane change. These applications

can be split into passive mode and active mode [47]. In passive mode, a distance calculation is made between vehicles involved in detecting changes in movement. Active mode entails communicating with other vehicles to check their proximity and detect any changes in vehicle behavior. In the case of a lane change and change in direction, the message is propagated to nearby vehicles.

- **Road Hazard Control Notification**. This involves notification by vehicles of events like landslides or changes in road layout, like a sharp bends a sudden downhill, for example [21]
- **Traffic Vigilance**. This refers to monitoring, through the use of cameras and other equipment installed along highways and roads, driver behavior, with the objective of verifying and detecting hazardous driving behavior for the purpose of reducing road rage and punishing drivers for infractions.

Some already developed works implement such applications related to road safety and safe driving in urban environments, for example Meneguette et al. [29], who proposed a data dissemination protocol called Autonomic Data Dissemination in Highway for VANETs (ADDHV). ADDHV informs vehicles about events happening within a given area of interest. This protocol uses only vehicle communication and involves only a slight delay that allows drivers in the area of interest (place of accident) to take action, such as take a detour to avoid possible traffic congestion. Akabane et al. [2] proposed an alerting information propagation mechanism called the suiTable URban Broadcast protocol (TURBO), which uses the communication coverage area of vehicles to propagate alerts within an area of interest. Following the same line of previous work, Souza et al. [13] also proposed an alert mechanism for vehicular networks called DRIFT, where, in addition to sending out notifications about highway accidents, the authors used a route exchange mechanism with the objective of allowing drivers to avoid congestion at accident sites. Figure 7.1 describes the operation of this alert mechanism. Figure 7.1a shows vehicle 5, which has been in an accident and starts propagating an alert about it. Neighboring vehicles (vehicles 1, 2, 3, and 4), upon receiving this alert, initiate a retransmission process. However, not all vehicles are within the retransmission zone, so only vehicles 2 and 4 pass on the alert. Thus, vehicles 1 and 3 cancel their rebroadcasts, avoiding redundant retransmissions. The process continues until all vehicles within the area of interest receive the alert.

These mechanisms use V2V communication to disseminate alerts on roads. However, some applications use V2I communication through cellular technologies to disseminate alerts not only to nearby vehicles but also to a control center, which will sends help. In [52] the authors present an application that makes use of an Android application and interactions with the onboard diagnostic (OBD) port of vehicles to detect accidents. If there is an accident, the application is activated and phones marked as emergency numbers are warned. In experiments, the authors showed that in less than 3 s the application reacts to alerts about events. In [35] offers numerous applications for drivers and passengers; one of the applications was for a system that sends notifications to a call center that forwards notifications to emergency responders who then go to the scene of the event.

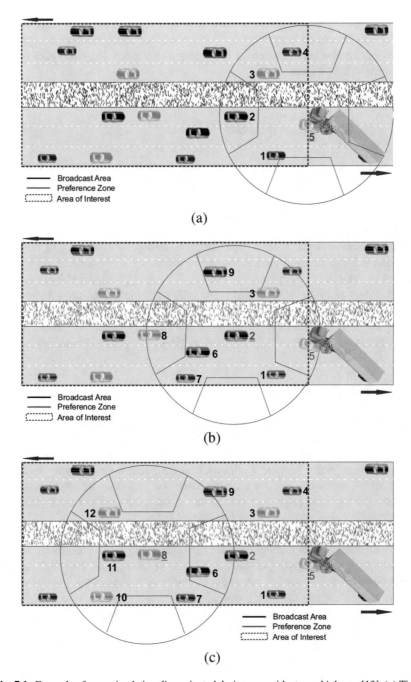

Fig. 7.1 Example of a warning being disseminated during an accident on a highway [13]. (**a**) Time instant 1. (**b**) Time instant 2. (**c**) Time instant 3

These applications can be aided by track monitoring systems. The camera system that informs the emergency response team about an accident maps out possible actions before the team arrives on the scene and notifies the team about traffic conditions in the vicinity.

7.2.2 Nonsafety Applications

The application classes of comfort, also called nonsafety applications, aim to make journeys more efficient and more comfortable not only for drivers but also for passengers, allowing interactions among passengers through messages, chats, and voice messages, among other applications.

These have very different communication requirements than security applications, where specific criteria regarding the timing of sending and receiving messages are not required [47]. These applications are more focused on meeting the requirements of the applications. Therefore, these applications aim at the desire of passengers and drivers to communicate with each other, both to make journeys more enjoyable and to provide drivers with tools to make their routes more efficient. Due to the large number of applications in this category, we could subdivide them into applications of traffic efficiency, road sensing, comfort, and entertainment.

7.2.2.1 Road Sensing

Using sensors, cameras, computers, and communication resources, vehicles can collect, transmit, and interpret information to assist in the acquisition of data to help drivers and devices take action. With the ability to sense and act in an environment, vehicles become a relevant tool for smart cities not only in vehicle traffic management but also for capturing relevant real-time information used in resource management [10]. This sensed data could become the richest collection and computing platform in urban environments [25].

The large number of vehicles that travel in cities and circulate in various regions of cities shows a significant benefit from using these vehicles as sensing agents capable of aggregating relevant information from regions. Therefore, sensing applications bring information about the state of roads through readings of vehicle sensors and the aggregation of the data of multiple vehicles and make it possible to contextualize the values obtained and make inferences about the conditions and state of city monitors [23, 27]. What follows are examples of applications that use data from multiple sensors and vehicles to construct images of environment variables.

Ganti et al. [18] developed a GPS-based navigation service called GreenGPS that shows drivers the most fuel-efficient route. GreenGPS collects vehicle data to estimate the fuel consumption of several vehicles to determine the expected fuel consumption on the streets of Urbana-Champaign. This collection is made using the onboard diagnostic (OBD-II) interface along with a typical scanner tool to enable collection and upload of fuel consumption data. The application uses prediction models for abstract vehicles and routes through the values obtained by the OBD-II scanner as well as the vehicle route generator. GreenGPS uses Dijkstra's algorithm to compute the minimum-fuel route. With a fuel-consumption map of the city, the authors have developed an application that traces the best route between two points from the point of view of fuel consumption, which can be reduced by up to 10% when choosing correct routes.

GreenGPS can work in two ways, through members and nonmembers. Members are drivers who have OBD-II adapters or scanning tools and who collaborate with the GreenGPS repository. They have accounts and derive additional benefits from the system. Nonmembers are users who only use GreenGPS to query about fuel-efficient routes. These users do not have OBD-II adapters, so the system only answers queries based on the average estimated performance for their particular vehicle.

Chen et al. [8] proposed a crowdsourcing-based road-surface-monitoring system, simply called CRSM. CRSM is composed of a set of hardware devices installed on vehicles for data collection and a central server for multisource data fusion. Figure 7.2 describes the system architecture. Each piece of onboard hardware has a microcontroller (MCU), GPS module, three-axis accelerometer, and GSM module.

Therefore, when a vehicle is traveling in Shenzhen, the microcontroller abstracts the speed and location through the accelerometer and GPS and transmits this information to the central server through the GSM module. This center then processes the information and makes it available to users. Thus, CRSM can effectively detect potholes and evaluate road roughness. As a case study, the authors installed this system on 100 taxies in the Shenzhen urban area and were able to find potholes with 90% accuracy. Also, the number of vehicles makes it possible to monitor the weather in a city with greater precision than weather stations.

Massaro et al. [28] used a data set of more than 1900 trips to estimate local temperature using vehicle sensors. The authors showed that vehicle temperature readings are consistent with temperatures measured by weather stations. However, the first readings had a higher frequency and resolution than the last ones, showing

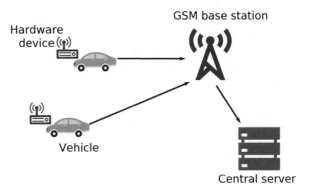

Fig. 7.2 CRSM system architecture [8]

that it is possible to monitor the climate of a region or city microscopically using data from sensors. An interest common to most drivers in large cities is traffic conditions on their intended routes. Although valuable, this information is difficult to obtain since it requires a complex and comprehensive infrastructure to monitor the state of a city's roads.

7.2.2.2 Traffic Efficiency

There has been an observable increase in the number of vehicles in cities in recent decades. The large number of vehicles, coupled with limitations in road infrastructure, has made traffic congestion a significant problem in major urban centers around the world. According to a report from the US Department of Transportation [41], congestion can result from certain events, for instance, accidents, road construction, major entertainment events, or infrastructure-related events like traffic light malfunctions. Such problems can be resolved not by improving road infrastructure but also through computational infrastructure that provides tools to help manage traffic cheaply and efficiently [6]. This class of applications aimed at the management of vehicular traffic is designed to assist in the management of traffic by obtaining, sharing, and deciding on traffic information abstracted from vehicles. This management reduces travel time and the costs of congestion.

The combination of several applications focused on vehicle traffic control and sensing forms a traffic management system (TMS) that aims to improve transportation systems through the integration of information, communication, and sensing technologies. Thus, these systems collect data from a variety of traffic-related sources, process and summarize the data, and merge the data to generate useful information, allowing applications and services to detect, control, and reduce congestion on public roads. Therefore, these traffic management applications must be widely accessible to drivers so drivers can make the most informed decisions about their journeys [11]. The following are some solutions that aim to improve traffic efficiency.

Meneguette et al. [31] proposed a mechanism for detecting congestion and suggesting new routes called the INtelligent protocol of CongestIon DETection for urban and highway environments (INCIDEnT). INCIDEnT is based on an artificial neural network (ANN) that classifies congestion levels and detects different levels of congestion. Also, INCIDEnT can suggest new routes to bypass congestion. Thus, INCIDEnT's main objective is to reduce congestion, with the following specific objectives: (1) allow for more significant traffic flow through collaborative information transfers between vehicles to reduce average travel time, (2) reduce fuel consumption, and (3) reduce CO_2 emissions.

INCIDEnT uses the vehicle speed and the density of neighboring vehicles as input parameters for the ANN. The multilayer perceptron type used in the ANN model aims to determine congestion levels on highways. To facilitate understanding of the ANN used in this proposed solution, Fig. 7.3 presents the ANN topology and how the input data are used for its learning. To tailor a multilayered learning of

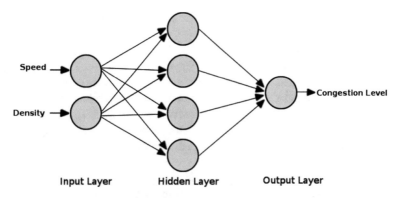

Fig. 7.3 ANN topology employed in [31]

congestion levels, the model's RNA was configured with the following topology: (1) input layer with two neurons, representing vehicle speed and density of neighboring vehicles; (2) hidden layer with four neurons, representing the protocol's ability to classify congestion levels; and (3) output layer with a neuron, representing the classification of congestion levels on roads. The output layer data are normalized, and the activation function used was the hyperbolic tangent ($tanh()$), with a backpropagation algorithm to train the network. Consequently, the results obtained from the output layer are in a range between 0 and 1.

INCIDEnT uses three levels congestion: free from congestion, moderate congestion, and congested. To instantaneously provide vehicles with information about current road conditions, the detection and classification of the congestion level are performed periodically every 2 s, avoiding any hastened imprecise result in the classification computation and allowing the classifier to perform a correct convergence in the level of congestion. This information is propagated on the network. Upon receiving the information disseminated in the network with the location of the congestion and the congestion level of the road, the vehicle checks whether it can pass through the signalized location. If not, the vehicle searches for a new route; otherwise, it maintains its route.

Souza et al. [12] proposed FASTER, a TMS traffic management system that classifies traffic conditions across the entire region using a probabilistic k-shortest path (PKSP) algorithm based on road weights. PKSP uses the Boltzmann probabilistic algorithm [1] to select a route for vehicles from among those in a set of possible routes.

FASTER relies only on V2V communication to gather traffic information, detect congestion, and compute alternative routes with low overhead. In FASTER, each vehicle gathers information from its one-hop neighbors to build a local knowledge base about traffic conditions. In FASTER, all vehicles need to send their information to their neighbors so that it can detect congestion and suggest alternative routes. When congestion is detected, FASTER employs a cooperative routing, which suggests alternative routes for vehicles heading for the congestion. This cooperative routing applies to load balancing to better distribute the flow of vehicles across the area.

Doolan and Muntean [16] introduced EcoTrec, a hybrid TMS that is based on periodic routing of vehicles. Because it is a hybrid solution, EcoTrec uses a central server to collect information from vehicles and build knowledge about the traffic conditions in the general area; then this knowledge is disseminated to vehicles so that they can calculate a route based on lower fuel consumption. To send information to the server, EcoTrec uses a broadcast protocol that does not use any broadcast suppression mechanism, whereby it could in turn introduce overhead into the system in dense scenarios.

Another way to manage traffic is by controlling devices that surround the mesh of the transport system, such as traffic lights along overall routes. The following are some solutions that aim to improve traffic efficiency by controlling traffic lights.

Younes et al. [50] proposed an Intelligent Traffic Light Controlling algorithm (ITLC). The algorithm aims to decrease the delay time at each intersection and increase its throughput. The traffic flow with the highest traffic density is scheduled first, without exceeding the maximum allowable green time for that phase. We defined the area around the signalized intersection where vehicles are ready to cross an intersection. The ready area is proposed to guarantee fair sharing of road intersections without exceeding the maximum allowable green time. The authors also proposed an arterial traffic light (ATL) control algorithm. The ATL uses real-time traffic characteristics of conflicting traffic flows to schedule traffic lights.

Younes et al. [51] proposed the context-aware traffic light scheduling (CA-TLS) algorithm. CA-TLS seeks to schedule the phases of traffic lights to allow vehicles to pass safely and smoothly through the shared intersection. This strategy reduces waiting time for the formation of congestion on roads. In the CA-TLS algorithm, traffic lights can be interrupted to allow emergency vehicles to cross signalized intersections fast. This method manages traffic lights, so emergency vehicles pass through intersections smoothly and safely. First, lights are configured based on the traffic density of all competing traffic flows at signalized road intersections. Thus, if an emergency vehicle is near the traffic flow with low density, CA-TLS protocol schedules and indicates the traffic flow to the vehicle.

7.2.2.3 Comfort and Entertainment Application

Applications related to comfort and entertainment aim to bring information that provides well-being and entertainment, as well as commercial activities for drivers and passengers. They are usually designed to provide convenience and improve the quality of trips. Typically these applications require that the requested information be made available when drivers need it. Applications in this category need to be connected to a shoreline infrastructure that provides Internet access to send and receive information. Within the class of applications that depends on Internet access, we can mention applications of information about the time, traffic in the network, and points of interest present in the route to be realized.

Another way to access these services and applications can be through a P2P connection. Such a connection allows information from a class of applications to continue to be sent and received even when there is an Internet connection failure or when the wired network is overloaded. Examples include applications for sharing files, music, images and video, and chatting and playing network games with other passengers from other cars.

Regardless of how these applications communicate, they have to deal with unique aspects of vehicle networks such as vehicle mobility and frequent disconnection. Within this category of applications are several types that can be applied. In what follows, we describe some types of application of comfort and entertainment.

- **Notification Services and Yellow Pages**. These types of applications provide information related to weather and traffic condition. In addition, these services can offer information related to comfort-related businesses, such as gas stations, restaurants, or pharmacies, for example. The information provided by this type of service can be directly through the Internet. Others can be obtained using V2V communication, where a vehicle passing through some point of interest disseminates relevant information to other vehicles.
- **Game, Chat, and Information-Sharing Services**. These are entertainment-oriented services that allow for the sharing of information of interest with passengers such as music, movies, pictures, or general files. Also, it can allow interactions between these users through games and chatting.
- **Vehicle Monitoring**. This service allows owners, car makers, and car shops to monitor a vehicle's operation remotely. These applications notify drivers about vehicle information and indicates irregularities that the vehicle may be experiencing. Thus, it is not necessary to worry about maintenance, since these applications inform the driver when the vehicle needs maintenance. These applications abstract information from the sensors embedded in vehicles to estimate the vehicles' operating time, rough mileage, fuel consumption, oil level, brakes, and tire pressure, for example, and this information is collected and sent to a central server or an app.
- **Automatic Parking**. In addition to obtaining information on parking spots, automatic payment of a fare, or scheduling of a parking space to be used, a vehicle can park without the supervision of the driver [36]. Some automakers have already introduced this convenience service [4, 5]. Such parking services can help in addition to providing information on empty parking spaces; they can offer a mobile cloud computing service with the joining of devices in vehicles parked on the premises [34]

Each type of application related to behavior and entertainment needs different treatment due to the requirements of each application. Applications of video exchange or streaming between vehicles need robust and real-time communication. On the other hand, event notification applications need Internet connectivity and low bandwidth. Automatic parking applications also require a high-precision location infrastructure, which includes sensors in cars and GPS utilization. In what follows, we provide more detailed information on solutions for comfort and entertainment applications.

Huang and Wang [20] proposed a collaborative system to perform content download. This system divides a network into cells to manage rapid changes in the topology of vehicular network. Each cellphone uses a P2P routing protocol to allow cooperation between vehicles to download content.

Castro et al. [7] developed an intelligent service based on wireless sensors to manage parking spaces in public or private spaces. The image-based service detects available parking spaces in a parking lot. Also, this service is integrated with an intelligent transport architecture that provides the structure needed to detect, manage, and notify units about these vacancies. These infrastructures aim to avoid heavy traffic in parking areas, thereby reducing time and fuel consumption, as well as pollution caused by vehicles looking for an available space.

The infrastructure uses sensors to detect parking spaces and cameras to record activities. Sensors and cameras are used to detect important parking information, allowing drivers to infer if there are available parking spaces. In addition, this infrastructure consists of a data center (cloud) that provides a good mechanism for data abstraction and image processing, as well as a good communication mechanism between drivers and sensors. Also, the data center provides a security mechanism that hardly anyone else has access to. Drivers have access to the data center through a mobile app that can run on a smartphone or tablet. Figure 7.4 displays an abstraction of the proposed infrastructure that is used to detect and notify users about free parking.

Therefore, the data center, from time to time or when a sensor detects a change in the environment, receives information about parking places. This information is processed by the system, which detects available parking spaces. After the information is processed, the system makes it available to driver applications. Accessing their mobile application, drivers can see the parking availability near their destination.

Li et al. [26] proposed a car search method based on a smartphone system. This method makes use of an internal location function and registered paths by navigation to search for and detect a vehicle parked in a large parking lot. The author has developed a QR code-based mobile application that is used to format information that assists in researching and detecting available parking spaces. The data coded in QR code consists of the parking space and its floor or floor and location. The mobile applications created are an offline map, reading QR code to record the parking place, planning the best way to get to the car, and real-time navigation. Thus, drivers can scan and decode QR codes using a smartphone and using the location app to find their vehicle in a large parking lot.

Tasseron et al. [42, 43] proposed a system for finding street parking to reduce congestion and time to find parking. The authors argue that works in the literature deal with reserving parking spaces. Thus, sensors are installed in cars and use V2V communication. The sensors monitor empty spaces and disseminate parking information to nearby vehicles. Early on de Olario et al. [34] and Floring et al. [38] had discussed the use of stationary vehicles in parking lots to create a vehicular

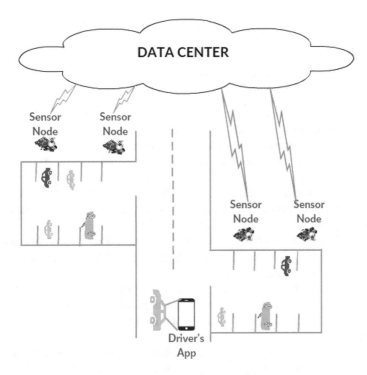

Fig. 7.4 Abstraction of infrastructure proposed by Castro et al. [7]

cloud for processing and storing useful information for ITSs in smart cities, thereby allowing for the development of new services and applications that aid in the management of intelligent city traffic systems.

7.3 Big Data in ITS

One of the obstacles to building a smart city is the processing and analysis of the large volume of data generated. Today the amount of data produced daily by humanity exceeds our ability to process them. These data are generated from a variety of applications, ranging from user activities on social networks to urban data sensors. One of the challenges encountered is the processing of this large volume of data, and there is also the challenge of doing so efficiently and at an acceptable cost. The traditional method is to use increasingly powerful machines and store the data in relational databases to be processed using SQL. However, when confronted with typical data loads of smart cities, these platforms are neither scalable nor suitable. New distributed processing models that go beyond traditional SQL are being developed under the generic name of NoSQL [22]. This research problem is currently referred to as big data [22], where one of the leading current solutions is the MapReduce model [14].

The term big data refers to a collection of data so large and complex that it becomes challenging to process the data using common database tools. Some important aspects of the big data concept that should be kept in mind:

- **Volume**. The scale is certainly a part of what makes big data big. The revolution of the mobile Internet, which has brought a flood of social media applications along with their updates, sensor data, and an explosion of e-commerce, means that all sectors are being flooded with data that can be extremely valuable if you know how to use them.
- **Speed**. This refers to the increase in the speed with which this data are created and the increased speed at which data can be processed, stored, and processed when analyzed by relational databases. The possibility of real-time data processing is an area that allows companies to do things like customize advertisement displays on web pages visited by particular users, based on recent searches, previews, and purchase histories.
- **Variety**. Of all data generated, 90% is "unstructured," coming from several sources and in a variety of forms. They can be GPS data, tweets with content and subjective information, or visual data like photos and videos, among other things.
- **Variability**. This aspect refers to data whose meaning is constantly changing. The constant changes are especially evident when data collection is based on language processing. Words do not have static definitions, and their meanings can vary widely according to context.
- **Veracity**. Data are practically useless if not accurate. This lack of precedence is particularly true in programs involving decision making by automated or unattended machine learning algorithms. The results of such programs are as good as the data they are processing.
- **Visualization**. Once processed, it is necessary to find a way to present data in a readable and accessible way. Visualization can entail dozens of variables and parameters, which go well beyond the x and y variables of standard bar graphs, and finding a clear way to present this information is one of big data's challenges.
- **Value**. The potential value of big data is enormous. In essence, data alone are practically useless. The value lies in the opportunity to conduct rigorous analyses of accurate data and in the information/insights such analyses provide.

Many governments are planning to adopt the smart city concept in their cities' design and implementing big data applications that support components of an intelligent city to achieve the required level of sustainability and improve the standards of living of their citizens. Smart cities use various technologies to improve health performance, transportation, energy, education, and water and other utility services, leading to higher levels of comfort for residents. These objectives involve reducing costs and resource consumption, as well as more efficient and active involvement of residents. The analysis and use of big data reflects recent technological advances that have enormous potential to improve services in a smart city. As digitization has become an integral part of everyday life, data collection has resulted in the accumulation of huge amounts of data, which can be used in various ways to benefit communities.

Using big data in a smart city is indispensable in many scenarios, such as public transport, health, weather monitoring, physical security, government administrations, and mobility, among others. In a smart city, the production, management, and diffusion of knowledge are essential, as is the management of the cities themselves and the data related to them. Thus, smart cities and big data are two sides of the same coin. One cannot work with one without considering the other. However, although indispensable, the application of big data in these scenarios presents many challenges: (1) the wide variety of data formats, (2) the wide range of data sources, (3) the large variations in data quality, (4) costs for deployment, and (5) adaptation and acceptance by the population.

7.4 Discussions and Future Applications

An efficient transportation system is composed of a combination of safety and nonsafety applications in which the quantity of vehicles is used in environmental sensing and abstraction of information and to help drivers and passengers have a safe and comfortable journey. To do so, applications must take advantage of the structure of vehicular networks, as well as of other technologies, so that the minimum requirements of these services can be fulfilled. The information and actions to be taken can be made available and executed within a reasonable time.

Currently several applications seek to reduce the impacts caused by congestion as well as bring greater collaboration and interaction among the users of these applications, providing greater entertainment for passengers as well as the comfort to drivers due to access to information about traffic conditions and service facilities close to its trajectory. Table 7.1 presents a summary of some applications studied that can be used by ITSs in cities to assist in the management of various function, services, and activities.

Through the applications studied, it is possible to observe the ability to abstract information from urban environments through both V2V and V2I communication. This information allows one to make inferences about road conditions as well as the conditions of vehicles through the use of the combination and interpretation of information received by sensors installed on vehicles. However, while these sensors and devices may aid in the abstraction of information, they are inherently subject to errors arising from a variety of causes, including sensor inaccuracy, failure of I/O access to data files, and even failures in the operation of both vehicles and sensors [37]. Therefore, it is necessary to verify data as they are obtained so that during the processing and analysis of virtual sensor data, the data from different sensors have no discrepancies and no conflicting, incomplete, or ambiguous information and correlates. Following such a check, it is possible to use fusion and data inference fusion methods, which allow one to obtain new values

Table 7.1 Availability and evaluation of applications

Application	Type	V2V	V2I	Environment	Safety communication
Meneguette et al. [29]	Post-Crash Notification	✓		Highway	No
Akabane et al. [2]	Post-Crash Notification	✓		City	No
Souza et al. [13]	Post-Crash Notification	✓		Highway	No
Ganti et al. [18]	Road Sensing		✓	City	No
Chen et al. [8]	Road Sensing		✓	City	No
Massaro et al. [28]	Road Sensing		✓	City	No
Meneguette et al. [31]	Traffic Efficiency	✓		City and highway	No
Souza et al. [12]	Traffic Efficiency	✓		City	No
Doolan and Muntean [16]	Traffic Efficiency	✓	✓	City	No
Younes et al. [50]	Traffic Light Control		✓	City	No
Younes et al. [51]	Traffic Light Control		✓	City	No
Huang and Wang [20]	Content Downlaod	✓		City	No
Castro et al. [7]	Parking Lot		✓	City	No
Li et al. [26]	Parking Lot		✓	City	No
Tasseron et al. [42]	Parking Lot		✓	City	No

with a more critical context than the raw data, so that the results of analyses are not corrupted by the information source. Therefore, it is a challenge to extract useful information from vehicular sensors to correlate them with internal and external variables, enabling the provision of personalized services to drivers and to an intelligent transportation system.

This contextualization is essential for understanding traffic patterns, driver behavior, and the mobility patterns of a city. Obtaining a more detailed characterization of driver behavior and mobility patterns within a city represents a very challenging problem. Several factors contribute to this issue. The most significant is the lack of massive public availability of data, which need to be generated by a substantial set of vehicle sensor readings to be statistically relevant. An example of a useful application of such models is the identification of and distinction between traffic jams, strikes, roadblocks, and accidents in urban environments. Therefore, one of the challenges facing these applications for use in smart cities is to understand the dynamics of cities.

With the increase in the number of devices with higher communication, as well as storage, capacity and the evolution of ITSs, a huge amount of data has been generated and made available to analyze the behavior of people and vehicles in cities. In addition to this increase in devices, another important point is the increasing availability of services that optimize resources and efficiently use means of transport, considering the particularities of each city such as territorial and population size, culture, economic assets, and commuting routines. Englund et al. [17]

describe some applications aimed at vehicular cloud and green transportation as future applications used by ITSs in cities. Among the applications described we can mention the following:

- **Vehicle temporary data center**. Junction of a group of vehicles to share computer resources in a vehicular network to offer services and applications focused on ITSs, as described in the works of Olario et al. [34].
- **Vehicle torrent network**. Content sharing, especially large volumes of data distributed among vehicles interested in the content. Communication is established through P2P communication between vehicles. An example of this future application is live video data.
- **Personal travel management**. A charging electric vehicle (EV) is handled automatically according to the owner's schedules. Autonomous algorithms manage the parking periods of vehicles, allowing better use of recharge islands.
- **Eco-driving**. This refers to vehicle sharing for individuals with the same or nearby destinations, thereby decreasing the number of vehicles on the roads. Users communicate with each other through a server or a cloud service.

Another major challenge encountered by any application is to provide security, privacy, and comfort information. Consequently, an error in information can have catastrophic consequences, like the death of a driver as a result of being directed to a dangerous location by a bad route suggestion. Misinformation can possibly be produced by malicious individuals or poorly calibrated applications. Another danger can considered much more significant to people: personal information can be inferred based on the movements patterns or data access requests over time. Thus, these applications must have security mechanisms to prevent information from being obtained without authorization so that erroneous information cannot be embedded in the system.

7.5 Final Discussion

In this chapter, we have described some applications of the vehicular networks used by ITSs. We used the standard classification of these applications as secure and nonsecure. Then we described each of them, presenting the main subclasses of each category. We discussed some works related to the main subclasses closely related to ITSs to assist in the management of urban traffic, as well as applications that bring greater comfort to travelers. Finally, we discussed the significant challenges and research opportunities in the field.

References

1. Aarts E, Korst J (1989) Simulated annealing and boltzmann machines. Wiley, London
2. Akabane AT, Villas LA, Madeira ERM (2015) An adaptive solution for data dissemination under diverse road traffic conditions in urban scenarios. In: Proceedings of the IEEE wireless communications and networking conference, pp 1654–1659

3. Allen H, Millard K, Stonehill M (2013) A summary of the proceedings from the united nations climate change conference in Doha, Qatar, and their significance for the land transport sector, Copenhagen: bridging the gap (BTG) initiative
4. Alfatihi S, Chihab S, Alj YS (2013) Intelligent parking system for car parking guidance and damage notification. In: Proceedings of the fourth international conference on intelligent systems, modelling and simulation (ISMS), Bangkok, pp 24–29
5. Reyher A, Naya M, Chiba H (2007) Parking assist system. US Patent US20100231717A1. Bosch Corporation
6. Brennand C, Boukerche A, Meneguette R, Villas LA (2017) A novel urban traffic management mechanism based on FOG. In: Proceedings of the ieee symposium on computers and communications, Heraklion, pp 377–382
7. Castro MRO, Teixeira MA, Nakamura N, Meneguette RI (2017) A prototype of a car parking management service based on wireless sensor networks for its. Int Rob Auto J 2:00021
8. Chen K, Tan G, Lu M, Wu J (2016) CRSM: a practical crowdsourcing-based road surface monitoring system. Wirel Netw 22(3):765–779
9. Cintra M (2013) A crise do trânsito em são paulo e seus custos. GVExecutivo 12(2):58–61
10. Cuff D, Hansen M, Kang J (2008) Urban sensing: out of the woods. Commun ACM 51(3): 24–33
11. da Cunha FD, Villas L, Boukerche A, Maia G, Viana AC, Mini RAF, Loureiro AAF (2016) Data communication in vanets: protocols, applications and challenges. Ad Hoc Netw 44: 90–103
12. de Souza AM, Villas LA (2016) A fully-distributed traffic management system to improve the overall traffic efficiency. In: Proceedings of the 19th ACM international conference on modeling, analysis and simulation of wireless and mobile systems, MSWiM '16. ACM, New York, pp 19–26
13. de Souza AM, Boukerche A, Maia G, Meneguette RI, Loureiro AA, Villas LA (2014) Decreasing greenhouse emissions through an intelligent traffic information system based on inter-vehicle communication. In: Proceedings of the 12th ACM international symposium on mobility management and wireless access, MobiWac '14. ACM, New York, pp 91–98
14. Dean J, Ghemawat S (2008) Mapreduce: simplified data processing on large clusters. Commun ACM 51(1):107–113
15. Domingos Da Cunha F, Boukerche A, Villas L, Viana AC, Loureiro AAF (2014) Data communication in VANETs: a survey, challenges and applications. Research Report RR-8498, INRIA Saclay; INRIA. https://hal.inria.fr/hal-00981126
16. Doolan R, Muntean GM (2017) Ecotrec - a novel vanet-based approach to reducing vehicle emissions. IEEE Trans Intell Transp Syst 18(3):608–620
17. Englund C, Chen L, Vinel A, Lin SY (2015) Future applications of VANETs. Springer, Berlin, pp 525–544
18. Ganti RK, Pham N, Ahmadi H, Nangia S, Abdelzaher TF (2010) Greengps: a participatory sensing fuel-efficient maps application. In: Proceedings of the 8th international conference on mobile systems, applications, and services, MobiSys '10. ACM, New York, pp 151–164
19. Hartenstein H, Laberteaux LP (2008) A tutorial survey on vehicular ad hoc networks. IEEE Commun Mag 46(6):164–171
20. Huang W, Wang L (2016) ECDS: efficient collaborative downloading scheme for popular content distribution in urban vehicular networks. Comput Netw 101:90–103
21. Kumar V, Mishra S, Chand N (2013) Applications of vanets: present and future. Commun Netw 5:12–15
22. Leavitt N (2010) Will NoSQL databases live up to their promise? Computer 43(2):12–14
23. Lee U, Gerla M (2010) A survey of urban vehicular sensing platforms. Comput Netw 54(4):527–544
24. Lee J, Chen W, Onishi R, Vuyyuru R (2008) Vehicle local peer group based multicasting protocol for vehicle-to-vehicle communications. In: Proceedings of the fourth international workshop on vehicle-to-vehicle communications

25. Lee U, Magistretti E, Gerla M, Bellavista P, Corradi A (2009) Dissemination and harvesting of urban data using vehicular sensing platforms. IEEE Trans Veh Technol 58(2):882–901

26. Li J, An Y, Fei R, Wang H (2016) Smartphone based car-searching system for large parking lot. In: Proceedings of the IEEE 11th conference on industrial electronics and applications, pp 1994–1998

27. Lo SC, Gao JS, Tseng CC (2013) A water-wave broadcast scheme for emergency messages in vanet. Wirel Pers Commun 71(1):217–241

28. Massaro E, Ahn C, Ratti C, Santi P, Stahlmann R, Lamprecht A, Roehder M, Huber M (2017) The car as an ambient sensing platform [point of view]. Proc IEEE 105(1):3–7

29. Meneguette RI, Maia G, Madeira ERM, Loureiro AAF, Villas LA (2014) Autonomic data dissemination in highway vehicular ad hoc networks with diverse traffic conditions. In: Proceedings of the IEEE symposium on computers and communications, pp 1–6

30. Meneguette R, Fillho G, Bittencourt L, Ueyama J, Villas L (2016) A solution for detection and control for congested roads using vehicular networks. IEEE Lat Am Trans 14(4):1849–1855

31. Meneguette RI, Geraldo Filho P, Guidoni DL, Pessin G, Villas LA, Ueyama J (2016) Increasing intelligence in inter-vehicle communications to reduce traffic congestions: experiments in urban and highway environments. PLoS One 11(8):e0159110

32. Nadeem T, Dashtinezhad S, Liao C, Iftode L (2004) Trafficview: traffic data dissemination using car-to-car communication. SIGMOBILE Mob Comput Commun Rev 8(3):6–19

33. Olariu S (2007) Peer-to-peer multimedia content provisioning for vehicular ad hoc networks. In: Proceedings of the 3rd ACM workshop on wireless multimedia networking and performance modeling, WMuNeP '07. ACM, New York, p 1

34. Olariu S, Khalil I, Abuelela M (2011) Taking vanet to the clouds. Int J Pervasive Comput Commun 7(1):7–21

35. Onstar (2017) Onstar. https://www.onstar.com/us/en/home.html. Last visited in June, 2017

36. Paromtchik IE, Laugier C (1996) Motion generation and control for parking an autonomous vehicle. In: Proceedings of IEEE international conference on robotics and automation, vol 4, pp 3117–3122

37. Rettore PHL, Santos BP, Campolina AB, Villas LA, Loureiro AAF (2016) Towards intra-vehicular sensor data fusion. In: Proceedings of the IEEE 19th international conference on intelligent transportation systems, pp 126–131

38. Ryan F, Syedmeysam A, Ghazi ZA, Stephan O (2017) Big data in the parking lot. In: Big data management and processing. CRC Press, West Palm Beach, pp 425–450

39. Sharef BT, Alsaqour RA, Ismail M, Bilal SM (2013) A comparison of various vehicular ad hoc routing protocols based on communication environments. In: Proceedings of the 7th international conference on ubiquitous information management and communication, ICUIMC '13. ACM, New York, pp 48:1–48:7

40. Sugiura A, Dermawan C (2005) In traffic jam IVC-RVC system for its using bluetooth. IEEE Trans Intell Transp Syst 6(3):302–313

41. Systematics C et al (2005) Traffic congestion and reliability: trends and advanced strategies for congestion mitigation. Final Report, Texas Transportation Institute. http://opsfhwadotgov/congestion_report_04/indexhtm

42. Tasseron G, Martens K (2017) Urban parking space reservation through bottom-up information provision: an agent-based analysis. Comput Environ Urban Syst 64:30–41

43. Tasseron G, Martens K, van der Heijden R (2016) The potential impact of vehicle-to-vehicle communication on on-street parking under heterogeneous conditions. IEEE Intell Transp Syst Mag 8(2):33–42

44. Texas Transport Institute, Schrank DL, Eisele WL, Lomax TJ, Bak J (2017) 2015 urban mobility scorecard, mobility report

45. Traffic IS (2015) EPA - united state environmental protection agency. http://www.ibm.com/smarterplanet/us/en/traffic_congestion/ideas. Last visited in January, 2017

46. US Department of Transportation (DOT), US Department of Transportation Statistics B (2017) National transportation statistics 2014, Technical Report

47. Vegni AM, Biagi M, Cusani R (2013) Smart vehicles, technologies and main applications in vehicular ad hoc networks. In: Giordano LG, Reggiani L (eds) Vehicular technologies - deployment and applications, chap 1. InTech, Rijeka

48. Villas LA, Boukerche A, Maia G, Pazzi RW, Loureiro AA (2014) Drive: an efficient and robust data dissemination protocol for highway and urban vehicular ad hoc networks. Comput Netw 75:381–394

49. Wischhof L, Ebner A, Rohling H (2005) Information dissemination in self-organizing intervehicle networks. IEEE Trans Intell Transp Syst 6(1):90–101

50. Younes MB, Boukerche A (2016) Intelligent traffic light controlling algorithms using vehicular networks. IEEE Trans Veh Technol 65(8):5887–5899

51. Younes MB, Boukerche A, Mammeri A (2016) Context-aware traffic light self-scheduling algorithm for intelligent transportation systems. In: Proceedings of the IEEE wireless communications and networking conference, pp 1–6

52. Zaldivar J, Calafate CT, Cano JC, Manzoni P (2011) Providing accident detection in vehicular networks through OBD-II devices and android-based smartphones. In: Proceedings of the IEEE 36th conference on local computer networks, pp 813–819

Chapter 8
Implementation and Testing Tools

Abstract The evaluation of services, applications, and protocols for intelligent transport systems (ITSs) is a complex task because such systems aggregate several technologies, where each technology has a set of limitations that need to be overcome. Also, the cost of evaluating such systems can be high because it involves allocating not only equipment but also the residents of a city. Assessments also need to consider the environmental conditions under which the system is evaluated. To reduce this cost and provide greater scalability in the evaluation of a new protocol, system or server, simulations are used that make it possible to examine conditions, come up with alternatives, and evaluate solutions while avoiding costly real experimental setups, mapping the complexity of the environment, and preventing interference with existing urban systems. This chapter describes the main simulation tools of an ITS for a smart city, as well as the concepts involved in such simulators.

8.1 Introduction

Intelligent transport system (ITSs) must overcome several limitations because they must coordinate several technologies simultaneously, such as vehicular networks, sensor networks, and cellular networks. Therefore, performing performance tests on protocols and services for ITSs may require large numbers of people, incur high costs, and still need favorable climatic conditions and environments. Also, repeating a given experiment in a multivariable environment is difficult [19]. The use of simulations is an attractive alternative because it makes use of a controlled environment and consumes fewer resources. However, the reproducibility of conditions similar to those found in the field poses a challenge.

Therefore, modeling and simulation are vital for determining the factors and forecasting the events that might affect urban traffic and are valuable for planning and addressing transportation issues. Simulations make it possible to examine conditions, produce alternatives, and evaluate solutions while avoiding costly real experimental setups, mapping the complexity of an environment, and preventing interference with existing urban systems.

© Springer International Publishing AG, part of Springer Nature 2018

R. I. Meneguette et al., *Intelligent Transport System in Smart Cities*, Urban Computing, https://doi.org/10.1007/978-3-319-93332-0_8

The simulation of vehicular networks is a complex task since it involves modeling signal propagation, media access protocol, and several other network protocols. In addition, a vehicular network is a mobile network for which specific mobility models must be developed. Thus, the problem shifts instead to the level of realism of the simulation, and the dominant aspect is that of mobility [18]. Thus, the use of an unrealistic model causes the simulation results to be biased, unreliable, or completely erroneous. Mobility models of road traffic consists of the description of the traffic flow of the traffic flow of a city, transit rules, and evaluating traffic management efficiency. The simulators are restricted to only the movement of vehicles or a single application domain.

Vehicular mobility can be described at three different levels [7]. (1) First is the macroscopic level, which represents road traffic. At this level, flows of cars move along roads at a certain speed and density and with a certain in-/outflow of vehicles, but there is no information about individual vehicles, just an aggregate overview. (2) Next is the mesoscopic level, which models at the individual vehicle level but determines the speed of each car using macroscopic measures. Thus, vehicles are not independent of each other in their movement. (3) Finally is the microscopic level, which models each vehicle as an autonomous entity. It describes the movement of each driver independently, providing the acceleration and the behaviors of drivers. These mobility classes have advantages and disadvantages by which they impact the modeling of a simulation environment of an ITS.

Modeling of new ITS environments requires incorporating features of communication paradigms, interaction methods, control, and decision making. To incorporate these elements, frameworks have been developed to merge traffic and network simulators, which are prone to performance loss and interoperability issues. Also, the valuable input of real-time sensed data into simulations to adjust and correct trends with the most up-to-date status of the actual environment is not contemplated in current simulation systems.

Most solutions proposed for the evaluation of applications, services, and protocols for ITSs use an already established network simulator in conjunction with a mobility simulator or other software that confirms the soundness of the preestablished standard for various technologies such as vehicular networks and wireless networks.

This chapter outlines some tools aimed at implementing and evaluating new services, applications, and protocols for ITSs. Such tools allow us to evaluate the solutions proposed in a scalar way, allowing us to stress the solutions to verify how efficient they are in a real environment. The rest of this chapter is organized as follows. Section 8.2 discusses the concept of mobility model and describes the main types of such models that are in use. Section 8.3 describes network simulators, focusing on the main types of simulators. Finally, Sect. 8.5 briefly summarizes the chapter.

8.2 Mobility Model and Simulation

To use all types of applications in an ITS, the whole system needs to be evaluated and a real test environment set up, considering all the limitations found such as the expense, network complexity, distributed environments, and high mobility [6]. To simplify the validation and verification of the new systems, the simulators can facilitate the evaluation of the new protocols and services allowing the use of any type of network and necessary infrastructure. For example, simulation allows users to emulate a network considering routing, security, vehicle mobility, and other factors that are similar to real-life situations. Therefore, one of the critical points of a simulation is to establish models and parameters that appear in the real world, so that the results obtained are consistent with real-world experience.

In simulations of an environment oriented to ITSs one of the significant challenges is related to the model of mobility of vehicles in a city. This model of movement must take into account not only the mobility of residents but also the flow of vehicles in the city. Therefore, the model should map a model of human behavior, as well as understand the unique characteristics of urban mobility as reflected in traffic regulations, restricted road patterns, and traffic. With the objective of obtaining a reliable result and for ITS simulations to be realistic, it is essential to generate a mobility model to stimulate the movement pattern of vehicles and people.

To generate a mobility model, several parameters are used, such as topological maps, emulation of the driver behavior to simulate the action of the drivers in the streets, as well as the car generation that emulates the mobility of the vehicle such as, direction, velocity, among others. These parameters cannot be chosen randomly because their values must reflect reality, such as a real mobility scenario. Due to the difficulty and complexity of obtaining values for these parameters, researchers have made simplifying assumptions and neglected various parameters [7]. Most models available today include a topological map, or at least a graphic, such as motion restrictions. Also, vehicle engine parameters are largely absent from all models and vehicle behavior is limited to smooth accelerations or decelerations.

According to [1, 7], the model of vehicular mobility can be divided into four different classes:

- **Synthetic Models**: all models based on mathematical models;
- **Survey-based Models**: mobility patterns from surveys;
- **Trace-based Models**: mobility patterns from real mobility traces;
- **Traffic Simulator-based Models**: mobility patterns from a detailed traffic simulator.

In the following sections, we discuss some works in the literature. We also describe how mobility models are validated. Finally, a discussion on the challenges of mobility models is presented.

8.2.1   Synthetic Models

The first kind of mobility modeling uses synthetic modeling. This mobility class is based on mathematical equations aimed at abstracting realistic mobility models. According to Fiore et al. [5], this template can be subdivided into five categories:

- Stochastic model: depends completely on random motions;
- Traffic stream model: checks the mechanical features of the mobility model;
- Car-following model: monitors car-to-car communication behavior;
- Queue model: roads are represented as queue buffers, and cars are assumed to be traveling on such roads;
- Behavioral model: checks the effects of social interaction on movement.

We can also classify synthetic mobility models based on certain criteria [8]. (1) At the traffic level, criteria details are given about streets, obstacles preventing vehicles on the road from communicating with each other, and the density of vehicles on roads. (2) The motion level establishes the topology between networks in vehicles and analyzes their behavior based on information collected at the traffic level. Furthermore, at this level, patterns of human behavior are identified.

Some researchers, such as Musolesi et al. [20], have developed a synthetic mobility model based on social network theory and then validated it using real traces. They showed that the model was a reasonable approximation of human movement patterns.

Hsu et al. [11] proposed the Weighted Waypoint Model (WWM) that tunes the parameters of a synthetic model using real traces. The WWM adds the notion of preferences to a random waypoint. The calibration of this "preference criterion" is performed based on mobility traces obtained inside the University of Southern California campus.

For this model, it is necessary to formulate a validating mathematical model to guarantee its realism compared to real mobility. Therefore, an abstraction of real traces is carried out to enable subsequent comparison with the synthetic modeling performed. The major challenge of this model lies in the complexity of modeling human behavior. The complexity corresponds to the volatility of individuals, who respond to stimuli and disturbances that may affect the mobility model. Thus, realistic mobility models should consider behavioral theories.

8.2.2   Survey-Based Models

These models are based on data collected on human behavior and actions people perform, both of which relates strongly to macroscopic mobility information. The most substantial performance surveys are provided by laboratories in the United States, where extensive statistics on American citizens' behavior are gathered, from the beginning of the work day or lunch time to commuting time or lunch preferences.

These statistics are included in models of mobility, which allows for generating generic mobility capable of reproducing the behavior of a city's residents.

We can cite the UDel Model for the Simulation of Urban Mobile Networks [16]. The mobility simulator monitored students of the Department of Labor and Statistics and abstracted time-use studies of pedestrians and vehicle mobility studies conducted by the urban planning and traffic engineering communities. With these data the mobility simulator models arrival times, lunch time, breaks, errands, pedestrians, vehicular dynamics, and workday time use, such as meeting size, frequency, and duration.

The agenda-based mobility model [34] adds both geographic movements and social activities. The movement of each person is based on an individual agenda, which includes all kinds of activities in a given day. Data from the US National Household Travel Survey have been used to obtain activity distributions, occupation distributions, and dwell time distributions.

One of the great challenges of this model lies in building an infrastructure for the abstraction and monitoring of human behavior so that it is possible to generate a generic model based on the abstracted data.

8.2.3 Trace-Based Models

Unlike the other models described so far, trace-based models do not involve the use of mathematical modeling and does not attempt to generate models from real mobility patterns. Models in this class use data from traces directly and extract generic mobility patterns from movement traces. Thus, these models can be used to monitor the movement of vehicles and humans in the analysis process to obtain generated traces according to their motion and location.

An example of this model can be found in the work of Tuduce et al. [29] that presents a mobility model based on real data from a wireless LAN on the campus of ETH Zurich. The authors used a simulation area divided into squares and derived the probability of transitions between adjacent squares from access point data.

Yoon et al. [33] used association data between Wi-Fi users and access points, with a map of the area over which traces were collected to generate a probabilistic mobility model representative of real movements. For this, the authors derived a discrete-time Markov chain that considers not only current locations but also previous locations, as well as the origin and destination of a given route.

The great challenge of this model is to extract a pattern directly from real traces. Furthermore, another challenge is to formulate a generate a vehicle-based mobility model based on the real traces with low computational cost.

8.2.4   Traffic Simulator-Based Models

These models can obtain traces of urban traffic rather than a realistic level of detail through realistic traffic simulators. These simulators can model microscopic urban traffic, energy consumption, noise level, and pollution, among others. These simulators cannot be used directly as network simulators, i.e., it does not have the implementation of the network interfaces. These simulators parse traffic and network simulator input files. Thus, users can validate traffic patterns and obtain a level of detail unobtainable by any current vehicle mobility model. Several simulators are described in what follows.

The MObility model generator for VEhicular networks (MOVE) automates the creation of mobility models for vehicular networks [15]. This tool uses a road map editor and a vehicle movement editor. With the map editor, the user can create maps manually, generate them automatically, or even import real maps. The vehicle movement editor allows the user to add the routes of each vehicle to the previously generated map.

Simulation of Urban Mobility (SUMO) [3] is a microscopic simulator of urban traffic used in some simulation solutions for vehicular networks. SUMO simulates the movement of different types of vehicles without the occurrence of collisions and supports multiple route ranges. SUMO's operation is based on a model of driver behavior combined with traffic controllers present on roads. Among the main features of SUMO, we can mention the following. (1) the granularity of simulation elements: in SUMO it is possible to model and control explicitly individual vehicles, pedestrians, and public transport systems; (2) importing and creating scenarios: SUMO contains a set of tools that allow the creation of different types of road networks, as well as the creation of road scenarios from mapping information previously obtained from other services, such as OpenStreetMap [23]; (3) online interaction: SUMO enables interaction with the elements of the simulation online. As a result, such functionality allows the use, for example, to change, in individual simulation time, individual vehicle routes and the timing of traffic lights, in addition to allowing integration of the traffic simulator with simulators of communication networks; (4) performance: SUMO makes it possible to simulate large networks, such as vehicle traffic in a large city. In addition to allowing the microscopic simulation of vehicle and pedestrian mobility, which is its main functionality, SUMO provides a set of tools and libraries that aim to facilitate the development of the most varied types of scenarios, allowing the study of issues involving vehicular and pedestrian traffic. For example, it is possible with SUMO to create different types of road infrastructure, to import a road infrastructure from mapping services, to define the demand for vehicles and their routes, to study the consumption of fuel, and to evaluate the emission of gases from vehicles.

Traffic simulators that send information to a network simulator and do not receive feedback are called network-centric. For some applications of vehicular networks, however, it is necessary for the driver to obtain information through the network to make route decisions. Traffic simulators whose traffic module gets information from the network module are known as application-centric. Most traffic simulators are network-centric. The Traffic and Network Simulation Environment (TraNS) [24], however, can be both network-centric and application-centric. TraNS is a simulation tool that uses NS-2 and SUMO. Also, with this tool it is possible to test the influence of applications in vehicular networks on the behavior of vehicles in traffic. This analysis is possible due to Traffic Control Interface (TraCI) [28], an interface module that connects the network simulator and the traffic simulator. TraCI sends mobility commands to the traffic simulator and can feed the network simulator with new mobility models. Another advantage of this simulator is the presence of a framework for application development.

The major challenge of this model is the configuration complexity of these traffic simulators; calibration usually requires a broad set of parameters. Furthermore, the level of detail needed for vehicular network simulators may not require as much detail for traffic analysis as other simulators such as traffic analysis, global vehicular mobility patterns and exact vehicular behaviors.

8.2.5 Validation

The results obtained by these models should be verified to determine how similar to reality the results are. Thus, the results generated by the models are compared with actual results.

Validation can be done by checking for errors between the trace generated by the mobility models and the real trace, if the actual trace is accessible. Another form of validation is called delegated validation. A comparison is performed through a validated model instead of real ones.

This validation is performed before performing an analysis of service or protocol used in ITSs.

8.2.6 Advantages and Shortcomings

We can observe the complexity and challenges of each class of mobility model used to evaluate the services and protocols used by ITSs. Thus, we can determine whether, depending on the complexity of the mobility pattern, the mathematical models can reproduce the mobility of the residents of a city with a high precision level. However, if the complexity of the model is high, individual monitoring can be used to generate a general mobility pattern, which is based on daily observations of the city to generate a pattern of mobility.

The use of these mobility classes may also depend on the type of service or application used, for example, the protocols of data dissemination are sufficient and traceable or a survey-based model may be envisioned.

8.3 Network Simulation Tools

Not only are mobility models essential for evaluating the performance of any service or protocol of an ITS; the entire stack of protocols for communication between elements that compose an ITS are essential as well. For this, one can also use simulators that allow for evaluating the performance of any network to highlight any issues that may exist; the most appropriate way to accomplish this task is to deploy simulations that provide the closest results to real-world observations [27].

Currently, several simulators are used to test and evaluate new protocols and applications for ITSs. We describe some of these simulators in what follows.

8.3.1 Network Simulator

Network Simulator (NS) [21] is a discrete event simulator resulting from a project known as the Virtual InterNetwork Testbed (VINT). Among others, this project is made up of DARPA, USC/ISI, Xerox PARC, LBNL, and the University of Berkeley. A great advantage of NS is that it is completely free and open source, which allows the user to make any necessary adjustments. The simulator supports the simulation of a large number of network technologies (wired and wireless) and different scenarios.

Currently, this simulator has two versions, NS-2 and NS-3. NS-2 is coded in two languages: C++ for the basic structure (e.g., protocols, agents) and Object-oriented Tool Command Language (OTCL) for use as a front end. OTCL is an interpreted language developed at MIT for effectively writing simulations. The reason for using two programming languages is based on two different needs. On the one hand, there is a need for a more robust language for the handling of bytes and packets and for implementing algorithms that run large data sets. In this context, C++, which is a compiled and traditional language, has proved to be the most effective tool. On the other hand, it is a fact that, during the simulation process, adjustments are necessary with certain frequency. Change the size of the link and conduct a test, change the delay and conduct a test, add a node and conduct a test. In short, there would be a lot of wear and tear if, with each parameter change (and there are many in a simulation), there was a need to compile the program to test it. The use of the OTCL language, which is interpreted, avoids this wear and tear on the part of the user since there is a simplification in the interactive process of changing and reexecuting the model. In NS-2, the network nodes have to be manually staked to find nodes that are moving around and that send and receive data to each other.

NS-3 made improvements over NS-2 regarding the programmability of simulation components. In NS-3, the entire simulator is written in C++ with optional Python support. In this way, simulation codes can be written only in C++ or Python. The results of some simulations can be visualized by Network Animator (NAM), but new forms of visualization are being developed. NS-3 generates packet trace files in pcap format so that other tools can be used for packet analysis. In NS-3 multiple objects can be linked together at run time, such as nodes. This aggregation model manipulates access between different objects and facilitates memory control.

8.3.2 JiST/SWANS

JiST/SWANS [14] programming code is open source and was released under the Cornell Research Foundation license. This simulator uses the scalable wireless network simulator SWANS built atop the JiST platform [2]. JiST is a high-performance discrete-event simulation engine that runs on a Java virtual machine (JVM). JiST converts an existing virtual machine into a simulation platform by embedding simulation time semantics at the byte-code level. Thus, JiST simulations are written in Java, compiled using a regular Java compiler, and run over a standard, unmodified virtual machine. The JiST design is used to achieve high simulation throughput, save memory, and run standard Java network applications over simulated networks.

SWANS leverages the JiST design to achieve high simulation throughput, save memory, and run standard Java network applications over simulated networks. In addition, SWANS implements a data structure, called hierarchical binning, for efficient computation of signal propagation.

8.3.3 OMNeT++

The OMNeT++ [22] discrete event simulation environment has been publicly available since 1997. OMNeT++ represents a framework approach that consists of an integrated development environment (IDE), a kernel simulation, and an execution environment. The IDE is based on Eclipse, which facilitates the configuration and development of new protocols and services. The simulation kernel has two aspects, module behavior and module description. The behavior of the module is written in C++ and describes the services and functionality that the module has to perform in a simulation, such as managing the channels of communication with other modules, managing their functionality, and sending control messages. The description module stores in plain-text Message Definition (msg) and Network Description (ned) files, the main parameters of the module. Thus, with these modules OMNeT++ can easily interface with third-party libraries and be debugged using off-the-shelf utilities; thus, it lends itself equally to rapid prototyping and developing production-quality applications [30].

The OMNeT++ discrete-event-simulation environment serves as an execution environment and can be divided into two functionalities. (1) The command-line-based environment targets unattended batch runs on dedicated machines. (2) The graphical environment better supports interactive interactions with components of a running simulation, making it possible to monitor or alter internal states directly.

8.3.4   Advantages and Shortcomings

Although these simulators have the main protocols for the communication of several network technologies, the configurations of these protocols, as well as their behavior, have to be similar to real-world operation and parameters so that the results generated are reliable. Also, these simulators do not have a mobility model in which to adequately simulate an ITS environment of a city, requiring aggregation and other protocols or methods to generate and manage the mobility of nodes in the network.

Therefore, one of the great challenges of these simulators lies in providing results that are in line with the real world. In addition, the simulators need to be able to interface with other simulators, such as mobility simulators, that would allow them to add new functionality to simulations.

8.4   Integrated Mobility and Network Module in Simulations

In this section we describe simulators and methods that integrate network simulators with simulators and methods of generation and control of node mobility in networks, seeking to create a simulation environment closer to the real world.

8.4.1   iTETRIS

An Integrated Wireless and Traffic Platform for Real-Time Road Traffic Management Solutions (iTETRIS) [12] was developed to integrate and simulate ITS applications. iTETRIS addresses certain challenges, such as those associated with (1) dynamic, distributed, and autonomous ITSs; (2) realistic vehicle-to-vehicle (V2V) and vehicle-to-infrastructure (V2I) communication; and (3) road traffic and wireless integrated open-source simulation platforms [25]. For these, iTETRIS integrates wireless communications and road traffic simulation platforms in an environment that is easily tailored to specific situations allowing performance analysis of cooperative ITSs at the city level [12].

iTETRIS provides a standard compliant, open-source integrated communication and traffic platform suited for large-scale scenario simulation through the use of four key modules: the network simulator NS-3, the traffic simulator SUMO, an ITS application simulator, and a central federating module called the iTETRIS Control System (iCS). iCS aims to handle interactions of multiple ITS applications with NS-3 and SUMO. Therefore, iCS consists of an interface connecting various modules,

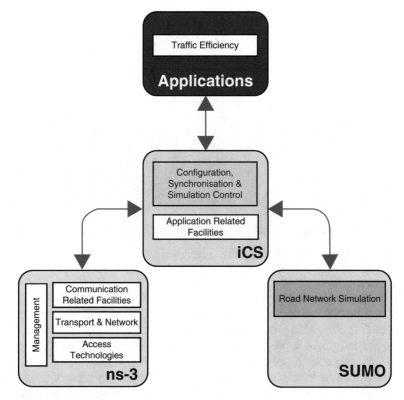

Fig. 8.1   iTETRIS platform architecture [10]

allowing interactions between mobility models and network models. Figure 8.1 describes an abstraction of the iTETRIS simulator architecture for ITSs.

For the applications and services of ITSs, iTETRIS implements the ETSI ITS architecture, which facilitates the development of new applications or the evaluation of new communication protocols directed at ITSs. The architecture of the ITS simulator is separated into two parts [27]. The first part manages all connection between the ITS application logic, the iCS, SUMO, and NS-3. The second part is a container for the ITS application logic. This layer was extended by Bellavista et al. [4] with an innovative, flexible higher-layer node architecture that supports necessary send and receive primitives, much like NS-3.

8.4.2   VSimRTI

The Vehicle-2-X (V2X) Simulation Runtime Infrastructure (VSimRTI) [32] is a framework for the assessment of new solutions for cooperative ITSs. Vehicle movements and sophisticated communication technologies like V2X communication and cellular networks can be modeled in detail. VSimRTI uses an ambassador concept

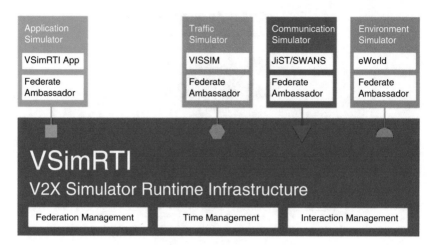

Fig. 8.2 An example of a VSimRTI simulator coupling [32]

inspired by some fundamental concepts of the high-level architecture (HLA) [27]. Thus, it is possible to couple arbitrary simulation systems with a remote control interface [32]. Figure 8.2 describes an abstraction of the VSimRTI simulator.

The architecture of the application simulator is based on the ETSI ITS standard. Besides the sandboxed application layer approach, it features a rich layer facility with application, information and communication support, enabling a set of applications and services that are ready to use, such as the traffic simulators SUMO and PHABMACS. VsimRTI also allows the use of other network simulators to perform communication simulation such as NS-3, OMNeT++ and a cellular communication simulator, and several visualization and analysis tools.

8.4.3 Veins

Veins [31] is a simulation framework of communication networks composed of a set of models specifically developed for the study of vehicular networks. The execution of these models is performed by the OMNeT++ 4 discrete-event simulator in conjunction with the SUMO traffic simulator. Figure 8.3 shows the general structure of Veins. Because it is a simulation framework, Veins serves as the basis for the development of specific applications. However, since Veins is composed of several models, it is possible to use it only by grouping the available models and modifying a few parameters, which facilitates the study of applications of ITSs.

In Veins, each simulation is performed by executing two simulators in parallel: OMNeT++, to simulate the communication network, and SUMO, to simulate vehicle and pedestrian traffic. Both simulators communicate through a TCP socket, and the adopted communication protocol is defined by TraCI, as presented in

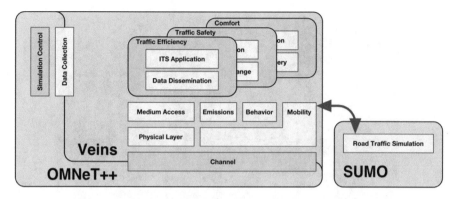

Fig. 8.3 Simulator architecture of Veins [31]

the previous section. This allows the joint simulation of both aspects of data communication as well as aspects of traffic and mobility. The movement of vehicles in the SUMO traffic simulator is reflected by the movement of nodes in the OMNeT++ network simulator. Therefore, interaction with the traffic simulator allows one, for example, to simulate the effect of communication between vehicles in traffic. The impressive fact about Veins consists of interactions between network simulators and traffic, which is entirely transparent to the user, facilitating the development of applications.

Veins includes a model for 802.11 wireless network simulation designed explicitly for network environments. This model is defined obeying the IEEE 802.11p [13] communication standard. Among the functionalities that exist in a Veins model, we can mention the existence of different access channels with quality of service that follow the EDCA, specific characteristics of timing, modulation and coding of frames for road environments, and various models of communication channels. Veins also includes a channel hopping functionality, which switches between control channels (CCH) and service channels (SCH) as defined by the DSRC/WAVE standard [17]. Also implemented in this model are manipulations of wave short messages, beacon exchange, base safety messages, or cooperative awareness messages.

Veins also includes a model of the Japanese communication standard for ITSs ARIB T109 [9]. This model implements both features of the physical layer and the medium access layer, which uses a combination of TDMA and CSMA/CA.

Precise signal propagation models are fundamental to the study of ITSs. Usually, it is assumed that a signal propagates under conditions free from any interference, which does not represent a realistic scenario. Therefore, Veins implements the Two-Ray Interference signal propagation model, which more realistically captures effects such as signal reflection [26].

Radio transmissions are greatly affected by signal attenuation effects. Accurately capturing these effects is of paramount importance in the study of applications of ITSs, especially in urban environments where buildings block the propagation of

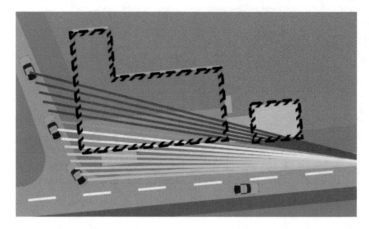

Fig. 8.4 Model of signal attenuation caused by obstacles are used in Veins [31]

radio signals. Given this, Veins includes a model of obstacle signal attenuation that realistically captures the effects of blocking signals caused by buildings, as shown in Fig. 8.4.

8.4.4 Advantages and Shortcomings

Like network simulators, these simulators that integrate mobility and network simulators have the challenge of not only presenting a real simulation environment but also using parameters and functionality that resemble the real world. This challenge is heightened since the environment has to consider not only the mobility and trajectory of nodes but also the entire physical environment that surrounds a city such as buildings, houses, trees, and objects that can interfere with the simulation environment.

Therefore, such systems have to take into account not only the behavior of the simulation but also the behavior of the elements that make up its scenery as well as the mobility of vehicles, people, objects, and contrivances that are part of this environment.

8.5   Final Discussion

In this chapter, we have described the main tools used to evaluate and validate new protocols and services for ITSs. We described one of the most important points that involve this evaluation, models of mobility, and discussed the main concepts that can be used to carry out modeling. Also, we described the main network simulators that simulate communication protocols, enabling the development and evaluation of a new communication protocol for ITSs. Finally, we listed the main simulators and tools that integrate mobility models with network simulators to allow the development of a more realistic scenario to obtain results that are closer to the real world.

References

1. Al-Sultan S, Al-Doori MM, Al-Bayatti AH, Zedan H (2014) A comprehensive survey on vehicular ad hoc network. J Netw Comput Appl 37(Supplement C):380–392
2. Barr R, Haas ZJ, van Renesse R (2005) Jist: an efficient approach to simulation using virtual machines. Softw Pract Exp 35(6):539–576
3. Behrisch M, Bieker L, Erdmann J, Krajzewicz D (2011) Sumo–simulation of urban mobility: an overview. In: Proceedings of the third international conference on advances in system simulation, ThinkMind
4. Bellavista P, Caselli F, Foschini L (2014) Implementing and evaluating v2x protocols over itetris: traffic estimation in the colombo project. In: Proceedings of the fourth ACM international symposium on development and analysis of intelligent vehicular networks and applications, ACM, DIVANet '14, pp 25–32
5. Fiore M et al (2006) Mobility models in inter-vehicle communications literature. Politecnico di Torino, p 147
6. Fiore M, Harri J, Filali F, Bonnet C (2007) Vehicular mobility simulation for vanets. In: Proceedings of the 47th annual simulation symposium. IEEE, Washington, DC, pp 301–309
7. Harri J, Filali F, Bonnet C (2009) Mobility models for vehicular ad hoc networks: a survey and taxonomy. IEEE Commun Surv Tutorials 11(4):19–41
8. Hasan S, Schneider CM, Ukkusuri SV, González MC (2013) Spatiotemporal patterns of urban human mobility. J Stat Phys 151(1–2):304–318
9. Heinovski J, Klingler F, Dressler F, Sommer C (2016) Performance comparison of ieee 802.11p and arib std-t109. In: Proceedings of the IEEE vehicular networking conference, pp 1–8
10. Hrizi F, Bonnet C, Härri J, Filali F (2013) Adapting contention-based forwarding to urban vehicular topologies for active safety applications. Ann Telecommun – annales des télécommunications 68(5):267–285
11. Hsu Wj, Merchant K, Shu Hw, Hsu Ch, Helmy A (2005) Weighted waypoint mobility model and its impact on ad hoc networks. SIGMOBILE Mob Comput Commun Rev 9(1):59–63
12. iTETRIS (2017) iTETRIS simulation platform. http://www.ict-itetris.eu/platform.htm. Last visited in Oct, 2017
13. Jiang D, Delgrossi L (2008) Ieee 802.11p: Towards an international standard for wireless access in vehicular environments. In: Proceedings of the IEEE vehicular technology conference, pp 2036–2040
14. JiST/SWANS (2017) Java in simulation time/scalable wireless ad hoc network simulator. http://jist.ece.cornell.edu/. Last visited in Oct, 2017
15. Karnadi FK, Mo ZH, Lan KC (2007) Rapid generation of realistic mobility models for vanet. In: 2007 IEEE wireless communications and networking conference, pp 2506–2511
16. Kim J, Sridhara V, Bohacek S (2009) Realistic mobility simulation of urban mesh networks. Ad Hoc Netw 7(2):411–430
17. Li YJ (2012) An overview of the DSRC/WAVE technology. Springer, Berlin/Heidelberg, pp 544–558
18. Manzoni P, Fiore M, Uppoor S, Domínguez FJM, Calafate CT, Escriba JCC (2015) Mobility models for vehicular communications. Springer International Publishing, Cham, pp 309–333

19. Meneguette RI (2016) A vehicular cloud-based framework for the intelligent transport management of big cities. Int J Distrib Sens Netw 12(5):8198597
20. Musolesi M, Mascolo C (2007) Designing mobility models based on social network theory. SIGMOBILE Mob Comput Commun Rev 11(3):59–70
21. NS (2017) NS - documentation. https://www.nsnam.org/. Last visited in Oct, 2017
22. OMNeT++ (2017) Omnet++ discrete event simulator
23. OpenStreetMap (2017) OpenStreetMap. https://www.openstreetmap.org/. Last visited in Oct, 2017
24. Piórkowski M, Raya M, Lugo AL, Papadimitratos P, Grossglauser M, Hubaux JP (2008) Trans: realistic joint traffic and network simulator for vanets. SIGMOBILE Mob Comput Commun Rev 12(1):31–33
25. Rondinone M, Maneros J, Krajzewicz D, Bauza R, Cataldi P, Hrizi F, Gozalvez J, Kumar V, Röckl M, Lin L, Lazaro O, Leguay J, Haerri J, Vaz S, Lopez Y, Sepulcre M, Wetterwald M, Blokpoel R, Cartolano F (2013) itetris: a modular simulation platform for the large scale evaluation of cooperative its applications. Simul Model Pract Theory 34(Supplement C): 99–125
26. Sommer C, Joerer S, Dressler F (2012) On the applicability of two-ray path loss models for vehicular network simulation. In: Proceedings of the IEEE vehicular networking conference, pp 64–69
27. Sommer C, Härri J, Hrizi F, Schünemann B, Dressler F (2015) Simulation tools and techniques for vehicular communications and applications. Springer International Publishing, Cham, pp 365–392
28. TraCI (2017) Introduction to TraCI. http://sumo.dlr.de/wiki/TraCI. Last visited in Oct, 2017
29. Tuduce C, Gross T (2005) A mobility model based on WLAN traces and its validation. In: Proceedings IEEE 24th annual joint conference of the IEEE computer and communications societies, vol 1, pp 664–674
30. Varga A, Hornig R (2008) An overview of the omnet++ simulation environment. In: Proceedings of the 1st international conference on simulation tools and techniques for communications, networks and systems and workshops, ICST (Institute for computer sciences, social-informatics and telecommunications engineering), Simutools '08, pp 60:1–60:10
31. Veins (2017) Veins – in-depth information on select components. http://veins.car2x.org/documentation/modules/. Last visited in Oct, 2017
32. VSimRTI (2017) VSimRTI – smart mobility simulation. https://www.dcaiti.tu-berlin.de/research/simulation/. Last visited in Oct, 2017
33. Yoon J, Noble BD, Liu M, Kim M (2006) Building realistic mobility models from coarse-grained traces. In: Proceedings of the 4th international conference on mobile systems, applications and services, ACM, MobiSys '06, pp 177–190
34. Zheng Q, Hong X, Liu J (2006) An agenda based mobility model. In: Proceedings of the 39th annual simulation symposium, p 8

Printed in the United States
By Bookmasters